Henry Miller: Full of Life

Also by Kathryn Winslow

Big Pan Out
The Story of the Klondike Gold Rush

Alaska Bound

Henry Miller:

Full of Life

Kathryn Winslow

An Ernest Scott Book

Jeremy P. Tarcher, Inc. Los Angeles

Distributed by

St. Martin's Press New York

The author thanks the following for their permission to reprint from copyrighted works:

Doubleday & Company, Inc., for excerpts from *Insomnia* by Henry Miller, copyright © 1974 by Henry Miller.

Bern Porter Books, for excerpts from *Murder the Murderer* by Henry Miller, copyright © 1944 by Henry Miller; *The Plight of the Creative Artist in the United States of America* by Henry Miller, copyright © 1944 by Henry Miller; and *What Are You Going to Do About Alf?* by Henry Miller, copyright © 1943 by Henry Miller.

Greenwood Press, for excerpts from the Preface by Henry Miller to *Life Without Principle*, copyright © 1946 by James Ladd Delkin.

Grove Press, Inc., for excerpts from *Black Spring* by Henry Miller, copyright © 1963 by Grove Press, Inc.; *Nexus* by Henry Miller, copyright © 1965 by Henry Miller; *Sexus* by Henry Miller, copyright © 1965 by Henry Miller; *Tropic of Capricorn* by Henry Miller, copyright © 1961 by Grove Press, Inc.; and *The World of Sex* by Henry Miller, copyright © 1978 by Henry Miller.

New Directions Publishing Corporation, for excerpts from *The Air-Conditioned Nightmare* by Henry Miller, copyright © 1945 by New Directions Publishing Corporation; *The Books in My Life* by Henry Miller, copyright © 1952 by Henry Miller; *Big Sur and the Oranges of Hieronymus Bosch* by Henry Miller, copyright © 1957 by New Directions Publishing Corporation; *The Colossus of Maroussi* by Henry Miller, copyright © 1941 by Henry Miller; *Remember to Remember* by Henry Miller, copyright © 1947 by New Directions Publishing Corporation; and *Sunday After the War* by Henry Miller, copyright © 1944 by Henry Miller.

Library of Congress Cataloging-in-Publication Data

Winslow, Kathryn.
  Henry Miller: full of life.

  "An Ernest Scott book."
  Bibliography: p.
  Includes index.
  1. Miller, Henry, 1891–   —Biography. 2. Authors,
American—20th century—Biography. I. Title.
PS3525.I5454Z95 1986   818'.5209 [B]   86–14376
ISBN 0–87477–404–7

Jeremy P. Tarcher, Inc.
9110 Sunset Boulevard
Los Angeles, CA 90069

Design by Linda Norlen

Manufactured in the United States of America

10 9 8 7 6 5 4 3 2 1
First Edition

In memory of
Henry Miller
and of those who were
with him in life and are
with him in these pages

Contents

Preface

As a boy growing up in Brooklyn, Henry Miller was a voracious reader, and the people he admired most were authors. He imagined how wonderful it must be to write books for others to read but never dared think of himself as one who could do it. Not until his late twenties did he put his name, Henry V. Miller, to a few reader-reviews published in a short-story magazine. Seeing his name in print pleased him, and he began experimenting with short pieces such as humorous incidents, character sketches, and social commentaries. He could get none of it published, but he continued to turn out whatever was on his mind. During a three-week vacation from his job, he wrote a book. It, too, was turned down.

When he was forty-two years old, he was still writing—and hoping to be published. By then he had left New York and was living in Paris, and it was there in 1934 that his friend Anaïs Nin paid the Obelisk Press to bring out his book *Tropic of Cancer*. After that there was no stopping him. Long books, short books, essays, articles, letters, portraits, critiques, "fragments," and more clattered from his typewriter. He mastered the short story (often presented within the longer book he was writing), the vignette, the saga, comedy, satire, imagery, characterization, dialogue, caricature—and he often put all of it into a single book.

Writing in the first person as honestly as he could, he freed himself from the literary clichés that he considered to be ruses for keeping reality out of focus, especially when they dealt with the sexual relationships between men and women. He gave his readers close-ups, some of which were too close for those weaned on romanticism, and he was reviled for it. It did not stop him. His zest for recording everything about the life he knew could not be quenched.

He had strong personal convictions. Disillusioned by social

injustices, he wrote a book on the subject. He hated war, the atom bomb in particular, and as early as 1946 he wrote that it would bring the civilized world to the brink of destruction. He predicted and described what today we call "Star Wars."

In 1961, an incomplete bibliography of his published work listed 421 titles, including translations and reprints. His work was appearing in print faster and in more places than a compiler could keep up with, and Henry had almost two decades of writing ahead of him. He wrote his last three books when he was in his eighties, not allowing the handicaps and infirmities of old age to stop him. This book about Henry Miller is about a man for whom writing was life.

Henry Miller was my friend. We met in 1944, when he first came to live in Big Sur, and four years later, when I was living in Chicago, he joined me in a venture for showing and selling his watercolors and encouraging people to buy his books. During the forties and early fifties, his books were not popular, and for necessary income he painted watercolors to sell for a few dollars apiece. He had a wife and two little children to support. To help him, I opened M, THE STUDIO FOR HENRY MILLER in Chicago's old Jackson Park art colony. It was both a gallery and a bookstore. Its only purpose at the beginning was to sell his work, and he received all of the money that came in. This was my idea. He often asked me to keep something for myself, and when I would not, he made me gifts of his watercolors. I thought that it would be a venture of only a year or two, but, as it turned out, the studio continued for ten years, from 1948 to 1958.

M became a gathering place for people who had read his books and admired his work, and for avant-garde painters, writers, poets, sculptors, and others who wanted to be part of the scene. If the Establishment was appalled by Henry Miller's work, many young people found it stimulating and fun. They called M "an oasis in the desert of Chicago." The studio also drew visitors from cities as far away as New York on the East Coast and San Francisco in the West.

After a while, Henry asked me to help Anaïs Nin by selling her books as well as the long-playing records of her reading from her work. Later he asked me to sell also the books of Kenneth Patchen, and we put on two successful benefits at M for the disabled poet. Michael Fraenkel, who had influenced Henry greatly in Paris, was another author whose work we sold eventually.

This book, then, is about Henry at Big Sur and as represented at M, and also about Henry at other places that figured in his life and work: Brooklyn, Manhattan, Paris, Bowling Green, Los Angeles, Beverly Glen, San Francisco, Monterey, Minneapolis, Hamburg, and Pacific Palisades.

Our friendship continued from 1944 until his death in 1980. During the last years of his life, I learned from him and from our mutual friends about his failing health, his operations and partial recoveries, the afflictions that plagued his body but not his spirit. In a last short note to me three months before he died, he seemed as indestructible as ever. He mentioned only that his eyesight was so poor in his remaining good eye that he was saving it for his painting. I thought he would live on for years.

Back in 1960, Henry had encouraged me to write a book about M and had given me permission to use his letters. But, before I could begin, a furor erupted over *Tropic of Cancer,* and arrests, confiscations, and trials to suppress the book went on throughout the country. It was not the time to write a book about Henry Miller.

As the years passed, other commitments kept me from working on the book. When Henry died I regretted that this had been so. For old times' sake I looked through his letters and my old notebooks, diaries, and folders containing long-ago information. I found old photographs. I was encouraged to try the book again. However, for a new generation of readers I needed to tell of Henry's early life and his years in Paris and to explain how he came to Big Sur and how he spent his first years there. I realized that the story of M would now be only a part of the book, and that the events of Henry's life from 1960 to 1980, after M had closed, must also be included.

In reconstructing conversations and personal comments, I have kept before me my notebooks and diaries as well as the many letters I received from Henry and others who are quoted in this book. While I remember quite clearly the content of the quoted conversations with Henry and others, I have necessarily taken liberties with the word-to-word reconstructions. Other quotations are taken from Henry's books, his unpublished notebooks and manuscripts that I own, his letters to me, and his published interviews with journalists.

While much of this book relies upon personal knowledge and participation, I am indebted to a number of people who were closer to Henry than I and who generously gave me information, corrected me when necessary, and added personal details to certain incidents.

In writing about the Big Sur years, I owe the most to Emil White, who came to Big Sur in 1944 at Henry's invitation and was for many years his neighbor and close friend. In 1981 he donated his home to the Big Sur Land Trust for preservation as the Henry Miller Library, and he contributed his own collection of Milleriana as its nucleus. While its focus is on Henry's work, the library is also maintained for the work of all writers who live and work on the Big Sur coast. Emil's assistance was essential.

I am also deeply indebted to Bern Porter, who was often with Henry during the time when he was publishing Henry's books. His interest in my book and his assistance in many ways are gratefully acknowledged. In addition, Virginia Varda Goldstein, who was Jean Varda's wife when I met her long ago, offered important details and suggestions, and Keith Evans, William Webb, and Edwin and Darlene Culver provided necessary links in the continuity of the Big Sur chapters. To all of these I am deeply grateful.

My gratitude is also due Richard French, Lynda Sargent's nephew and the conservator of her estate, for his generosity in supplying pertinent facts, and also for permitting me to quote from Lynda's newspaper column.

For assisting me in the sequences dealing with the Colt Press in San Francisco, I wish to thank Sherwood Grover, Polly Black, and Arvilla Seligman.

I owe much to Miriam Patchen for her permission to use her letters to me concerning Kenneth Patchen and herself during our years of warm friendship. For more about the Patchens when they first came to live in Palo Alto, California, I am most grateful to Gordon Claycomb, an old friend of mine who became a good friend of theirs.

In writing about the Henry Miller Literary Society and Henry's visit to Minneapolis in 1962, I was assisted in many details by my good friend the late Edward P. Schwartz. He made many contributions to this book and also permitted me to quote from his correspondence with Henry and from issues of the society's newsletter. As a cofounder of the society, he was able to give me many details. While my appreciation was often extended to him during the writing of this book, I wish to write of it again here.

I am also indebted to the other cofounder of the society, the late Thomas H. Moore, who, with Schwartz, visited M and whose letters provided additional information.

I am deeply indebted to the eminent attorney Elmer Gertz of Chicago, who permitted me to quote from three of his books that relate reminiscences of his personal friendship with Henry and also of his professional role on Henry's behalf in the Illinois trials of *Tropic of Cancer*.

Others I wish to thank are Wallace Fowlie, for providing me with books and other writing of his that concerned Henry, and for other assistance with this book, and Phil Nurenberg, for supplying me with transcripts of interviews he taped with Emil White, Bern Porter, and Edward P. Schwartz.

For the past forty years, certain of my friends have kept me supplied with clippings and photographs from newspapers and magazines, as well as book reviews, obituaries, advertisements, and so on, that concerned Henry and other people who appear in this book. For this huge amount of material, all of which I saved because of my interest in these individuals, I am in debt to Gustave Dorn, Laurie Hildebrand, Anna and Margaret Shipley, and the late Ruth (Bobby) Ferro.

I wish to thank especially Valentine Miller for sharing with me certain family details.

The most interesting parts of this book, the quotations from Henry's books, would not have appeared had it not been for the generous permission of his publishers. Those to whom I owe much are Barney Rosset, James Laughlin, Bern Porter, James Ladd, and Jack Stauffacher.

I am also indebted to the Anaïs Nin Trust for permission to include excerpts from letters of Anaïs Nin.

Finally, for the use of photographs that appear in this book, I wish to thank Emil White, William Webb, Bern Porter, Virginia Varda Goldstein, Miriam Patchen, Noel Young, Gunther Stuhlmann, and the family of Edward P. Schwartz.

K. W.

Sonoma, California
April 1986

Part One

Brooklyn

Paris

Manhattan

Los Angeles and Beverly Glen

1

*In the past every member of our family did something
with his hands. I'm the first son of a bitch with a glib
tongue and a bad heart.*

Black Spring

When Henry Miller was forty-five years old, he wrote: "My
people were entirely Nordic, which is to say *idiots*. . . . In my
bitterness I often search for reasons to condemn them, the better
to condemn myself. For I am like them, too, in many ways. For a
long time I thought I had escaped, but as time goes on I see that
I am no better, that I am even a little worse, because I saw more
clearly than they ever did and yet remained powerless to alter my
life."

The family was German. His grandparents on both sides
had emigrated from Germany and settled in Yorkville, a German
neighborhood on the Upper East Side of Manhattan, and both of
his parents, Heinrich Miller and Louise Nieting, had been born
there. On December 26, 1891, he, too, was born in Yorkville and
baptized Henry Valentine after the anglicized first names of his
father and his mother's father, Valentin Nieting. While he was still
an infant, the family moved to Brooklyn, where a sister Lauretta
Anna was born three and a half years later. There were no other
children.

His father and grandfather Nieting were tailors, and it was
expected that Henry would follow the trade. When he was sixteen
years old, his father opened a tailor shop in Manhattan and named
it Henry Miller & Son.

The Williamsburg neighborhood of Brooklyn, where the

Millers lived until Henry was almost ten years old, was lower middle class and only partly residential. The family, including grandfather Nieting, lived above a barbershop with a fish market next door and, down the street, a Chinese laundry, a burlesque house, and a corner saloon. The red glow from the furnaces of an ironworks could be seen from the Millers' windows, and only a little farther away there was a tin factory where the incendiary hazards required frequent visits from the fire station's horse-drawn wagon. To little Henry's terror, it came on the gallop, the bell clanging fiercely. Directly opposite the Millers' flat was the office of a veterinarian who found it necessary to castrate horses out of doors, a gory sidewalk performance that always drew a crowd of onlookers. In 1901, the family moved to the better neighborhood of Bushwick in Brooklyn's Fourteenth Ward.

Henry was bright in school, which pleased his parents, especially since Lauretta was severely retarded and unable to apply herself to the simplest lessons. When he was eleven, his parents bought a piano and had him take lessons. They were surprised at how quickly he learned to play. Physically he was rather frail, had trouble with his eyes and wore glasses, and was deaf in one ear because of improper medical attention to early ear problems. But poor eyesight did not keep him from reading. He was given books from an early age, the children's classics and the currently popular titles for boys. Books became his prized possessions, and in high school his favorite classes were in literature. He liked Emerson best and, after him, Victor Hugo. He disliked Shakespeare as much as the Goethe that he had to read in his German class and Virgil's *Aeneid* that he had to study in Latin.

He spent hours at the public library in search of new authors to read. There he discovered Knut Hamsun, Rider Haggard, Oscar Wilde, and more of Walt Whitman than was in his class assignments. He tried to borrow Rabelais's *Gargantua and Pantagruel*, but the librarian would not let him have it. At the library he also read unabridged dictionaries and began to keep lists of words that intrigued him—*chthonian, cotyledon, occiput, chape, acromegaly, brumous, stoup*. It was a search he never tired of and followed throughout his life.

Authors were the people he admired most. He was in awe

of their gifts and liked to imagine himself as a noted writer too, although he did not really expect to be one. While he filled notebooks with passages that he copied from books, it was clear to him that he could never write anything as good. But he did not want to be a tailor.

At seventeen he graduated from high school second in his class and announced to his parents his intention of going on to college. His father had already accepted the fact that his son was not going to join him at the tailor shop. He applied for a scholarship to Cornell University but was turned down. Then he enrolled at New York's City College, where the course he took in English literature bored him so much that he did not stay long. "It was Spenser's *Faerie Queene* that drove me away," he said.

To get out of going to work at his father's shop, Henry took a clerical job with the Atlas Portland Cement Company, which had offices in lower Manhattan. His father was hurt because he needed Henry to help with the clerical work at the tailor shop and also to collect the overdue bills that his customers ran up. Many of his customers were his friends and drinking cronies, and he could not dun them himself.

Each day as Henry rode the trains to and from work, he turned his thoughts to an imaginary novel. He did not put a word on paper, still not thinking of himself as a writer. He just passed the time giving his characters dialogue filled with emotional stress. It seemed to ease the tension that he felt at home as well as relieve the monotony of his life. "Each time . . . I was truly alone . . . the book commenced to write itself, screaming the things which I never breathed, the thoughts I never uttered, the conversations I never held, the hopes, the dreams, the delusions I never admitted."

His mother was distraught when he left home to move in with a widow twice his age.

When Henry was twenty-one, he made up his mind to go to California. He spent less than a year there, mostly picking fruit, working as a ranch hand, and doing other work for which he was unsuited. He had hoped to save enough money to go north to the goldfields of Alaska, but after nine months he had only enough for the train fare back to New York.

His mother begged him to join his father at the shop in order to keep an eye on him. Henry's father was drinking so heavily that he was in danger of losing the business. Henry did go to the shop, and he tried to get new orders and collect old bills. At times he helped the tailors cut out patterns. He often had to go out looking for his father, drag him out of some saloon, and take him home.

He began playing the piano again and even thought of making it a career. His teacher was a talented young woman named Beatrice Wickens. When a tepid romance developed and she hinted at marriage, he fled to Washington, D.C., to take a job sorting mail in the office of the War Department. It was 1917 and the country was about to enter the war against Germany. When he registered for the draft, he asked for deferment on the grounds that he was the sole support of his parents and sister. And then he quickly married Beatrice.

His parents expected him to settle down, but he didn't because he did not know what to settle down to. The idea of making the piano his career faded when he saw that he was not nearly the pianist his wife was and that even she could make a living only by giving lessons. He had no plans for steady employment of any kind. There was really nothing that he wanted to do unless, perhaps, it was to write, and he had misgivings about that.

Beatrice did not encourage him to write, which she saw as an excuse to stay home all day. She accused him of laziness and of being unwilling to support her. Each morning she handed him carfare and lunch money and pushed him out the door to look for work. There was no tailor shop to go to. His father had lost the business. Henry picked up work as a dishwasher, bartender, door-to-door salesman, grave digger, streetcar conductor, and so on. He was usually fired after a day or two. He didn't care. If he ran into a friend who would stake him to a meal or a matinee ticket, he would spend the day that way. Sometimes a friend would have a car, and they would spend the day at the beach.

"When I woke up to the fact that as far as the scheme of things goes I was less than dirt I really became quite happy. I quickly lost all sense of responsibility. And if it weren't for the fact that my friends got tired of lending me money I might have gone on indefinitely pissing the time away." He felt that it was easier to accept menial jobs because it left his mind free. What he needed, he said, was not work but a life more abundant: "After I was fired from the garbage trucks I remember taking up with an Evangelist who seemed to have great confidence in me. I was a sort of usher, collector and private secretary. He brought to my attention the whole world of Indian philosophy."

Henry salvaged the big pigeonholed desk and the brass spittoon that had been at the tailor shop. He had them delivered to the third-floor flat in Brooklyn where he and Beatrice were living, and he had the movers leave the desk in the middle of the room. He stood the spittoon beside it. ". . . I put my feet up on the desk and dreamed of what I would write if I could write. . . . All the pigeon-holes were empty and all the drawers were empty; there wasn't a thing on the desk or in it except a sheet of white paper on which I found it impossible to put so much as a pot-hook."

He always found time to read and he was engrossed with the books of Sherwood Anderson, Theodore Dreiser, Marcel Proust, and Fyodor Dostoyevski. He was still filling notebooks with excerpts from what he read. He was also dipping into the philosophies of Oswald Spengler and Friedrich Nietzsche.

One day he saw a notice that the editor of a monthly magazine of "clever short stories" called *The Black Cat* wanted to hear from its readers what they thought of the stories being published. A reply judged worthy of printing would appear in the magazine and be paid for at a penny a word, which was the same rate paid to the authors themselves.

Henry mailed in $1.50 for a year's subscription, since only subscribers were eligible, and, when the next issue arrived, he looked it over and then wrote a lengthy review about the lead story. The editor was looking for an increase in subscriptions and didn't expect to get any "reviews," especially not from someone like Henry whose years of reading gave him a know-it-all attitude. But Henry did make several interesting points, and the editor published his article. Henry was delighted. He sent in four more reviews before the editor withdrew the offer. All were printed and paid for, which gave Henry the right to call himself a professional writer whose work had appeared under the byline, Henry V. Miller.

On September 30, 1919, a daughter was born to Beatrice and Henry. They named her Barbara. Six months later Henry went to work for the Western Union Telegraph Company as the messenger employment manager. It was a job he described as uninterrupted pandemonium "from the moment I arrived at the office. . . . Before I could take my hat off I had to answer a dozen telephone calls. There were three telephones on my desk and they all rang at once. They were bawling the piss out of me before I had even sat down to work."

The hiring office was always jammed with applicants begging for work. Some were businessmen, salesmen, professional people who had held good jobs but were now down and out and in need of this menial employment. However, most were drifters, Bowery boozers, ex-convicts on parole, psychopaths, screwballs, half-wits, the unemployable and infirm, some who could neither read nor speak English, all of them derelicts in one way or another.

The company kept records of every person who had ever been hired by them, records that included how many times they had been fired and perhaps rehired and fired again. Red marks beside their names indicated some delinquency, "a theft, a fraud, a brawl, or dementia or perversion or idiocy." Some of the names showed as many as six aliases.

All of the pages were heavily scratched with red ink, but there was no time for Henry to consult them with fifty men in front of him "weeping, begging, beseeching, imploring, cursing, spitting, fuming, threatening" him. He took on as many as he could but had to turn away at least half.

Some that were hired didn't last through the day. They got lost on the subway or in the underground labyrinths beneath the office buildings, or they threw the telegrams away and rode around all day on the subway and elevated trains, their uniform allowing them to ride for free.

Every ten days or so I was put on the carpet and lectured for having "too big a heart." . . . Be firm! Be hard! they cautioned me. Fuck that! I said to myself, I'll be generous, pliant, forgiving, tolerant, tender. In the beginning I heard every man to the end; if I couldn't give him a job I gave him money, and if

I had no money I gave him cigarettes or I gave him courage. But I gave! The effort was dizzying. Nobody can estimate the effects of a good deed, of a kind word. I was swamped with gratitude, with well wishes, with invitations, with pathetic, tender little gifts. If I had had real power, instead of being a fifth wheel on a wagon, God knows what I might not have accomplished.

Some of the messengers got into trouble. Some were sent to prison, or they committed suicide, or they were killed in an accident, or murdered. When he read of it in the newspaper, he clipped the articles and filed them with a journal that he kept about his job. He had more than enough material for a book of "case histories," a project that was always in the back of his mind. Then, "by chance one day, when I had been put on the carpet for some wanton piece of negligence, the vice-president let drop a phrase which stuck in my crop. He said that he would like to see someone write a sort of Horatio Alger book about the messengers; he hinted that perhaps I might be the one to do such a job."

It was just the goad that Henry needed. He would write a messengers book, one such as they never imagined. It would not be a Horatio Alger story about the unlikelihood of any messenger ever getting to be manager, chief, or superintendent. He would dwell on the hardships, degradations, and humiliations of destitute men grateful to be taken on for the lowest of jobs. And to spice it up he would add how the Hindu boy Guptal got his throat slit one night; how Olinski got whipped to a pulp in a neighborhood where Jews were not welcome; why Clausen beat his kids' brains out with a blackjack; and how Schuldig, gone mad, crashed his head into a stone wall—messengers all.

He looked through his journal and selected an even dozen cases to write about, choosing those with the most distressing details. He had two weeks' vacation coming up soon, so he asked for another week, and during this time he wrote the book. Typing five, six, sometimes eight thousand words a day, he finished more than three hundred pages of grief and mayhem. He titled the book *Clipped Wings*.

Remembering it years later, Henry wrote, "It was a colossal tome and faulty from start to finish. But it was my first book and

I was in love with it. If I had had the money, as Gide had, I would have published it at my own expense. If I had had the courage that Whitman had, I would have peddled it from door to door. Everybody I showed it to said it was terrible. I was urged to give up the idea of writing."

At the time he thought enough of the manuscript to show it to a publisher. It was rejected.

He was disappointed but he was not discouraged. He continued to write whenever he could find the time, turning out character sketches of the men and women he knew, some philosophical monologues, panegyrics, prose poems, humor, many essays on one social or private gripe or another. No magazine would publish any of it. Yet he kept on, for writing helped him to dismiss the realities of his everyday life.

He was thirty-one years old. As a writer he saw himself a failure. He loathed his job. His marriage had long since fallen apart, and his sexual diversions with a number of women, including the mother of his wife, only made it more difficult to come to terms with himself. He wanted to change his life, but he did not know how: "I knew very well I'd have to make a break someday. . . . but I knew also that there was nothing I could do about it— yet. Something had to happen, something big, something that would sweep me off my feet. All I needed was a push, but it had to be some force outside my world."

He did not expect a woman to be that force.

2

The woman's name was June Mansfield. That is the name
she gave Henry, but he was never sure if it really was her name,
any more than he could tell who she was. "Knowing only a frac-
tion of her life, possessing only a bag of lies, of inventions, of
imaginings, of obsessions and delusions, putting together tag
ends, coke dreams, reveries, unfinished sentences, jumbled dream
talk, hysterical ravings, ill-disguised fantasies, morbid desires,
meeting now and then a name become flesh, overhearing stray
bits of conversation, observing smuggled glances, half-arrested
gestures . . . ," he could only try to guess the truth. If he asked
her who she was or where she lived, or anything about her personal life, she would not hesitate to tell him, revealing even more
than he had expected to hear. And while he listened he would
know that not a word of what she was saying was true.

The subject of all her conversations was herself, and while
he listened, mesmerized by her soft, low voice, he searched the
impassive innocence of her face for some clue to reality. He found
none. Everything she said was spoken with detachment, as if she
were describing something she had read in a book and what she
was telling him had happened to the heroine, not to herself.

She confided in him the most lurid events of her life. They
made his mouth go dry. Yet whenever she paused, as if unable to
continue with the details, he would beg her, "Go on! Go on!" The

disclosures were of childhood rape, of her numerous seductions, of being forced to accept the attentions of numerous lovers because she was hungry, destitute, abandoned, or whatever. The erotic details sent him into paroxysms of jealousy, for now he was also one of her lovers.

They had met in a dance hall near Times Square. She was twenty years old, one of the taxi dancers. "Standing on the edge of the dance floor I notice her coming towards me; she is coming with sails spread, the large full face beautifully balanced on the long, columnar neck. I see a woman perhaps eighteen, perhaps thirty, with blue-black hair and a large white face, a full white face in which the eyes shine brilliantly. She has on a tailored blue suit of duveteen. I remember distinctly now the fullness of her body, and that her hair was fine and straight, parted on the side, like a man's. I remember the smile she gave me—knowing, mysterious, fugitive—a smile that sprang up suddenly, like a puff of wind."

When the dance hall closed that night, they met across the street in a Chinese restaurant, and as they sat in one of the booths he thought to himself, "One can wait a whole lifetime for a moment like this. The woman whom you never hoped to meet now sits before you, and she talks and she looks exactly like the person you dreamed about."

They took a furnished room together in the Bronx, but when he told Beatrice about it she only ridiculed him, calling June another one of his whores. She would not agree to a divorce. Perhaps because she believed that someday he would "settle down." Perhaps because of little Barbara. Perhaps because she loved him.

But Henry was in love with June. Her fabrications made her only more mysterious, more exotic. He really did not want to know the truth, whatever it was. The intricacies of her deceptions intrigued him. He wondered if she was of gypsy blood. Or a Jewess? He thought she might be Jewish because she denied it so vehemently. "She could have passed for a Portuguese, a Basque, a Roumanian gypsy, a Hungarian, a Georgian, anything she chose to make you believe. . . . She had her own wave length: it was short, powerful, disruptive. It served to break down other transmissions, especially those which threatened to effect real communication with her." He had listened to so many lies that he no longer tried to keep anything straight. It had in no way diminished his love for her.

June was infatuated with Henry, whom she called Val. He had told her that he was a writer, and, since he was the first one she had known, he was as attractive to her as her chameleonlike personality charmed him. She left the dance hall and attached herself to the Theatre Guild, claiming to be an actress. In no time she became the understudy to the leading woman, and she told Henry that the director and the leading man, who were both "madly in love" with her, had said she had a great future in the theater.

From the Bronx they moved in temporarily with friends on Riverside Drive. Henry was still working at Western Union. June said, "I want you to quit that awful job. I'll find a place where you can write. You won't need to earn any money. I'll soon be making lots of money. You can have anything you want. . . . Maybe you'll write a play—and I'll act in it!"

Beatrice knew that they were living together but she was still trying to get Henry back, and she refused to give him a divorce. Then one day when Henry thought Beatrice and Barbara were out of town, he brought June to the Brooklyn flat and they stayed all night. Early the next morning Beatrice returned and found them in bed. She was as outraged as she was hurt but it changed her mind about giving him his freedom. A few months after the divorce, Henry and June were married.

They moved at once into an unfurnished apartment in Brooklyn Heights. At ninety dollars a month, it was far beyond their means, but June was determined to have it, and they put down a ten-dollar deposit. As for the remaining eighty dollars and the money to buy furniture and everything else that was needed, June said to leave it to her. He learned that she got three hundred dollars from one of her admirers, who turned out to be a room clerk in a hotel. She had demanded five hundred, but he had protested that his bank account was almost exhausted. She assured Henry that he was "perfectly harmless."

They were all "harmless," he said to himself. It was hard for him to understand what prevented these gallant lovers from looking her up, but he told himself that it was better not to pry too deeply. He assumed that, as she had told him, she told them she was living with her parents, that her mother was a witch and her father bedridden, dying of cancer.

He walked off his job without giving notice and tried to be what June wanted him to be—a successful writer. He couldn't get started. The more he needed to impress her, the harder it was for him to accomplish anything. They were soon in debt, and he was in arrears with his alimony payments. His writing, he knew, even if he could produce something, would not pay the rent.

If he spent too much time at the typewriter she scolded him for ignoring her. She was gone at night, to return in the early hours of the morning, sometimes staying out all night. When he was alone and free to work he could not while imagining what she was doing and whom she was with. It was useless to question her.

Between the time she took off and the time she returned I lived the life of a full blooded schizerino. It was not eternity which elapsed, because somehow eternity has to do with peace and with victory, it is something man-made, something earned: no, I experienced an entr'acte in which every hair turns white to the roots, in which every millimetre of skin itches and burns until the whole body becomes a running sore. I see myself sitting before a table in the dark, my hands and feet growing enormous, as though elephantiasis were overtaking me at a gallop. I hear the blood rushing up to the brain and pounding at the ear-drums, like Himalayan devils with sledge-hammers; I hear her flapping her huge wings, even in Irkutsk, and I know she is pushing on and on, ever further away, ever further beyond reach. It is so quiet in the room and so frightfully empty that I shriek and howl just to make a little noise, a little human sound. I try to lift myself from the table but my feet are too heavy and my hands have become like the shapeless feet of the rhinoceros. The heavier my body becomes the lighter the atmosphere of the room; I am going to spread and spread until I fill the room with one solid mass of stiff jelly. I shall fill up even the cracks in the wall; I shall grow through the walls like a parasitic plant, spreading and spreading until the whole house is an indescribable mass of flesh and hair and nails. I know that this is death, but I am powerless to kill the knowledge of it, or the knower.

One day she told him that she had given up the theater and was working as a hostess in a Greenwich Village speakeasy, making more money than she ever had. His suspicions and jealousy increased in proportion to the amount of money she made and the frequency with which she stayed out all night. They quarreled violently.

She had an idea, though, that appealed to him. She suggested that he condense some of the things he had written, or write new pieces, each one to fit exactly onto a single sheet of paper, and to put her name on them as the author. She would pose as a struggling young writer and offer the work to her customers. He put together about three dozen pieces, which he called "Mezzotints," and had them printed on different colors of paper. She sold them easily.

She saw no reason why they should not open a speakeasy, and, when Henry reluctantly agreed, they moved to a basement apartment in Greenwich Village and opened for business. His job was to serve drinks and sandwiches, and hers was to offer the customers her company.

He soon fled in disgust, hitchhiking to Florida, where he expected to get in on the land boom. When he discovered that he was too late for that, he wired his father for train fare and returned to his parents' home. It was Christmastime. His thirty-fourth birthday was on December 26, 1925.

He tried to write, striving for acceptance by one of the popular weeklies, the *Saturday Evening Post, Liberty,* or *Colliers.* He carefully studied the styles of work they published, but he was unable to sell to them. His mother was ashamed to have him home all day and apparently unwilling "to do a day's work." Whenever a visitor came to the door, she made him hastily pick up his typewriter and his work and hide them in the bathtub while he himself hid in a closet.

The editor of *Liberty* liked the work Henry submitted, but he could not use it for one reason or another. He thought that Henry could write an interesting article on words and asked him to try. He was only too happy to do so and an interview was arranged with the editor of *Funk and Wagnalls Dictionary,* on which he was to base his essay. The interview was such a momentous experience for him that he could not stop at the five-thousand-word limit and wrote three times as many. Besides its length, the way he wrote it was not in a style likely to appeal to the readers of *Liberty,* and so was not used. However, Henry was paid for his work, and with the money he moved out of his parents' home and returned to June.

She urged him to write stories that she could sell to the pulps under her name. Two of her admirers were editors of pulps that published romantic stories, and when she talked to them about "her" work they readily agreed to look at it. She then sold all the stories that Henry wrote for her. His opinion of the magazines was so low that after the first story or two he did not try to be original and just lifted the plots from stories that had been published a few years earlier.

Writing for the pulps was not what he wanted to do, yet nothing else of his got into print. He still saw himself as a failure and wondered if it was worthwhile continuing to make the effort.

June was working again as a hostess in a Greenwich Village dive and had given him orders never to come there. A husband hanging around was not an asset in her business. She also forbade him to tell anyone that she was his wife lest the word get around and put an end to the various schemes she used to get money out of her "suckers." Her pay was considerably less than the money she took in on the side.

It was clear to him that his wife had many lovers but he was unprepared for Jean Kronski, a poet and painter who had been in and out of asylums. She was a year or two younger than June, and June adored her. She insisted that Henry allow Jean to live with them in their basement apartment. And he was not to tell Jean that they were married.

He became the third party, always in the way, a wet blanket who scolded them for their untidy ways and laziness, who complained when he was hungry and they had forgotten to bring home anything to eat. When he flew into rages and smashed the furniture, they burst into hysterical laughter and called him a nut. He halfheartedly looked for work in order not to be alone so much.

Waiting for June to come home, it infuriated him to see that Jean was always with her. He was never alone with June.

After months of humiliation he ran away, hitchhiking as far as New Jersey before he returned, unable to bear the thought of a final separation from June. Coming home that night, he planned to sneak back inside "the cellar," as he called it, expecting them to be out. He would "crawl in like a dog with his tail between his legs." He resolved that he would never again annoy them with his jealous scenes:

> I would be grateful for any crumbs that were handed me. If she wanted to bring her lovers in and make love to them in my presence it would be all right too. One doesn't bite the hand that feeds one. . . . Oh, I know how to be quiet now and obedient. I had learned my little lesson. I would curl up in a corner near the hearth, just as quiet and gentle as you please. They would have to be terribly mean to kick me out. Besides, if I showed them that I didn't need anything, didn't ask any favors, if I let them carry on just as if they were by themselves, what harm would come by giving me a little place in the corner?

When he reached his door he slowly and noiselessly partly opened it; he could hear voices. Yes, they were home. Jean was talking.

> She sounded maudlin, hysterical, as though she had been drinking. The other voice was low-pitched, more soothing and caressing than I had ever heard it. She seemed to be pleading. . . . There were strange pauses, too, as if they were embracing. . . .

Suddenly Jean shrieked.

> "Then you do love him still? You were lying to me!" "No, no! I swear I don't. You *must* believe me, *please*. I never loved him." "That's a lie!" "I swear to you . . . I swear I never loved him. He was just a child to me." This was followed by a shrieking gale of laughter. Then a slight commotion as if they were scuffling. Then a dead silence as if their lips were glued together. Then it seemed

as if they were undressing one another, licking one another all over, like calves in the meadow. The bed squeaked. Fouling the nest that was it. They had gotten rid of me as if I were a leper and now they were trying to do the man and wife act. It was good I hadn't been lying in the corner watching this with my head between my paws. I would have barked angrily, perhaps bitten them. And then they would have kicked me around like a dirty cur. . . . I crept upstairs on all fours and left the house as silently as I had entered it."

He decided to kill himself. In the note that he left for June he wrote that if he could not have her he preferred death. He took the pills and lay down on the bed to die, but the friend who had supplied the drug had substituted a nonlethal variety and he only went into a deep sleep.

Not long afterward the women began raising money in order to go to Paris. He overheard them making plans but didn't expect it to happen. When he came home one day and found that they had left, he broke down and wept. He did not expect ever to see June again but in a few days she cabled him for money, and to get it he found a job as a grave digger.

During the nearly four months that she was gone, he began working on a book about his life with her, filling page after page with notes. He had not yet started to write the book when she suddenly returned, telling him that she and Jean had quarreled and separated. She now wanted to take Henry to Paris, and an elderly admirer of hers whom she called "Pop" was to supply the money. "He's got plenty of dough, Val. We should let him do this for us."

Her plan was simple. She began by telling Pop about a novel that she was writing, letting him know how difficult it was to be a writer when there was no money coming in. She couldn't write and work, too, could she? He offered to provide the money if she wanted to stay home and write. He had read "her" stories that appeared in the pulps and agreed that she should do something with her talent.

Henry began writing the book for her. It was not the one he had been working on while she was gone. As she showed "her progress" to Pop she convinced him that if she could return to

Paris for a while she could really turn out something very good. He gave her the money, and she and Henry sailed at once. For the next nine months they idled about Paris and central Europe; then returned to New York and the same old jealousies, accusations, and reprisals.

When Henry started to work again on the book about himself and June she insisted on reading everything he wrote, and she bitterly criticized whatever was uncomplimentary to herself. There were certain subjects that she demanded he leave out. She also told him that there were things she could now "tell him the truth" about, things that at one time she had wanted him to believe but, she now admitted, were untrue.

Finally he put the book aside. Everything seemed hopeless —his writing, his marriage, his chance of getting something out of life. There were lengthy periods when he was too low in spirit to get out of bed.

June hated these "spells" and decided to do something about it. Her solution was to buy him a one-way steamship ticket to Southampton. From there he could take the train to London or cross the channel to France. She didn't care which. She tried to make him believe that the separation would do him good and would help him get started again on his book. She promised to send him money.

He took the ticket and sailed in February 1930. He stayed in London less than two weeks while he waited for her to send him a little money, and the day it arrived he set out for Paris.

3

There is only one great adventure and that is inward towards the self, and for that time nor space nor even deeds matter.

Tropic of Capricorn

At the American Express in Paris, small sums for Henry arrived infrequently and finally not at all. But he had made friends from whom he could cadge a meal now and then or be given a place to sleep.

From the day that he arrived in Paris, he began to fill notebooks with his impressions of the city—the sights, sounds, smells. He wrote about the people he ran into and his conversations with them, and he described his hunger pains and his search for shelter.

He had come to know Alfred Perlès, who was a proofreader working for the Paris edition of the *Chicago Tribune*. He was a friend of June, and Henry had met him in 1928 when he and June had stayed awhile in Paris. Through Perlès he met Wambly Bald, who wrote a weekly column for the *Tribune* called "La Vie de Bohème."

Bald was impressed with Henry's enthusiasm for Paris, and he envied the liveliness and color of his writing, while wishing that he could do as well. Bald was not much of a writer, and the chore of producing a column by deadline was always a harrowing experience for him. When he was particularly distressed, he would get in touch with Henry, who would turn out a column for him in no time.

Now and then Henry also wrote a feature for the paper which appeared under Perlès's name, for members of the staff were encouraged to write for the paper. Later Perlès got Henry taken on as a proofreader, but this was a skill he lacked, and he was soon fired.

During the winter of 1931, Richard Osborn, whom Henry had known for a few months, invited him to share his large and well-furnished apartment. Henry accepted gladly. The apartment was at 2, rue Auguste-Bartholdi in the Champ de Mars district. A Russian "princess" was already sharing it with Osborn.

There was a typewriter, for Osborn had literary aspirations and sometimes turned out an altogether unpublishable piece. Henry used it all day, writing short pieces, essays, stories, whatever was on his mind. Later the *New Review,* which had recently appeared on the scene, would buy his "Mlle. Claude," a short story. Aside from the purloined stories that he had written for the pulps under June's name, this would be the first time in his life that substantial work of his was published.

Osborn was a lawyer working in the legal department of the Paris branch of the National City Bank of New York. As soon as he had graduated from Yale Law School, he had come to Paris to live for a few years before returning to New York, where he knew he would be tied down to a law office forever. He was acquainted with Anaïs Nin, the wife of Hugo Guiler, one of the bank's officers, and he knew that she was a writer. Her first book, *D. H. Lawrence: An Unprofessional Study,* had just been published. One day he took Henry along on a visit to the Guiler home in Louveciennes.

In Anaïs, Henry found the most intelligent and the most intellectual woman he had ever met. She was twenty-eight years old and beautiful in a delicate doll-like way. He fell in love with her. Later, when they were alone, he showed her what he was writing, and she soon afterward shared with him part of a diary that she had been keeping since the age of eleven. She was a student of the psychologist Otto Rank, and she urged Henry to pay him a professional visit. Henry went once, but he was unwilling to undergo analysis. She urged him then to examine his subconscious drives, which she saw surfacing in his work. She suggested that what was buried in his psyche might be the fuel that set him on fire.

The idea of delving into his subconscious motivations intrigued him, but *he* would do the probing, not Rank. He decided that the interpretation of his dreams was the way to begin, and he trained himself to write them down as soon as he awakened. As the months went by he filled 247 typed pages with analyses of his dreams, accompanying them with explanatory notes and references for Anaïs's benefit. He did not keep the dreams a secret from her, but he felt that she should have a guide to go with them.

He remembered dreams from his boyhood and wrote that after reading *Grimm's Fairy Tales* he had often had nightmares. Other early dreams were of illnesses, broken bones, ear troubles. In one, he is standing before a mirror trying in vain to put back pieces of his jaw that have broken off from his face. There were hostile dreams about his mother. In one of them, he watches as her hands burst into flame, and, when he is asked to send for help and medication, he takes his "long, sweet time about it."

Then his dreams became "mainly sexual . . . a kind of obsession with the genital organs." Women with soft breasts comfort him. There are many seductions. In one dream he is in bed with a homosexual psychologist and is being strangled with the bed sheets.

He dreamed of Greta Garbo, of watching her in a movie. In the margin of the page he wrote, "I hate the droop of Garbo's lips, the lidless character of the eye, like a lizard's, the eternal romancing instead of sensual, sexual behavior, the constant evasiveness, the boy figure, the swagger and strut, the Scandinavian Ibsenesque quality of her acting."

He often dreamed of Anaïs. In recording one of these dreams he described a scene at Louveciennes: "when she jumped up, saying, 'There's H.' . . . he was already in the house and coming up the stairs and . . . just as he was giving her a crack, I saw myself standing there in my pjamas [*sic*], pushing him off . . . but it seems to me that I rather enjoyed the glimpse of H. giving A. a harmless little crack. . . . Why? Because it seemed as though H. was incapable of doing such a thing, and secondly, subconsciously, the feeling that A., by her recklessness, almost merited this."

There are no marginal notes with this dream of February 12, 1933, but he underlined the words *I rather enjoyed the glimpse of H.*

giving A. a harmless little crack and *the feeling that A., by her recklessness, almost merited this.*

He had a dream of Anaïs's mother taunting him for "destroying her daughter's life" and calling him a worthless, good-for-nothing who never accomplishes anything. The dream ends as he is strangling her.

He dreamed mainly of people he knew long before, who joined him now in jumbled, disconnected, impossible situations that were too tangled for him to understand completely.

When he had written all he cared to about his dreams he fastened the pages into a blue paper binder and on the cover pasted a sticker that read "Dreams, Original Versions." On an inside page he did a watercolor portrait of himself and wrote "To Anaïs from Henry Miller." He added a short column of characters pretending to be writing in Chinese. He kept the carbons for himself.

Because of Anaïs's interest in Lawrence, Henry began to read his books. She encouraged him and was pleased when he kept copious notes. He told her that he was planning to write a book of his own about Lawrence. To keep him supplied with paper, she brought him the discarded sheets of the New York Stock Exchange quotations from her husband's bank; Henry wrote on the backs.

This work was interrupted when, after the New Year in 1932, he found employment as an English teacher at Lycée Carnot in Dijon. It was a short-lived, dispiriting experience, and he was back in Paris by spring.

Another of Miller's early friends in Paris was Michael Fraenkel, who, at the age of forty, had decided to become a full-time writer. He had been a well-to-do businessman in New York when he wrote a book of poems, *Death in a Room.* That accomplishment turned his life around. To better follow his literary bent, he moved to Paris, and when Henry met him he was living on rue Villa Seurat. He had bought a two-story house and furnished it expensively.

When Fraenkel was a boy, he came to America from Russia with his parents. He attended school and later worked his way through college and became an English teacher. Then he left the academic world because he wanted to make money, and he had success in a book-distribution business. Wise investment of his income brought him a small fortune. Successful and rich, he began to see himself as having committed "spiritual suicide," and from then on he wrote essays and poems on the subject of "the bastard death."

He was well read in literature, philosophy, ancient history, religion, psychology, and the arts, among other interests, and what he liked about Henry was his volubility as a conversationalist on any of these subjects. Fraenkel liked nothing better than to discuss his death-in-life theme while working into the conversation examples from obscure, erudite sources. With all the reading that Henry had done he was a fair match wherever Fraenkel chose to begin. Theorizing, analyzing, supposing, repudiating, the talks were never finished. Fraenkel gave Henry a place to sleep—a couch in the corner of his living room.

Henry, of course, agreed with Fraenkel that to struggle to get ahead, to get to the top, to acquire wealth and possessions, to fit the mold, was "to die" while one was still alive. "Active negation" was Fraenkel's term for avoiding such a death.

Fraenkel was slight of build, bony and thin. He had a heavy shock of wiry, black hair and a Mephistophelean goatee that brought his pale face to a sharp, black point. When indoors, he lived in a dressing gown. When he left the house he wore striped trousers and a frock coat. He was inflexible, proud, and penurious. Because of Fraenkel's monastic attitude toward food Henry could find little to eat in the house, and, when Fraenkel went out to eat he did not invite Henry to join him. Henry solved the problem by going through Fraenkel's pants pockets and helping himself to the loose change.

Fraenkel had now written *Werther's Younger Brother*, which he described as an approach to the understanding of spiritual death, and he was finishing a second book, *Bastard Death*, which had an exchange of letters between him and Henry as its foreword. It was as discursive and abstruse as any of their conversations. The book was published by Carrefour, a firm that Fraenkel owned in partnership with Walter Lowenfels, a poet friend.

Although Fraenkel's own style of writing was verbose and

pedantic, it was his advice that showed Henry how to write *Tropic of Cancer*. Many years later Henry admitted this. "Write the way you talk!" Fraenkel told him, explaining that the reason Henry had failed as a writer before was because he was writing as if he were someone else. When Henry talked with friends, relating some scene or event in which he had taken part, he always drew his listeners into the experience with him. His colorful, rushing way of speaking gave life to his words. "Write the way you talk!" Henry would never forget that advice.

He put aside his first and second drafts of *Tropic of Cancer*. He would hold back nothing; he would let "the naked, throbbing present" burst from him. The result was a chaotic and obscene book, and as he was writing it he knew it was unpublishable. Yet now he could write it no other way.

Fraenkel said that Carrefour would publish it if he let them have it anonymously. Henry had no intention of letting them have the book, knowing that the obscenities would become asterisks and that with so many pages full of them the book would be unreadable.

Before Fraenkel took a trip to China in the fall of 1933 he talked with Henry and Alfred Perlès about writing to one another letters on the death-in-life theme. Perlès was not interested but Henry was, and when Fraenkel said that Carrefour would publish the letters, Henry said the book's title should be *Hamlet*. "Hamlet," he said, "is the drama of man's inner duality, the drama of his swerving allegiance, his irresolution. . . . If there is any success in our endeavor it will be in laying the ghost, for Hamlet still stalks the streets."

Henry moved with Perlès to an inexpensive flat in Clichy, where he continued to write and rewrite *Tropic of Cancer*. At the same time he did other work, including short pieces that would later appear in *Black Spring*. He also kept on with the D. H. Lawrence book. Anaïs was usually at the flat, for now she and Henry were inseparable. When she read the third revision of *Tropic of Cancer*, she convinced him that it was ready for publication.

She found a literary agent for him, William Aspenwall Bradley, an American who was known to be favorable to new writers.

After reading the book, which he liked very much, he told Henry that, because of the subject matter, he had little hope of finding a publisher for it. However, he would try Jack Kahane, whose Obelisk Press published paperback books of a teasing, titillating, risqué variety, giving them erotic covers.

Kahane had published Frank Harris's notorious *My Life and Loves*, but he was unprepared for Henry's book. Nothing like it had ever been seen in print. Although he, like Bradley, was impressed with Henry's powerful style, he was reluctant to take the book. He did not want trouble with the police.

When Anaïs pleaded with him—and paid the six-hundred-dollar printing cost—he drew up a contract that gave Henry a 10 percent royalty on sales. He did not intend to advertise the book.

Anaïs and Henry worked together on a preface that would appear under her name. In introducing a book of this kind, which they expected to shock and confuse many of its readers, they wrote: "To regard a naked book such as this with the same critical eye that is turned upon even such diverse types as Lawrence, Breton, Joyce, and Celine is a mistake. Rather let us look at it with the eyes of a Patagonian for whom all that is sacred and taboo in our world is meaningless."

Kahane did not want to pay an artist to illustrate the book's cover and had his sixteen-year-old son Maurice draw a picture of a crab for it. He chose a crab because it is the zodiac's sign for Cancer. A supine figure of a nude woman clutched in the crab's claws was added.

Tropic of Cancer was published on September 1, 1934, and immediately Henry gave autographed copies to Anaïs and to all of his friends. He mailed one to Fraenkel in China, and in the letter that accompanied it he wrote, "These are good times for me. I move with the changing climate. I move with the sun and light. With the birds. With the wild flowers. Dear Fraenkel, I don't know what to say. I am so happy."

Tropic of Cancer has been described as a novel, but it is not a novel in the usual sense, nor is it strictly a narrative. It is a street scene, a burlesque show, a noisy, many-ringed circus. The contents follow no order or sequence. Events, character sketches, soliloquies, conversations, narration, marvelous descriptive passages that stand alone as prose poems, diatribes, caricatures, the wildest gaiety and humor, reveries, and confessions of excruciating despair all rush pell-mell at the reader in a torrent of rich, racing prose.

Swarms of characters move in and out of the pages, bringing with them their neuroses and eccentricities, vanities, and shabbiness. They leave behind them sweat and the scent of cheap perfume, boozy breath, semen, vomit, and blood. In the telling Henry omits nothing. Like the Seine's sweep through the city his Paris carries everything with it: passengers on pleasure craft, bargeloads of freight, the flotsam of the sewers, the floating scum of rubbish and debris, corpses, "the whole damned current of life."

For the most part these people were the expatriates of the twenties and thirties who were living in France because it was cheap to do so. They were writers, poets, and painters in varying degrees of pretense and success. Some were dilettantes and hangers-on. "The rustling presence of whores" was everywhere within this fugitive fellowship.

Henry sent a copy of the book to Ezra Pound, who lived in Rapallo, Italy. Henry had never met Pound nor read his poetry, but he knew that he was admired in literary circles, and he wanted him to read his book. Pound read it and then handed it over to a young friend who was visiting him, saying, "Here's a dirty book that's really worth reading." The visitor was James Laughlin, who was so interested in Henry's writing ability that he made a note of his name and a few years later became his American publisher. Pound also brought the book to the attention of a friend of his in London, T. S. Eliot, an editor with the publishing house of Faber and Faber.

Little notice was paid to the book in Paris. A few dozen copies were sold in shops where it was necessary to demand a copy before one was nervously produced. The then-exorbitant price of fifty francs ($2.50) was also a drawback.

Only two magazines carried reviews. One was written by Henry's friend, the young novelist Raymond Queneau, who reviewed the book for *Nouvelle Revue Française*. The other was written by Blaise Cendrars, a popular writer in France, who looked up Miller before he wrote his review for *Orbes*.

The United States and England refused to allow the book through customs. Nevertheless, copies got into the hands of writers, critics, and editors. Aldous Huxley wrote Henry to tell him that his book "made him feel swallowed to an extent that no El Greco could ever do." T. S. Eliot wrote him to say that he believed *Tropic of Cancer* to be a better book than *Lady Chatterley's Lover*. England's leading literary critic, Herbert Read, praised the "vivid indignation" and the lyricism of the writing in a column he wrote for the *New English Weekly*. A young author, George Orwell, whose *Down and Out in Paris and London* had recently been published, and who wrote book reviews for the same weekly, stated that Miller was more successful in his book than Joyce had been in *Ulysses*, in that "*Tropic of Cancer* is not complicated by feelings of horror and repentance."

Anaïs surprised him by renting the second floor of Fraenkel's house for him to have as his own studio. He had hardly moved in when she told him that she was leaving soon to go to New York to help Rank open a practice there. After she was gone Henry was so unhappy in his letters to her that she sent him the money for a steamship ticket so that he could join her.

4

I do not have to look in my vest pocket to find my
soul; it is there all the time, bumping against my ribs,
swelling, inflated with song.

Black Spring

Henry returned to Paris after a few months, but Anaïs called
him back, this time to assist her in conducting psychoanalysis with
patients that Rank turned over to her. It seemed to her a good way
for Henry to earn a living. He worked at it for a few months, and,
though he later wrote how easy it was to be a success as a psychoanalyst, he was soon bored and returned to Paris. He had with him
a book-length "letter" addressed to Perlès that he called "Aller
Retour New York." It was a long, rambling report intended to
give Perlès "a good clear picture of America."

In it he ridiculed, among other things, the Empire State
Building, Gypsy Rose Lee, Sophie Tucker, the Radio City Music
Hall chorines, the new young whores with strips of monkey fur
or skunk slung around their necks, red and green traffic lights,
electric-eye doors that opened when he stepped on a treadle, Ex-
Lax, Alka-Seltzer, and life in the suburbs. New York City itself
was colossal, monotonous, ugly, and covered with bird lime. He
wrote, "I would still be leading a dog's life if I had to depend on
America for inspiration. . . . New York crushes you."

June had by now divorced him, but seeing their old haunts
and feeling again the stings he had endured while they were married did not put him in a warm frame of mind. He avoided visiting
his parents, and he could not find the friends he had known in the
past.

At home now, in Paris, he composed another letter, this one as a joke, which he addressed "to all and sundry" and called "What Are You Going to Do About Alf?" "Alf" was Alfred Perlès. Henry asked each of the letter's recipients to send him twenty-five francs ($1.25) a week for the next six months so that he could see that Perlès quit his job at the *Tribune* and went to Ibiza to finish writing his novel. "Think of it in this light: 25 francs a week from you would enable Alf to live like a prince in Ibiza. The point is, how long are we to keep him going? Three months, six months, a year? I should say, roughly, somewhere from three to six months. In that time Alf ought to complete the novel which he has begun. That is, if he's the genius I take him to be. If he's not then the hell with him! Let him rot in Ibiza!"

He sent the letter to T. S. Eliot, Aldous Huxley, Ezra Pound, and Jean Cocteau among others, but neither they nor anyone else sent the requested francs. When word of the cheeky letter got around and people began asking for copies of it, he had it printed and sold it for five francs. It was bought as a piece of tomfoolery.

The Ibiza idea was entirely Miller's. Perlès had never intended to quit his job and go to Ibiza for any reason. Henry admitted that, had he received any money, he would have kept it for himself.

Pound sent him a postcard asking if he had ever thought of money, what makes it, and how it gets that way. In answer he wrote a fifty-page letter addressed to Pound, which he called "Money and How It Gets That Way." He wrote that, until Pound had put the subject to him, he had never thought of it, but since then he had thought about it "night and day."

After Anaïs returned to Paris, she and Henry began working on a Siana (*Anaïs* spelled backwards) series of books, which she would finance and Obelisk would publish. *Aller Retour New York* was the first book to come out, followed shortly afterward by one of hers, *The House of Incest.*

At this time *Tropic of Cancer* was having brisk sales, much to Kahane's surprise. He brought out a second printing and began paying Henry a thousand francs a month (fifty dollars) in royalties. This was plenty for him to get by on. For the first time in his life, Henry was earning a living from his writing.

He continued to exchange lengthy *Hamlet* letters with Fraenkel while also writing short pieces about his father's tailor shop, his pleasure in bicycling around Paris and its suburbs, public urinals, painting watercolors. Now he planned to put them together in a book he thought of calling "Tropic of Capricorn." By the time he showed it to Kahane, he had titled it *Black Spring*. Obelisk published *Black Spring* in June 1936. It was dedicated to Anaïs.

Black Spring is a very different book from *Tropic of Cancer*. Instead of the exuberant flow and "crazy jig" of the first book, it is structured into ten separate parts and is a showpiece of Miller's strongest talents. He wanted to please Anaïs, to show her that he was indeed more than an outrageous raconteur. It is not a book to be scanned for its shock effects, although all of the forbidden words can be found in it. And they were found because the book was immediately banned by the United States and England.

He opened the book with material that he had revised from his "Dream Book," the record of dreams that had taken him back to his boyhood in Brooklyn. The Fourteenth Ward had provided him with a rich mixture of sights, sounds, smells, and experiences that as an impressionable child he had absorbed in all its abundant detail. It was a rough, noisy neighborhood, raw, vigorous, at full stir with a life of its own. He had loved it and would never forget it. Now, at the age of forty-four, thinking about his boyhood chums, the neighbors, the passing crowd of misfits, imbeciles, drunks, hangers-on, and others, he saw them through a veil of nostalgia. Describing it, he slipped into poetry:

> We live in the mind, in ideas, in fragments. We no longer drink in the wild outer music of the streets—we *remember* only. . . . If we are stirred by a fat bust it is the fat bust of a whore who bent over on a rainy night and showed us for the first time the wonder of the great milky globes; if we are stirred by the reflections on a wet pavement it is because at the age of seven we were suddenly speared by a premonition of the life to come as we stared unthinkingly into that bright, liquid mirror of the street. If the sight of a swinging door intrigues us it is the memory of a summer's evening when all the doors were swinging softly and where the light bent

down to caress the shadow there were golden calves and lace and glittering parasols and through the chinks in the swinging door, like fine sand sifting through a bed of rubies, there drifted the music and the incense of gorgeous unknown bodies.

The second piece is filled with Miller's anger toward "the whole modern world." Into the vitriol he stirred dollops of hellfire and prophecy, serving it up in an oracular style.

"A Saturday Afternoon" is the title of the third piece. Here he is in Paris, riding his bike on a Saturday afternoon and as he bumps along over the cobblestones he remembers how he hated studying Virgil and Goethe when he was a schoolboy. Then he recalls the books that he really liked to read, ranging from *Robinson Crusoe* to *Leaves of Grass*.

A stop at a street urinal starts him off on pages about urinals, ones he has known in Paris, Carcassonne, and Avignon. With each of these scenes he includes the sights and sounds of the neighborhood or immediate countryside. He describes the people who live nearby, and he adds a little local scenery. The most colorful of these vignettes takes place at a urinal outside the old papal palace in Avignon where, inside, he imagines scenes of the long-ago past when the walls were covered with frescoes "of hunting, fishing, gaming, of falcons and dogs and women and flashing fish." He smells whole animals roasting on the spit, and he sees a Pope sitting at a writing table with a tankard at his elbow and a fat wench on his knee.

"The Angel Is My Watermark!," the fourth piece, is Miller at his best as a writer of humor. It is a stroke-by-stroke description of a man trying to paint a horse that, because of his lack of skill, threatens to turn into a landscape, a cemetery, a volcano, or various other subjects as he struggles with the drawing and the application of paint. He fights off Crusaders and penguins, he brings in Michelangelo, Mahomet, Turner, the New York Bowery, the Twenty-third Psalm, Seminole Indians, and the tomb of Belshazzar, to name a few of the appearances in this lunatic episode.

Henry had been experimenting with watercolors off and on for the past twenty years, taking suggestions from his artist friends and learning something of the technique. He did not claim any proficiency in the art. This piece satirized his attempts to paint recognizable subjects.

In "The Tailor Shop" he wrote with tenderness and great affection about his drink-addicted father and about his father's cronies and the oddball customers who came into the shop. These thoughts led him to other memories of his childhood, to scenes with his family and relatives. In one he is riding on a streetcar with his Tante Melia, who is on her way to being locked up in an insane asylum. Henry's mother had forced him to take her there and Tante Melia "went with him for a ride" because he was the only one she trusted. The memory scalds him.

A piece that he called "Jabberwhorl Cronstadt" is a caricature of Walter Lowenfels, who, besides writing poetry and looking after business affairs at Carrefour, carried on a variety of other enterprises including an importing business and a house-rental service. Henry wrote that Jabberwhorl Cronstadt's nameplate beside the bell-pull at his door read: "poet, musician, herbologist, weather man, linguist, oceanographer, old clothes, colloids." When he read *Black Spring*, Lowenfels was not amused.

Miller went again to his "Dream Book" for a nightmare episode that he described as a "Coney Island of the mind" and that he titled "Into the Night Life . . . ," taking the phrase from Freud, who had used it in *The Interpretation of Dreams*. Freud's complete sentence is "Into the night life seems to be exiled what once ruled during the day."

The remaining essays are bitter monologues about himself as a young man, when he saw himself as a misfit "in the hideousness of a life in which I had no part." Returning to the scenes of his early life, he writes: "Sitting before the house in which I was born I feel absolutely unique. I belong to an orchestra for which no symphonies have ever been written. Everything is in the wrong key."

Of "the city" he writes: "The crowd moves compact, elbow to elbow, each member of the great herd driven by loneliness, breast to breast towards the wall of self, frustrate, isolate, sardine upon sardine, all seeking the universal can-opener."

These sour meditations, which he titled "Walking Up and Down in China," "Burlesk," and "Megalopolitan Maniac," mirror his insecurities and his feelings of standing apart from others in spite of his outward show of bonhomie.

In *Black Spring* the critics saw that Miller was a master of many styles. Dialogue, characterization, satire, comedy, allegory, drama, reverie—he was in full command of them all. Paul Rosenfeld wrote in the *Saturday Review of Literature:* "Surely the largest force on the horizon of American letters: Henry Miller of Paris." H. L. Mencken wrote: "His is one of the most beautiful prose styles today." The first edition was soon sold out, and Kahane printed a second.

Publishers in New York and London asked to bring out an expurgated edition, and they wanted to see new work of his. He refused to allow then to bowdlerize *Black Spring* but he gathered together another collection of short pieces to send them. Most of these had been published in literary quarterlies, and *Scenario: A Film with Sound,* a surrealist play inspired by Anaïs's *House of Incest,* had been published by Obelisk.

The collection included an angry attack on the American way of life; his judgment of certain films and of filmmaking; an open letter to surrealists; a comparison of the works of Joyce, Proust, and Lawrence; and a paean to Anaïs's as-yet-unpublished diary. She was then beginning the fiftieth volume. In the essay "Un Etre Etoilique," he wrote that her diary would eventually take its place beside the revelations of St. Augustine, Petronius, Abelard, Rousseau, Proust, and others. The essay had been published in *Criterion* and afterward printed as a booklet at Henry's expense. "Etoilique" is a word that Anaïs invented for herself. "We have *lunatique* (moonstruck), why not *etoilique* (starstruck)?"

Henry wanted to see all of this work in permanent form as a book. He titled it *Max and the White Phagocytes.* (Phagocytes are cells that ingest other cells circulating in the human bloodstream.) A story about Max, a beggar on the streets of Paris, was the only new work.

Henry knew the real-life Max and always tried to avoid running into him, but one day he relented and took Max home. At that time Henry was living with Fraenkel. He thought that since both Fraenkel and Max were Jews, Fraenkel would do something to help him—give him money, anyway. Max had already confided in Henry that he wanted to go to Argentina, and if he could get there he would become "a new man" and would no longer need to beg on the streets. Henry didn't believe him because he was sure that Max liked his life as it was. He just wanted to see if Fraenkel would believe him and turn over the necessary thousand francs. Fraenkel did not give him the money.

So Henry saw to it that Max took a bath, and then he gave him clean underwear and a suit of clothes that had been given to him but was too large. He took him to a café for a meal, and left him.

Henry worked these generally unpleasant details into a story, but before sending off the book, he added two more sketches in a brighter mood. One was about his friend the artist Hans Reichel, who had a "cosmological eye." The other was about a Hungarian friend, Brassai, a photographer. Finally, for good measure, he included an episode from *Tropic of Cancer*.

No publisher accepted the book. They could find nothing in it that readers wanted from Henry Miller. He was puzzled and angry for a time, but it did not keep him away from his typewriter. He turned again to writing about his personal life, tearing himself wide open with painful confessions.

The five years that he had spent as an employment manager for Western Union, "The Cosmodemonic Telegraph Company of North America," provided blistering experiences. Writing of his boyhood, he picked random reminiscences of one distressful incident or another. He described numerous sexual encounters. In spite of their lusty details, reading some of them is like watching a slapstick bit in an old-time, two-reel silent movie. Mixed up, speeded up, and daffy.

The years with June had been the most traumatic of his life, and once again he tried to write what it was like in the "black hole" of their life together, where "in the sky above us there hung the huge black star which never twinkled." His memories of her were interspersed with the other chapters. Finally, "in the tomb which is my memory I see her buried now, the one I loved better than all else, better than the world, better than God, better than my own flesh and blood. I see her festering there in that bloody wound of love."

Occasionally a pleasant memory took over that freed him from June. He remembered a time when he was a child playing the piano on a Sunday morning, working the pedals with his bare feet:

> Towards eleven or so the folks used to rap on the wall of my bedroom for me to come and play for them. I would dance into the room like the Fratellini Brothers, so full of flame and feathers that I could hoist myself like a derrick to the topmost limb of the tree of heaven. . . . What a velocity I would work up, riveted to the piano stool! . . . I used to take a fist-full of chords and crash the piano from one end to the other. . . . the greater my euphoria the more tranquil the folks became. Even my sister who was dippy became calm and composed. The neighbors used to stand outside the window and listen, and now and then I would hear a burst of applause, and then bang, zip! Like a rocket I was off again.

5

*Love is something that brings two people together.
What is to hold them together they never ask
themselves. Love has to take care of itself, and usually
does, by dying a natural death.*

The World of Sex

During the summer of 1937, Henry had a visit from a young English novelist, Lawrence Durrell. The two men had been corresponding for more than a year, ever since Durrell had come upon a copy of *Tropic of Cancer,* had admired the exuberance and power of the writing, and had written Henry to tell him so. Durrell and his wife Nancy Myers lived in Greece on the island of Corfu and were in Paris on vacation when they called at Henry's Villa Seurat studio. His warm welcome encouraged them to stay on. They found his circle of friends so congenial that they remained for a year and a half.

Besides Anaïs and Perlès, who were closest to him, Henry had many more friends who visited him in his studio at number 18. Among them were Raymond Queneau, Hans Reichel, Brassai, the astrologer Conrad Moricand, a young Chinese poet Tcheou Nien-Sien, William Saroyan, the painter Hilaire Hiler, Betty· Ryan, who was an American heiress taking painting lessons from Reichel, and David Edgar. Fraenkel was back from China and living on the first floor of his house. His *femme de charge* was Daphne Moschos, who, besides keeping house for him, assisted him in the operation of Carrefour Press.

Betty Ryan was the granddaughter of Thomas Fortune Ryan, whose dealings in streetcar lines, insurance, tobacco, gold, and Congo diamonds provided his heirs with a $200-million legacy.

Her background, so different from that of her neighbors , did not keep them from feeling that she was one of them. She had great charm, and she was a generous dinner hostess. She always kept a well-stocked bar.

Edgar was slightly unbalanced, but he had an innocent nature and he was cheerful. Henry was always glad to see him, hoping that he would open up with one of his dissertations, which he delivered with great earnestness, although little that he said made sense. Among his favorite topics were interplanetary forces and their effect upon vegetable matter; Oriental wisdom; alchemy; Zen Buddhism; and the lost continent of Atlantis. It was impossible to follow his train of thought, especially when he invented words as he went along.

Not all of Henry's friends lived on rue Villa Seurat, but the others were only a few minutes' walk away.

There was talk of bringing out a Villa Seurat series of books. Anaïs had a new one, *Winter of Artifice*. *Max and the White Phagocytes* was still waiting for a publisher. Durrell had finished a second novel, *The Black Book*. When Nancy offered to pay Kahane for the printing costs, the three books were published and, in gratitude, Anaïs had Durrell's manuscript bound in red buckram and leather.

Henry dedicated *Max* "To Betty Ryan securely enthroned in her own cathedral of light and space."

Another group venture was the publishing of a monthly magazine, one that had unexpectedly fallen into the hands of Perlès. It was a small publication put out by the American Golf Club of France, and it was called *The Booster*. Perlès had taken the job of editing it after the *Chicago Tribune* had closed its Paris bureau and left him without work. Elmer Prather was the club's president and owner of *The Booster*. Suddenly, in the summer of 1938, he tired of the chores connected with its publication and gave the thing to Perlès. All Perlès was asked to do was to keep up the social notes. Otherwise, as the new owner, the contents were up to him.

"You're a writer, aren't you?" Prather asked. "You have writer friends, haven't you? Get them to contribute. Make it something really good." Perlès was also reminded to keep up the advertisements, but he had no intention of selling ads.

The Booster was little more than a few pages of social notes contributed by club members and some sports news copied from the Paris newspapers. The remaining space was filled with ads for golf equipment, golf clothes, liquor, cigarettes, steamship travel, cosmetics, gifts, and food specialties. Only the club's five hundred members read it.

When Perlès hurried to Henry's place to tell him the news he found the Durrells already there busy with preparations for dinner, and he waited until the meal was over before saying anything. He was disappointed when Henry did not share his enthusiasm. "But we can do whatever we want with it. It'll be ours. We can publish our work," insisted Perlès.

The chance to publish whatever they wanted appealed to Durrell. He mentioned wacky stuff that would put life into the old *Booster*. To him it was an opportunity too good to miss. Finally Henry agreed.

They sat around the table having fun naming the editorial staff. Perlès agreed to take over as managing editor while Miller, Durrell, and Saroyan would be the literary editors. Anaïs was to be society editor. Durrell, writing under the name of Charles Norden, would write up sports and, as Patrick Evans, be the turf editor as well. Henry took on the role of editor of men's fashions, relishing what he would write as the Earl of Selvage.

They made Fraenkel editor of metaphysics and metempsychosis and gave Lowenfels "butter news." Their Chinese friend Nien-Sien was to head the Oriental department. Reichel was to be editor of aquarelles and gouaches, Brassai was to be photography editor, and Hilaire Hiler was made travel editor. Edgar was named the publicity director. Nancy would be art editor, and one of her paintings would be reproduced on the cover of the first issue, which was planned for September 1. The names of the editorial staff would run on the first page.

Henry, Anaïs, and Perlès supplied the articles and fiction for the September issue. Two were written in French, for this was to be a bilingual publication. "Charles Norden" included in his sports comments the fact that Gene Tunney was a "profoundly Chinese boxer." As promised, Perlès ran several pages of social notes about club members. Nien-Sien wrote a poem in Chinese characters that took up all the space on the back cover.

A page of notes on contributors stated that Nancy Myers was the wife of both Charles Norden and Lawrence Durrell, describing the first as an English songwriter and the second as a Tibetan writer; also that Patrick Evans was "the drunken son of a drunken horse dealer and a poet when sober."

Some club members enjoyed the gags and flippancy, while others were not so sure and hesitated about sending in their social notes for the next issue. "By all means do," urged Perlès, thinking to himself that there was nothing like club notes to add a touch of surrealism.

Prather was baffled. He told Perlès to "soft-pedal it." Lowenfels wrote Perlès an angry letter over the use of "his good name" in connection with the magazine's "butter news," whatever was meant by that.

By the time the October issue came out, Prather was furious. He wrote Perlès a letter stating the club's dissociation from *The Booster*, and demanded that Perlès publish the letter in the next issue, making it clear that the club was blameless for the magazine's contents. Perlès published the letter.

What was so objectionable to Prather was the reprinting of an Eskimo legend that was part of an anthology collected in Greenland in 1884. Perlès and the others considered it "an innocent little prose poem." It was about a young girl into whom an old man disappears by way of her vagina while he is making love to her.

Following explicit details, the legend ends with "at last he gave a great shout and vanished in her completely. . . . In the morning the beautiful girl came out of the igloo to make water . . . and the skeleton of Nukarpiartetak came out." This was too much for Elmer Prather. It didn't matter that the rest of the issue was blameless with Durrell's poetry, essays by Saroyan, Anaïs, and Perlès, and the Earl of Selvage's fashion nonsense.

There were no club notes in the third issue, for none were sent in. Again Anaïs, Henry, Saroyan, Perlès, and Durrell were among the contributors. In a suddenly serious mood, seeing that the war was likely to be fought soon in France, Henry's essay was a bitter "Epilogue to Black Spring." He wrote: "If the war comes it will be a carnage . . . a procrastinated orgy of annihilation in which everything will be mopped up clean. There will come a bright, jolly morning when suddenly the celluloid sky will fall and the whole living world will swab its throat with a last mouth-wash of corrosive sublimate. Aye, it will come—and there will not even be time to say Amen! The sky will fall and bury us flat as pancakes."

The combined December-January "Air-Conditioned Womb Number" was the fourth and final issue of *The Booster.* The contents were not uterine, as might have been expected. Anaïs wrote about her diary as a "paper womb," and Saroyan wrote about his birthplace, Fresno, California. Durrell's piece was a fantasy about the afterlife of his "Aunt Prudence" traveling on the River Styx in an air-conditioned canoe. Henry's article was not much different from one of his *Hamlet* letters, although it was entitled "The Enormous Womb."

The group had already announced the publication of what they called *Booster Broadside,* each a booklet of work by Miller, Perlès, Fraenkel, and Durrell. *Money and How It Gets That Way* had come out in January.

When Prather threatened legal action if Perlès persisted in calling the magazine *The Booster,* the name was changed to *Delta.* Its first issue came out in April 1938 and was a poetry number with contributions from Dylan Thomas, Kay Boyle, Nicholas Moore, Fraenkel, Durrell, and others.

The third issue of *Delta,* and its last, was a Christmas "Peace and Dismemberment Number with Jitterbug Shag Requiem." The cover had a black funereal border.

In 1938, *Tropic of Cancer* went into a third printing and was also being translated for a Czech edition to be published in Prague with a cover by Henri Matisse. Critics had said that the book's tribute to the art of Matisse was among its most lyrical passages and showed Henry's sensitive perception of the artist's achievements.

As the war progressed and the Germans drew closer to Paris, many foreigners left the city. The Durrells were home in Corfu, Perlès was in London, and Fraenkel was in Ibiza. Knowing that it was only a matter of time before he, too, must leave, Henry sorted through his manuscripts and notebooks and stored a trunkful of them outside Paris where he thought they would be safe until after the war. He expected to return.

The troubled times did not keep Kahane from publishing another Miller book, his sixth, in February 1939. Henry had given it the title he had been saving, *Tropic of Capricorn*. The book's background is New York, and again Henry used a kaleidoscope technique in which episodes shift, slide into each other, disappear, and reform in coalescent patterns as the part of the past that he wishes to recall flashes by. In the sections about June, the words seethe with rancor and self-abasement. "She was double-barreled, like a shot-gun, a female bull with an acetylene torch in her womb. . . . I remember everything, but like a dummy on the lap of a ventriloquist. . . . I was better than a ventriloquist's dummy because I could act without being violently jerked by the strings . . . I learned to take my cue; no matter how swift the metamorphosis I was always there on her lap . . . the lap of laps, the lip of lips, tip to tip, feather to feather, the yolk in the egg, the pearl in the oyster, a cancer clutch, a tincture of sperm and cantherides." Then he remembered that "now and then we had fits of laughter, crazy, batrachian laughter which made the neighbors shudder."

He dedicated the book to her, not using her name but simply writing "To Her."

It is in this book that he describes how he first became interested in what he called "automatic writing." It was a new kind of writing for him, in which word associations came to him involuntarily. "It was just about this time that the Dadaists were in full swing, to be followed shortly after by the Surrealists. I never heard of either group until some ten years later. I never read a French book and I never had a French idea. I was perhaps the unique Dadaist in America and I didn't know it."

Tropic of Capricorn was immediately banned by the United States and England.

Henry's first book published in the United States also came out in 1939 when New Directions took *Max and the White Phagocytes,* changing the title to *The Cosmological Eye.* This was the title of a sketch about the painter Hans Reichel that was in the original book. New Directions did not use the sketch, and the book's contents were slightly different, with selections added from *Black*

Spring and other pieces that had been published in magazines. The edition was a small one of two thousand copies and Henry was given a two-hundred-dollar advance on the royalties.

In June 1939, Carrefour published the first 234 pages of the *Hamlet* letters exchanged between Fraenkel and Henry. That month Henry left Paris for the south of France to spend a few weeks with friends before leaving the country, and Anaïs joined him in Aix-en-Provence for a last good-bye. He had given up hope of marrying her for she would not leave Hugo and financial security.

Obelisk published fourth and fifth editions of *Tropic of Cancer* while Henry was still in France.

That year Victor Gollanz in London published a book of George Orwell's literary criticism. A major part of the book was about *Tropic of Cancer* and *Black Spring*. What Orwell found exceptional about Henry's writing was the lingering effect it had upon him, how he continued to recall many of the details long after he had put the book down. Passages rooted themselves in his memory.

Henry's ability to communicate with his readers had also impressed Orwell: "It is as though you could hear a voice speaking to you, a friendly American voice, with no humbug in it, no moral purpose, merely an implicit assumption that we are all alike. For a moment you have got away from the lies and simplifications, the stylised, marionette-like quality of ordinary fiction, even quite good fiction, and are dealing with the recognisable experiences of human beings."

Of the style he wrote, "Granted their utter worthlessness as social types, the drunks and dead-beats of the cafés are handled with a feeling for character and a mastery of technique that are unapproachable in any recent novel. . . . the prose is astonishing."

Orwell had not finished writing the book in 1936 when civil war broke out in Spain. He set the book aside in order to go there and fight on the side of the republic. En route he stopped in Paris to look up Henry in the Villa Seurat.

The two men did not discuss Henry's work because almost immediately they took sides on the justification for war, and the argument continued during the rest of the afternoon. For Orwell there was no question of whether or not to fight in a just cause, even if one had to sacrifice one's life. Henry believed that all war was unnecessary and that to prove by force of arms that one side or the other was right or wrong contributed nothing to the understanding of the meaning of civilization. He was not a coward. He said he was willing to be shot for his refusal to bear arms, his refusal to kill in cold blood for whatever reason.

Sometime later Orwell finished his book, and, while he did not delete the pages he had written about Henry's work, he now felt the need to add his opinion of the man. He began by pointing out that Western civilization was likely to be torn to pieces by the war and that in the future writers would have to adopt a passive attitude toward totalitarianism if they hoped to be published. He wrote that Henry had already shown this passiveness, this acceptance of things as they are, and that he, Orwell, believed that passiveness, because it was nonpolitical, was amoral. "To say 'I accept' in an age like our own is to say that you accept concentration camps, rubber truncheons, Hitler, Stalin, bombs, aeroplanes, tinned food, submarines, spies, provocateurs, press-censorship, secret prisons, aspirins, Hollywood films and political murders. Not only *those* things, of course, but those things among others. And on the whole this is Henry Miller's attitude." To Orwell, Henry was in the belly of the whale. He titled his book *Inside the Whale.*

This was Henry's phrase, used many times in his books, but it was not original with him either. He took it from Aldous Huxley, who had written that all of the people in El Greco's paintings looked as if they were inside the bellies of whales. Orwell saw this visceral position as "a womb big enough for an adult . . . yards of blubber between yourself and reality."

Henry was in Marseilles in mid July 1939, expecting to board a ship for the United States. Meanwhile, passage on a Greek ship bound for Piraeus became available and, because the Durrells had urged him to come to Corfu to wait out the war with them, he sailed for Greece on July 14. Two months later his income stopped. Jack Kahane had dropped dead, and when his son wrote Henry about it he did not enclose the usual thousand francs.

6

What sustained me more than anything else during my residence abroad was the belief that I would never be obliged to return to America.

Sunday After the War

Henry had not been in Greece six months when the American consul ordered all American civilians to leave that country. A cargo ship brought him back to New York, where he arrived in January 1940. He had about ten dollars on him, and his heart was as empty as his pockets. Anaïs had preceded him and was settled in Greenwich Village with her husband. Henry had written her that he was arriving on the *Exochorda* and begged her to meet the boat. But she was not there. When he saw her later, she explained that she had been ill that day and was unable to meet him.

Hugo Guiler, now assistant vice-president in the bank's New York office, was devoting his spare time to the study of copper engraving. He had never had time for this in Paris. Later, with achievement in the art, he would drop his last name and become Ian Hugo.

The small second-floor apartment where Anaïs and Hugo lived was far different from their house and garden in Louveciennes, which, at times, Henry had regarded as a second home. In New York he stayed away.

His parents, who were still living in Brooklyn, were only a subway-ride away, but he could not bring himself to see them. He especially dreaded to face his mother, remembering how she had scorned his efforts as a writer, predicting that he would never make a living at it. "Get a job!" she had nagged. She didn't care what kind of job it was, so long as he wasn't wasting his time writing. Neither of his parents had read his books. They had no idea of what he had accomplished. When he came home he knew that all his mother would see was that, as usual, he was broke.

He did want to see his father, having come to care deeply for him over the years. But he was determined not to go home empty-handed. He knew that they were having a hard time, somehow managing to get along on very little money. In Paris he had received pathetic letters from his father telling him how things were at home and asking him to send any money that he could spare. He had sent them money when he had it. The worst of it was that his father was terminally ill with cancer. Henry had not expected to see him alive.

While putting off the family reunion, he went down to Virginia to visit an old friend, the painter Emil Schnellock, who was teaching art at Mary Washington College for Women in Fredericksburg. They had known each other since boyhood, when they attended the same elementary school. From Paris, Henry had written him often, long letters about what he was doing, his new friends, the books he was reading, about his hopes and dreams, his inner thoughts. He had often enclosed carbons of his writings. Now their visit helped him to get his bearings and to plan ahead. He also returned to New York with some much-needed money.

In New York he took his manuscripts to dealers, hoping they could sell something to collectors. When the first fifty dollars came to him, he spent it on gifts for the family and went home. The gifts he had brought them from Paris had been surrendered to customs when Henry did not have the money to pay the duty.

Approaching the house, "I saw my father sitting in the armchair by the window. The sight of him sitting there, waiting for me, gave me a terrible pang. It was as though he had been sitting there waiting all these years. I felt at once like a criminal, like a murderer."

The family met him at the door and greeted him warmly. They were truly glad to see him, and it was soon evident that they expected him to stay with them now that he was back. He knew that he couldn't live at home, but he promised to visit them often, which he did, coming almost every afternoon for the next month or so to sit with his father and listen to the old man talk. His father brought him up to date on everything that had happened in the neighborhood during the last ten years.

During these visits he also discovered that his mother always put off his father's visits to the doctor for the necessary irrigation treatment, waiting until his pain was unbearable and she simply had to take him. She did this to save money. "It's five dollars a crack, you know," his father explained.

Another of her economies was to deprive him of a package of cigarettes every day. "By God, Henry, I have to do something to while away the time, don't I? Of course, it means fifteen cents a day . . ."

Aside from the warm relationship with his father, the visits were an ordeal for Henry. His mother's pitiless remarks about his father's illness and incapacities, about which she felt no embarrassment in expressing in his presence, enraged Henry. His angry replies as she whined about the extra work and the need to deprive herself and Lauretta of this and that in order to economize left a sour taste in his mouth. In his view, she was implying that the only real economy ahead was for his father to die.

Whenever Henry slipped his father a dollar or two for cigarettes, he had to give it to him when his mother was not around. "Better not to let them know you gave me anything—they'll take it away from me. They say I don't need money."

His mother put Lauretta through the same treadmill of overwork as she did herself, and most of it, as Henry observed, was unnecessary and done only to have more to complain about. Lauretta's inane chatter and inappropriate interruptions of every conversation made the arguments and emotional scenes unnerving.

While his father was the subject of most of these scenes, his mother did not overlook Henry, letting him know what she thought of him as a writer. "Can't you write something like *Gone With the Wind* and make some money?" she shot at him.

Henry took a suitcase filled with work to an agent. Some of it was new writing that he had finished in Paris before he left, and some of it had been published in various of the "little" magazines.

He suggested that one or two books could be brought out from these sketches and essays. The agent tried but was unable to sell even one piece.

Henry finally appealed to James Laughlin. Although *The Cosmological Eye*, in spite of good reviews, had not yet earned the two hundred dollars that had been advanced to him on royalties, Laughlin looked over the work and selected eighteen pieces for a book to be titled *The Wisdom of the Heart.* He gave Henry another two-hundred-dollar advance. When Henry gave the money to his mother, she was at first reluctant to take it. She thought he had stolen it.

At that time he was living in the spacious Manhattan apartment of Caresse Crosby on East Fifty-fourth Street. He had known her in Paris, where she and her husband, the poet Harry Crosby, had founded the avant-garde Black Sun Press in 1927. Henry's work had not appeared in any of their *Portfolio* publications, but he and Caresse had a friendly relationship. Now, when he went to her with his story of bad luck with New York publishers, she invited him to take up residence in her apartment. She was often in Washington, D.C., which was now headquarters for the Black Sun Press, and she also had another residence, a large estate in Bowling Green, Virginia. In New York Henry could work undisturbed.

During the few months that he lived in the apartment, he wrote *The World of Sex,* in which he explained why he had put so much sex into his books: "When I think of sex I think of it as a universe, part of which has been explored, but the greater part unknown, mysterious, possibly forever unknowable. . . ."

He wrote: "From the very beginning I took an abnormal interest in the fauna and flora of this sexual world which I had chosen to inhabit." He described some of his discoveries and added:

> When I got to Paris some years later the sexual side of life began to assume another character for me. . . . in Paris . . . sex is in the air. Sex is everywhere, in everything, and it's all quite natural, quite gay, quite innocent, I might say. You can have a woman for the price of a meal, or if you are well off you can take

her on after a meal, like a liqueur. Or if you are bored you can drop into a bordello and have a chat with a naked woman over a glass of beer. . . .

Some take it as a tonic, some take it tragically, some take it flippantly, some take it fearfully. It is an algebraic symbol, the x which is equal to anything you choose to make it equal. But in this it is like everything in life—a person, a thing, an event, a relationship. Everything depends on the view which is taken. . . . If there is something wrong with our attitude towards sex you may be sure there is something wrong with our attitude towards bread, towards money, towards work, towards play, towards everything. One can't enjoy a good sexual life if his attitude is faulty in other things.

It was April 1940 when he finished elaborating on these themes and brought the book to a close. Then he looked through his notes on Greece in order to prepare another book, which would be about the few months he had spent in that country and would be called *The Colossus of Maroussi.* Finally he went down to Bowling Green where Caresse's estate was open to resident writers and artists in need of seclusion and hospitality. When he arrived, he found Salvador Dalí and his wife Gala already settled in.

In Henry's "Dream Book" there are several pages copied from the writings of the surrealists, Dalí among them. One of Dalí's phrases that Henry thought had unusual power was "the numerous species of animals in heat upon the backs of which were painted famous lakes and other kinds of twilight." It was "other kinds of twilight" that especially pleased him. He had seen the film *Un Chien andalou,* which was the work of Luis Buñuel and Dalí, and it was to prove to himself that he could write surrealism as well as anyone that he had written *Scenario: A Film with Sound* in 1937.

Another surrealist whom he admired was the poet Paul Eluard. He filled a notebook with metaphors that he copied from Eluard. From time to time he was tempted to use one in the columns he wrote for the *Tribune* under the name of his friend Wambly Bald. He didn't, lest someone recognize it.

However, he did not hesitate to use a phrase of Dalí's in *Black Spring.* The phrase "The post-mechanical open street where the most beautiful and hallucinating iron vegetation" is on the first page of the book in quotations, but it is not identified.

Dalí had never heard of *Black Spring* or of Henry Miller. When the two men met at Bowling Green, it was a moment of instantaneous fire that smoldered fitfully for the next three months. Their personalities were wholly antagonistic.

There were others living and working at Bowling Green when Henry and the Dalís were in residence, and everyone found out soon enough that the Dalís did not wish to make friends. Gala, in flutters of protective supervision, made it clear that they were not to be annoyed by interruptions. Consequently, they were avoided as much as possible.

Henry stayed on until fall, completing *The Colossus of Maroussi, Quiet Days in Clichy,* and the first hundred pages of a new book about himself and June that he planned to call *The Rosy Crucifixion.* The chatter of his typewriter was seldom silenced except for meals and sleep.

When he returned to New York, he gave *The Colossus of Maroussi* to an agent who offered it to one publisher after another, a dozen in all, before he gave up. Was it a travel book about Greece? No. Was it a novel? No. Was it a biography of the "colossus" of the book's title? No. It is a book of lyrical prose describing Henry's personal experiences and impressions of Greece, and of what being there meant to him in a joyous visit of discovery. No publisher could accept that as a book anyone would want to read.

One of the publishers who saw the book asked Henry's agent why his client didn't take a look at his own country and write something about it that people could understand. When Henry learned of the possibility of writing a book about the United States, he was happy to discuss it with the publisher. The idea of traveling over America from coast to coast was not a new idea for him. In Paris, when Perlès had plied him with questions about the United States, he had always told him that if he ever returned he would stay only long enough to take a good last look at his native land and then head for China.

Negotiations for a contract opened with Henry's demand of a thousand dollars in advance. He was given five hundred. Henry brought up the subject of illustrations, explaining that he had an artist friend who could go along and do the sketches. He was thinking of Abraham Rattner, a Paris friend who was then living in New York, who had mentioned to Henry that someday he would like to make a sketching tour of parts of the United States.

The publisher said no, it would cost too much to publish such a book. But Henry and Rattner talked it over and decided to start the trip together anyway, Rattner to be on his own in the matter of expenses. A 1932 Buick sedan was bought for a hundred dollars, and Henry took a few driving lessons. On October 24, 1940, they headed south to begin what became *The Air-Conditioned Nightmare.*

7

*I had to travel about ten thousand miles before
receiving the inspiration to write a single line.
Everything worth saying about the American way of
life I could put in thirty pages.*

The Air-Conditioned Nightmare

Henry and Abraham Rattner journeyed as far south as St. Augustine, Florida, before turning west to New Orleans, which they reached early in January 1941. They had been in no hurry, stopping at one place or another to look up people they knew or had been asked to call on by mutual friends. These visits lasted from a day to a few weeks, and while the hospitality they received eased their financial burden and the necessity of putting up in motor courts, the layovers were looked forward to more as a relief from the monotony and strain of driving. Henry did the driving, which he loathed. He was a poor driver, and he suffered from eyestrain.

From New Orleans, Rattner returned to New York to assist with the preparation of a one-man show of his paintings. Henry went on to Natchez, Mississippi; while he was there, he received word that his father was near death and that he should come home at once. He flew back and hurried to the hospital, but his father had died two hours earlier.

My father died alone in a Jewish hospital during a peaceful sleep. A few hours after his death he had already been embalmed and was lying in the parlor of our home wrapped in a bed sheet. The expression on his face was one of utter serenity, due in part no doubt to the undertaker's art. It was while the undertaker was clothing my father's body in a pair of woolen underwear which I had brought from Greece . . . that my mother insisted that I run to the Chinese laundry and have my father's white shirt re-laundered.

The weather was bitter and raw, but Henry often walked to the cemetery to visit the grave, thinking back over the old man's life and of the many times he had failed his father, hurt him, and neglected him. He grieved there in tears.

His mother told Henry that there was a place reserved for him in the family plot. "But something tells me that I shall never occupy it. I have the sure conviction that I shall die in a foreign land, in a very remote spot, and that my remains will never be found."

In March 1941 he set out again, this time by train to Chicago where he would see his friend Ben Abramson, whose Argus Book Shop sold his books, including those from under the counter. Abramson had also befriended Henry financially from time to time. Henry brought him the manuscript of *The World of Sex* and asked him to print it for private circulation, which Abramson agreed to do.

The only part of Chicago that Henry thought worth writing up was the city's black South Side, where he found poverty and dilapidation. "Chicago's South Side . . . is like a vast, unorganized lunatic asylum. Nothing can flourish here but vice and disease."

He had one happy encounter in Chicago. He met Emil White. Emil was walking on Michigan Avenue when he saw a man coming toward him who was wearing his fedora tipped jauntily to one side of his head and the brim turned down over one eye. Like Abramson, Emil owned a bookstore and through the grapevine had heard that Henry was in town. He had read *The Cosmological Eye,* and he admired its author. He was hoping to meet him. As the man in the hat was about to pass him, Emil turned and asked, "Are you Henry Miller?"

"Why, yes, I am," answered the surprised Henry.

Emil's face lit up in a great smile, which so warmed Henry's heart that he threw his arms around him. The rapport was instant.

From then until he left town, Emil was his frequent companion, yet when he left the two men hardly expected to see each other again.

Henry took the train south to Natchez, where he picked up the car and headed west. He had given his itinerary to friends from whom he hoped to receive a few dollars now and then, and to wait for these communications he made rather lengthy layovers in Little Rock, Tulsa, Santa Fe, Albuquerque, and the Grand Canyon before he arrived at last in Los Angeles in midsummer.

He looked up two old friends of his from the Paris days, Man Ray and his wife Juliet, and through them met a young couple, Gilbert and Margaret Neiman. The Neimans had been living in Mexico, and now Gilbert was writing a novel with Mexico as the background. Henry spent much of his time with them in their tiny house in the seedy neighborhood of Los Angeles known as Bunker Hill. He had to sleep elsewhere because the place was too small to take in a guest.

He rented a room and began writing his book. All the while he knew it was unlikely to be published, for he had seen almost nothing he wanted to write about during the miserable trip. When he looked over his notes, he read such adjectives as *hideous, appalling, rust-bitten, morbid, suffocating, phony,* and *dead.* The trip had been in many ways a nightmare for him. The driving had been exhausting, his eyes sore and stinging, his stomach suffering from the poor food he had eaten in the cheapest cafés and beaneries. The car was always breaking down. He had been out of money all the time, depending upon handouts from those who replied to his letters. He had not had the energy to take detours to those places that make travel writers' copy. He had liked the Deep South, but there, too, he had seen decay and oppression. The only notes that he wanted to use were those describing the people he had met who were not the "American type" but were idle dreamers, eccentrics of one kind or another, or artists. In his notes he wrote: "America is no place for an artist: to be an artist is to be a moral leper, an economic misfit, a social liability. A corn-fed hog enjoys a better life than a creative writer, painter, or musician. To be a rabbit is better still."

He happened to see a newsletter put out by the Colt Press, a small new publishing venture in San Francisco. When he read that Colt was dedicated to the printing of good books and that it wanted to publish titles deserving better-than-ordinary treatment, he went to San Francisco to offer them *The Colossus of Maroussi.*

His arrival surprised the people at Colt, who had not expected Henry Miller of all people to walk in the door. But there he was with his high spirits and vagabond air, letting everybody know how glad he was to be among people who understood good writing, a special kind of writing that was good for its own sake, not necessarily because it had market value.

They sat around a table and listened to him tell about his recent travels in the United States. Then he told them about Greece and the book he had brought them. When they read *The Colossus of Maroussi,* they liked it so much that they agreed to bring it out at once.

Colt Press had been started in 1938 by Jane Grabhorn, a woman with an educated literary taste and a genius for creating books that in their design and typography were gems of the bookmaking art. She was the wife of Robert Grabhorn who, with his brother Edwin, owned the Grabhorn Press, a printing business with a long-established reputation for the handsome and innovative qualities of its work. They printed a number, but not all, of the Colt books.

Colt's small, crowded office was at 617 Montgomery Street, a dreary location with an unobstructed view of the city morgue. Colt published the obscure writings of such authors as Jane Austen, Robert Louis Stevenson, Thomas De Quincey, and Edward Everett Hale; the letters of Anthony Trollope and Rudyard Kipling; *The Fables of Esope;* Hawaiian, Chinese, and Mexican epicurean cookbooks; a songbook of the ballads of the 1848 California gold rush; a poetry series. Among its contemporary authors were Edmund Wilson, William Saroyan, Oscar Lewis, and Franklin Walker. *The Colossus of Maroussi* became its twentieth title.

During the next few months Henry went back and forth between Los Angeles and San Francisco several times while the book was in production. The last time, he autographed a hundred copies that had been printed on special paper and bound in boards of blue-and-white flowered wallpaper. The regular edition was bound in blue cloth and had a blue and white striped dust jacket to suggest the Greek flag.

The book came out in October 1941. On the inside flap of the dust cover was this factually askew account:

> This magnificent book about Greece is written by one of the finest and most astonishing writers of our time. Henry Miller, author of *The Tropic of Cancer* and *The Tropic of Capricorn,* is a New Yorker who has long lived in Paris. Today, this great figure, following in the truly American tradition of Whitman and Wolfe, is recognized by critics at home and abroad as one of the prose masters of the modern age. Having just completed a harrowing voyage from Greece, Miller is currently traveling through the West, writing a book on America. He has just had published a critique of *Hamlet* written in collaboration with Michael Fraenkel, and New Directions will issue a volume of his essays, *The Wisdom of the Heart,* this Fall. Miller's medium is the strong, free personal narrative, and his faith is the reality of people and of living.

Henry was eager now to return to New York in order to finish his "Nightmare" book. He chose a northerly route, driving through parts of Nevada, Utah, Wyoming, Nebraska, Iowa, Wisconsin, Illinois, Indiana, Ohio, and Pennsylvania. When he reached Chicago, he detoured north for a brief look at Detroit, which, with cities he saw later in Ohio and Pennsylvania, gave him an opportunity to see mill towns and factory centers. In their industries he saw only profits for the bosses and "the utmost servitude for the worker." He described the waste products as "slag heaps which look like the accumulated droppings of sickly prehistoric monsters which passed in the night." The more worn-out he became from the trip, the worse everything looked to him.

These hostile impressions did not disappear when, back in New York, he again set doggedly to work. He wrote more than five-hundred pages before he gave up. Realizing that harsh criticism and denunciations of stupidity, greed, artificiality, and hypocrisy, which he seemed to find everywhere, were likely to label him as "un-American," he decided not to submit the manuscript to the publisher and promised to repay the advance that had been given to him. Repayment would, of course, have to take place sometime in the future.

He wanted to get back to *The Rosy Crucifixion*, which he had not touched since had begun writing it in Bowling Green. When the Neimans wrote that they had moved to a larger place and invited him to come back to California and make his home with them, he went, this time by train. He was looking forward to 1942.

8

Henry settled in happily with the Neimans in their cottage
in Beverly Glen and began again to work on *The Rosy Crucifixion*.
Some income was needed. He could not expect to collect royalties
from *The Wisdom of the Heart*, which had been out just two months,
until the book earned the advance he had been given two years
earlier. Royalties from *The Colossus of Maroussi* were being credited
against Colt's hundred-dollar advance payment. As for his Obelisk
books, since the Germans had marched into Paris there had been
no further word from Kahane's son, although Henry learned that
he had inherited the business and taken his mother's maiden name
of Girodias.

Hollywood seemed the best place to look for work, and
Henry hoped to be taken on as a scriptwriter. He made the rounds
of the studios, but he got nothing except an offer of a writing job
from a private individual who offered him 15 percent of the even-
tual sale of the script, providing they could sell it to studio. He was
to write a screen adaptation of Jacob Wassermann's 1928 novel,
The Maurizius Case, using the English translation by Caroline New-
ton. Wassermann's theme is justice: What is it? Can it ever be
rightfully achieved?

The novel recalls a famous trial that took place years before
in the German courts, when an innocent man was convicted of
murdering his wife and given a life sentence. The novel opens as

a trial is about to begin for the release of a man called Maurizius, who is serving his eighteenth year of such a sentence. Everyone connected with the case is called to testify before the court, and in doing so a web of distressing passions and motives is revealed that involves them all. As the novel continues, all but one of them meet tragic ends. The one spared is the woman above suspicion who committed the murder for which her lover was punished. When Maurizius is pardoned and released, he looks her up, only to find a shallow and worthless person for whom he had been willing to sacrifice his life. He commits suicide.

Henry was drawn as much to this Dostoyevskian plot as he was to Wassermann's portrayal of the failed role of justice in modern society. While he worked on the film script, he kept a notebook to record his own thoughts about justice, vengeance, and morality.

When the script was finished, every studio turned it down. No one wanted to make a German picture when the United States and Germany were at war.

Out of work, Henry again saw himself a failure. He was already fifty years old and could see nothing for himself in the future. To shake off his depression, he turned to painting watercolors, a diversion he had resorted to many times before. At the art shop where he went for supplies, he got into a conversation with the owner, Attilio Bowinkel. A great deal of Henry's appeal was in his voice, in its flowing cadence and warmth, in the confidentiality expressed in "don't you know?" and "do you see?" He seldom hesitated to bring up whatever was on his mind, even when talking to strangers, and at that time his thoughts were on his considerable misfortunes.

Bowinkel listened sympathetically and then insisted that Henry lay aside the selection of cheap paints, paper, and brushes that he had chosen and take the best the shop had to offer. A few days later he went to the Beverly Glen cottage to see what Henry had painted and liked what he saw so much that he took several watercolors back to the shop to mat and offer for sale. They were soon sold, and his customers were asking for more.

People liked the watercolors for the joy of looking at them. Hardly anyone could look at one without breaking into a grin.

Most of the time Henry painted faces, drawing them in outline, simply, the way a child draws, but they were never childlike. Askew, distorted, the ears missing, the eyes open, the eyes shut, or astonished, or blank, crossed, or in the wrong places, his bald-headed nymphs and spellbinding jinns materialized from the non-sense whirling in Henry's head. There was seldom any way to tell which faces were male and which were female. They might even be "self-portraits," of which he did many.

He also drew frontal nudes, again in outline without sides, misshapen, winking at the beholder from a fleshless frolic of nav-els, nipples, and weedy pubic hair. They were never carnal. They were just joyful.

While his bodies were bare, his heads, if they were not bald, were covered with pharaonic headpieces such as only he could think up. Bonnets, helmets, crowns, Turkish turbans, skullcaps, shakos, and bandannas were designed with gimps and crimps and plumes, panicles, feathers, bangles and beads, tassels, papillotes, ruching, and whatever else sprang to mind in the enjoyment that filled him as he stroked paint on paper. All of his watercolors appear to have been painted while he was smiling from ear to ear, feeling full of glee and mischief.

The reason Henry painted nude figures and covered up heads was because clothing and hair were too difficult for him to do. He omitted ears for the same reason. The emphasis was on the eyes, which he especially liked to paint—in his way, as orbs with-out lids or lashes. Sometimes he threw in a few extra eyes here and there on the paper.

He did not waste space. In the area surrounding a figure he might add, in addition to the extra eyes, a few curlicues, some serpentine, confetti, or a tattoo of dots. Or an Easter egg, some postage stamps, a seashell, bottles, an angel, or the head of a fish. Henry was a wizard of droll embellishment.

If he painted houses, boats, or landscapes, the houses never rested on the ground, the boats tiptoed in seaweed, and the land-scapes came from dreamland. "I do not paint from life," he ex-plained. "I paint from the head and what's inside it. Now and then, of course, I have done a still life or a portrait or a landscape—by looking at it and trying to reproduce it. The results are usually quite harrowing. Nobody, not even myself, can ever detect what is called a 'resemblance.' "

If his paintings were unreal, they were also irresistible. People liked having them on their walls because they made them happy. They also liked their color, which was fresh and strong, in combinations not usually seen in watercolors. Pink and tangerine with turquoise. Chartreuse and periwinkle with hyacinth and indigo. Pink and vermilion with lemon. The brightest greens, blues, violets, purples were washed across the paper. The figures were outlined in black.

At the end of the summer of 1943, when the Neimans moved to Colorado, Henry took over the cottage and invited an artist friend of his, John Dudley, to move in and share the rent. Henry was painting full time, and, to announce "the permanent exhibition" of his work, he had a handbill printed. The cottage was now The Green House, and the show was both inside and out, weather permitting. The leaflet stated that due to perpetual impoverishment no refreshments would be served, which did not stop anyone from arriving with a bottle to be shared. There was a crowd there at almost any hour of the day or night, and the watercolors were sold as fast as he could paint them. The American Contemporary Gallery in Hollywood gave him a show that was a sellout.

Holve-Barrows, a firm in Fullerton, California, was preparing to bring out *The Angel Is My Watermark* using a special photographic process. Along with the essay of that title, which first appeared in *Black Spring*, several photographs of Henry's watercolors and one original one would be included. The book was to be priced at fifty dollars.

Aside from painting, Henry had done some writing for magazines, but it was the watercolors that brought him an income. He was paying off his debts and hoping to get enough ahead to go to Mexico and write. To attract even more buyers for his paintings, he composed "an open letter to all and sundry" and sent it to Ben Abramson to mimeograph and mail for him from Chicago.

Henry also sent one of the letters to the *New Republic*. His five-page letter was too long for the magazine to use in its entirety, but in the "Mailbag" section of November 8, 1943, there were two long paragraphs stating that Henry Miller "by common consent of the critics one of the most interesting figures on the American literary scene" was frequently hard up because of his refusal to compromise with what he considers the outrageous prudery of American publishers.

"We have received a communication from him in which he suggests that he will sell some of the watercolors which he paints, as a hobby, to our readers . . . with the understanding that the buyer may name his own price."

The piece included Henry's postscript to his letter: "Anyone wishing to encourage the water color mania would do well to send me paper, brushes, and tubes, of which I am always in need. I would also be grateful for old clothes, shirts, socks, etc. I am 5 feet 8 inches tall, weigh 150 pounds, 15 1/2 neck, 38 chest, 32 waist, hat and shoes both sizes 7 to 7 1/2. Love corduroys."

When the appeal began to bring results he wrote again to the magazine.

Time could not resist picking up the story. Under its own "Life by Mail Order" department of December 13, the following paragraph appeared:

> Henry Miller, whose Paris-published novels *Tropic of Cancer* and *Tropic of Capricorn* have stirred intelligentsiacs to as much prurient curiosity and as much sour criticastery as any novels since James Joyce's *Ulysses,* published an appeal for charity in the *New Republic.* He said he wanted contributions of old clothes ("love corduroys") and watercolor material. In Beverly Glen, near Los Angeles, the 52-year-old free-loving, free-sponging American-from-Paris had been destitute for months. Recently he had taken up painting.
>
> In a second open letter to the *New Republic,* Miller reported that his appeal had brought unorthodox seals of approval plus clothes, paints, brushes, and money in sums up to $100 from Mid-western women, a "little businessman," a WAC, soldiers, a 15-year-old boy, and other admirers. He repeated his earlier refusal to take any regular job. "Why don't I do as other men, other writers? . . . Because I am different for one thing. . . . This may seem like quite a tirade . . . yet if by tomorrow, by a decision of the Supreme Court [a] half-dozen terrifying words were restored to currency, if I, like the great English writers of the past, were

permitted to use them, I should undoubtedly be sitting in clover."

In Los Angeles there was a growing demand for Miller's watercolors. Soon he might be able to return to *Air-Conditioned Nightmare*, his book-in-progress on the immitigable crassness of the U.S.

It was around this time that the painter Jean Varda visited Henry. When Varda was living in London he read the *Tropics*, and now he wanted to meet the author, as well as see what kind of a painter he was.

Varda, or Yanko as he was called, was born in Smyrna, Turkey, of Greek parents, and he had lived among Greeks, Turks, Armenians, Alexandrians, Algerians, French, and English. He had been living in the United States since 1939.

When he was just a boy, his mother, a distinguished painter, saw that her son showed exceptional promise as a portraitist, and when he was a teenager he was sent to Paris to study. But there he turned away from the conventional style of painting to that of the modernists. He was especially won over by the cubists and painted in that style for several years. By 1943 he had begun to work in mosaics, embedding prepared pieces of mirror in a gessolike base. The effect was fire-bright. He was in Los Angeles because a show of his mosaics was at one of the galleries.

As a young man Yanko had danced for a few years with a ballet company and ever after he walked with lightness and grace. He often appeared to be on tiptoe, ready to spring out of sight. His face was full and tanned, the nose sharp, the mouth sensual, the brown eyes inquisitive and smiling. His hair was capped to his head, the bangs dropping over the brow.

Gregarious, warm, he had a personality that charmed everyone. He seemed always to be bubbling with a private joy that he could not hold back. He loved to talk, to tell stories, to reminisce for the benefit of his listeners, and his voice was musical with the lilt and syllables of all the people he had lived among for the past fifty years. Both men and women were drawn to him, wanting to be touched by his shine.

Henry fell under his spell at once. When they talked about his difficulties in getting to Mexico, Yanko dismissed Mexico and told him about a wild and beautiful California coast to which a road had only recently been completed.

"It's a beautiful place, Henry. You will be inspired. You will be happy."

Shacks that had been occupied by the convict laborers during the road's construction years were now abandoned and available for rent for five dollars a month. "You can live there for pennies, Henry."

Yanko was telling him about Big Sur, a seventy-five-mile stretch of precipitous coastline that begins about two-hundred miles north of Los Angeles. The shacks were at a place called Anderson Creek. For a time Yanko and his wife Virginia had lived and worked there. She was blonde and young, very pretty, and they had been married for four years. Her artwork included ceramics and jewelry.

When war was declared on Japan the Vardas had to leave this remote section of the coast because of Yanko's alien status. They moved north about forty-five miles to the town of Monterey and after a few months bought a barn to live in. They liked barns because they were spacious and, they believed, were more aesthetically pleasing than the boxes that most people lived in.

Theirs was an old horse barn painted red and was located on the outskirts of town in a section called New Monterey. The Vardas left the stables and troughs as they were, to use for storage and work areas, while the upper story, formerly the hayloft, was transformed into a merry-go-round of color and caprice. A little surreal, a little funky, it was filled with surprises. With scarcely any money to furnish the place, Yanko went to the junkyard, the garbage dump, the beach, anyplace where he could hunt for other people's discards. Broken ladders, broken chairs, broken windows, broken dishes, tin cans, torn sail, wire, rope, old bottles, driftwood, discarded lumber, nails, boxes, barrels, corks, pipes and tubing, car seats, fenders, tires, windshields—anything he came upon that could be transformed into something beautiful and useful was brought to the barn and given a new life.

Chair rockers became arched window frames. Windows

twinkled with gem light contrived from chips of colored glass. Hammered and stenciled tin cans disguised the battered surfaces of doors. Telephone transformers functioned as blue glass door-knobs. Virginia hung pieces of sail for curtains and painted them with Neptunian scenes befitting their past voyages. Yanko's mosaics, paintings, collages, papier-mâché masks, and other artwork scattered fragments of color and light over the walls. In the middle of the huge room he built a fireplace of boulders, bricks, and green wine bottles.

At one end of the room, high up, safe from the hot sparks that sometimes snapped out of the open bowl of fire, was Phoebe. She had been a damaged and discarded department-store mannequin before Yanko rescued her and carried her home to become an angel. She was now suspended by wires from a rafter and was afloat in the air, her arms outstretched in a swan dive. Virginia had made her a red and blue dress, put stockings on her, and carefully combed her long yellow hair—real hair, it turned out to be. She could close and open her eyes, and her cheeks in her pretty bisque face were rosy.

Aromas reached her of fresh paint and wet clay, of burning wood, glues, inks, oils, snuffed-out candles, and cigarette smoke, and often of garlic boiling in an Arabic stew. She watched people coming and going, a crowd there most of the time, talking, laughing, dancing, singing, eating together, finally falling asleep. Many of them called out her name.

Yanko invited Henry to visit him and Virginia at their barn and to look over the situation at Anderson Creek. Henry wanted to leave Los Angeles. He wanted to write, not paint all the time, and if he didn't have the money for Mexico perhaps this Big Sur that Yanko talked about would be the place to stay for a while. Early in January 1944 he took the train to the valley town of Salinas where Yanko met him and drove him back over the hills to Monterey.

Part Two

Big Sur

The Log House

Partington Ridge

9

As quietly and naturally as a twig falling into the Mississippi I dropped out of the stream of American life.

Black Spring

"Nothing in Monterey could possibly have drawn me to its environs, except Varda," wrote Henry.

Hardworking, bustling, ambitious Monterey was, in 1944, the largest commercial fishing port in the United States in annual tonnage, and it was proud to be called the sardine capital of the world. About the turn of the century, Italian fishermen had arrived to catch the numerous varieties of fish, especially sardines, that were abundant off the coast. When more Italians moved in to work in the fish canneries, Monterey became a little Italy.

The city is about 125 miles south of San Francisco and overlooks a scenic bay. Its history dates from 1602, when a Spanish navigator discovered the bay and named it for his patron, the viceroy of New Spain, Gaspar de Zuniga, count of Monterey. Later the settlement was made the capital of Spain's Alta California and remained the capital after the Mexican Revolution. In 1846, the United States took the city, but the Mexican flavor lingered on.

Monterey was also a soldier's town, as it had been for more than a hundred years. Enlisted men from Fort Ord, four miles away, looked to it for girls, entertainment, and liquor, and they were not disappointed.

This mix of Mexicans, Italian fishermen, and soldiers did not appeal to Henry.

Monterey was not a painter's or writer's town, although a few lived there. More moved into cottages among the pines and cypresses of Pacific Grove, a quiet, churchy community on the southern cusp of Monterey Bay. The land had been purchased in 1875 as a seaside resort for members of the Methodist Church, but, after a town was built there, members of other denominations had moved in. There was an early curfew, and the blue laws regarding liquor, tobacco, and public conduct were strictly obeyed in an atmosphere of piety and virtue.

The place that attracted the most people working in the arts was Carmel-by-the-Sea, five miles farther south on the coast. It was only two-thirds of a square mile in area and was nestled on piny slopes between the highway and a small bay of bright blue water.

Poets, writers, and painters had arrived after a development company had laid out and named Carmel in 1903. San Francisco's poet George Sterling had a small cottage built for him and his wife Carrie. It was too small to accommodate guests, who had to sleep out under the trees, but that was all right because all of the action was outdoors: the abalone feasts, the nightlong gabfests around a bonfire, the drinking and singing. There was plenty of abalone to eat. They pried it off the rocks along the shore, and sometimes they cooked it on the beach for a moonlit picnic. There was no swimming because of the undertow.

Sterling's cherished friend Ambrose Bierce visited once, didn't enjoy himself, and never returned. However, Gelett Burgess, Jack and Charmian London, James Hopper, Arnold Genthe, Xavier Martinez, Chris Jorgensen, Mary Austin, Maynard Dixon, and many others found Carmel idyllic in its free, wild beauty.

In December 1908, a well-known sister team of writers, Alice and Grace MacGowan, arrived from Missouri. They were the authors of a number of books, and their short stories, articles and poetry appeared in the leading periodicals. When they found themselves in need of a secretary, and of a possible collaborator on a book, they wrote to an aspiring writer friend in New York, asking him to come out and help them. They would pay his railway fare. Hal Lewis came at once. He was tall and skinny, blue-eyed, pimply faced, and fiery-haired. Nobody knew that his middle name was Sinclair. The sisters rented a shack on the beach for him, and he sometimes shared it with a Carmel visitor, Bill, who was William Rose Benét.

Later the sisters changed their minds about writing the book. Lewis began to concentrate on his own work and in July sold a short story to *Sunset*, then a literary magazine. The editors asked for other work of his, and he sold them an article about his impressions of San Francisco. He had worked on two newspapers and been fired, but, now that a popular magazine had accepted him, he felt that he could make creative writing his life's work.

Carmel began to change. In a few years it was no longer a rustic bohemia. In 1922 its main street, Ocean Avenue, was paved. Before that it had been a dirt road full of potholes that had to be covered with tree branches to make it passable in rainy weather. Groceries, fruit stands, the shoe repair shop, and others that had been located on Ocean Avenue for convenience were moved to side streets to make room for specialty shops selling silver teapots, Chippendale chairs, fine jewelry, and expensive clothing.

Not everyone who lived in Carmel was working in the arts, either seriously or as a hobby. Those who could afford it but were not painters or writers lived there because of the beauty of Carmel's setting and the relaxed atmosphere. There were art shows, little-theater productions, musical recitals, interesting people to meet, a charm that would have been hard to find anywhere else.

Everyone lived in small cottages set in flower gardens. Numbers were not permitted; instead, the cottages had such names as Wind Song, Moon Gate, or Sea Glimpse. The streets for many years had no names and wound through the pine forests. Trees were greatly admired and were not allowed to be cut down. There were no streetlights, and after dark the residents made their way by flashlight. In earlier years they had carried lanterns.

There were no deliveries of mail. Everyone had a box at the post office on Ocean Avenue, and the daily trip to pick up mail was also a social ritual for meeting friends and hearing the latest gossip, none of which got into the two weekly papers. These were the *Carmel Pine Cone*, which began publishing in 1915, and the *Carmel Cymbal*, which came along in 1926. Each paper had a staff of two or three and had no trouble filling its pages with stories about local social and cultural events. Both papers had unpaid columnists, all local writers, and it was their work that distinguished one paper from the other.

Two women who arrived in Carmel from San Francisco in 1922 brought it more renown than it had ever had as an art colony. They were Dene Denny, a concert pianist, and Hazel Watrous, a painter who had a flair for costume and stage design. During their first ten years in Carmel, they produced eighteen plays, put together an orchestra, and presented numerous concerts and recitals. They also had an art gallery.

It was in the summer of 1935 that they launched their most ambitious undertaking, a three-day celebration of the works of Johann Sebastian Bach. They called it a Bach Festival. It was so successful that it was repeated the next year, and again the year after that. It would become an annual weeklong event attracting the attention and esteem of the entire music world.

In 1944, Henry knew nothing of this or of Carmel. One day Yanko drove him there to look up a sculptor friend who lived in a cottage near the beach. Yanko knew a few of Carmel's painters, but he did not admire their traditional style of work, and he did not intend to bore Henry by taking him to see their seascapes, bouquets of flowers, and pretty portraits.

He could not recall the name of the sculptor's cottage. Was it White Caps? Sea Foam? Perhaps it was Surf Echoes. They could not find the place, and Henry was annoyed at the need to rely on playful names in order to locate someone. He could not understand why the cottages did not have the names of their occupants on their gates or doors.

What he had seen of Carmel as they drove down Ocean Avenue from the highway was a corridor several blocks long that had giant pine trees growing out of the sidewalks, with shops tucked in behind them. Many of the shops were built in a fairy-tale style of architecture that was meant to be quaint. In the midstreet traffic island there were more tall trees. As the car rolled along and he looked into the shop windows and saw how people were dressed, he judged correctly that this was not a place where an indigent artist or writer would fit in.

At the bottom of Ocean Avenue, Yanko turned the car to the

left, where Scenic Road follows the beach. He wanted to show Henry the picturesque bay. But the sky was overcast, dulling the usually sapphire water to the dark of unpolished silver. In the bay's half circle, the gentle incoming combers did not look any different from other bays that Henry had seen, although the sand was exceptionally white. He watched the flutter of shorebirds as they dropped down to pick into the wet sand, then flew up again. Neither the screeching of the birds nor the tide's soft surge could be heard above the strain of the car's engine.

The car was an old Model A Ford coupe that Yanko had restored. When he had acquired it, the top had been missing, and the one he had made for it gave it a jaunty gypsy air.

10

*People often ask how on earth I managed to keep my
head above water during the black years of famine and
drought. I have explained . . . that at the last ditch
someone always came to my rescue.*
    Big Sur and the Oranges of Hieronymus Bosch

The highway south of Carmel leads to the strip of coast
known as the Big Sur country. Leaving Carmel Point, the road
skirts the foothills of the Santa Lucia Mountains, where a few
white-faced cattle may be grazing, and then it rises and tightens
itself against the hills. The shoreline becomes a rubble of crags and
coves where surging tides burst and spew up great billows of
spray. A few miles more and Big Sur comes into view, a gargantuan spectacle of mountains falling from the sky in a tumult of
ridges, rolling hills, ravines, and knolls, the steep descent plunging
abruptly into the sea. The ocean swells and throbs against the
headlands, thrusting and hammering at them until the granite
cracks; then it sucks out the debris and casts it aside. The ever-
accumulating detritus of boulders and rock fragments can be seen
for many miles. Some of the buttresses have been wedged apart to
form canyons that allow thin streams to reach the sea. A road turns
in and out, gouged out of the mountainside.

The idea of building a coast road had come before the California legislature many times from as early as 1870, but it was
always rejected because of the extreme topographical difficulties
and the cost. In 1872, homesteader Charles Bixby pushed a rough
wagon road for thirteen miles through the wilderness, from the
Carmel River to his ranch near Bixby Creek. Later John Pfeiffer
moved the road to his place on down the coast, over another haz-

ardous thirteen miles of hairpin turns, hard climbs, and steep descents.

Finally, in 1919, a bill was passed authorizing the construction of a direct road, not to be built in the mountains but lower, above the shore. The work began the next year, using convict labor and some civilian workers. It took seventeen years to build. Among the many challenges was the task of spanning the canyons, which was accomplished by building thirty-one bridges. Not all of the road was so difficult; some of it swung inland through groves of redwood trees.

Big Sur is inhospitable, but it is neither barren nor grim. Along with the redwoods there are forests of pine, oak, and fir. The grass is green in January, and soon afterward the wildflowers come out. Spring is watercolor bright, except when the fog rolls in. Rain may come down in stinging bolts between November and March.

In the late 1930s and early 1940s there were less than a hundred people living within several hundred square miles. Some of them were the third and fourth generations of families that had settled the coast in the 1870s and 1880s, coming in to claim the timber, tanbark, and lime. Their lumber mills and limekilns had flourished for many years, until the canyons were stripped.

Once the settlers came in there was little contact with the outside. A few schooners arrived during the year to bring in freight and some supplies and to take out the lumber and other products. The unloading and loading operations were done by cables strung from the beach to the vessels as they lay at anchor off the mouths of certain canyons called "landings." There was no other way to come or to go except on the back of a horse or mule, following a trail through the Santa Lucias.

The isolation bred introversions and eccentricities among the people. Odd behavior, except for a distressing incident such as murder, was hardly noticed. In the repeated telling of tales that had been heard and passed along over the years, the stories of these early settlers became a kind of folklore.

The poet Robinson Jeffers had heard these stories, and he knew Big Sur. He and his wife Una had been living on Carmel Point, which is just south of the city of Carmel, since 1919. The scenes of many of Jeffers's long narrative poems are set on the Big

Sur coast. If he changed the names of places to those of his own inspiration, it does not matter. If the tragedies are sharpened to suit the fervent style of classical Greek drama, that does not matter. The poems have truth in them about a separate people clinging to a landscape of granite, sea, and stars.

Occasionally someone who wanted to leave civilization would make his way into the country. One of these was the Spanish-born aristocrat Jaime d'Angulo, who came in 1913 to homestead a piece of land on the slopes above the Big Sur River. He was a man of mystery; it was not known, until the United States went to war in 1917 and d'Angulo volunteered as a surgeon, that he held a medical degree from Johns Hopkins University.

From time to time he left the coast, only to reappear and resume his role as a hermit. It was said that he was an authority on the languages of American Indians and that he had written a book on the subject, although no one had seen the book. It was said that the young woman who once came to live with him was his daughter. It was said that he lived like an Indian, cooking his meals over an open pit dug into the earth that served as a floor in his crude habitation. It was known that he rustled cattle for his larder. He had been arrested for it and had paid a stiff fine to avoid a jail sentence.

On the day that Yanko and Henry drove down the coast to Anderson Creek, Yanko pointed out every sign of life that was visible from the road. It all looked desolate to Henry. Not even a wild animal made an appearance. To their right the sea and sky were an identical colorless nowhere. A light wind began to blow grit across the road, making the tires scratch around the curves.

"Aren't we there yet?"

"Pretty soon, Henry." Yanko turned on the windshield wiper. "We'll be there before the fog closes in."

When they reached Anderson, the fog was already fingering the canyon walls. Some of the shacks had fallen down, and those that remained were empty.

"Where is everybody?" asked Yanko. "Of course," he added, turning to Henry, "it's January. A bad month. It will change as soon as summer comes. You will see. There won't be room then for everybody."

They got back into the car for the drive home. When they had gone about seven miles, they turned off the road to visit a friend of Yanko, Lynda Sargent. She was glad to see them.

"Come in! Come in!" she said. Fat logs were burning in the big fireplace. She urged the dog Frigga to move so the men could bring their chairs close to the fire. Sir Thomas, the cat, had already leapt to a table and was watching them. Lynda went to the kitchen for a jug of red wine.

The house was a large one, built of logs, and it sat on top of a high knoll above the highway. A bramble of oak trees and shrubbery followed a cut of road to the front door. Because of its size and prominence the coast people always referred to the place as The Log House. It overlooked the ocean seven hundred feet below and was palatial by Big Sur standards, with its large living room, two bedrooms, bath with a shower stall, kitchen, and connecting guest quarters. Lynda rented it for thirty dollars a month, completely furnished.

"This is quite a place," said Henry, looking around.

"Come, I'll show you," Lynda said.

After they had been through the bedrooms and Henry had admired the shower, they came back through the living room and went to the kitchen. There Lynda added a thick piece of wood to the fire in the old-fashioned iron stove.

"That door," she said, pointing to it, "leads to my maid's room."

"You have a maid?"

"When I can keep one." She giggled. Lynda punctuated everything she said that was longer than a few sentences with a giggly laugh. "They stay about two months and then they want to go back to Monterey or Salinas or wherever. They say they want to hear a little noise. You can't even slam the doors around here. They just squeak shut. And they miss the radio. I don't have one. The reception's terrible."

When they returned to the fireside, Yanko continued telling her about their trip to Anderson. "Nobody there at all! Can you believe it?" Then he turned to Henry. "Henry is a very famous writer."

Lynda glanced at Henry, who was watching the flames.

"How many books is it now, Henry?" Yanko asked.

Henry counted. "Eleven, I think."

"Eleven!" said Lynda. "I'm struggling along with one." Later she told me, "He's the last person in the world you'd take for a writer."

She asked him politely, "What kind of books do you write?"

"I have been writing the story of my life. I may never finish it, but that doesn't bother me, you know."

Eleven books about himself! Lynda simply couldn't believe it. She couldn't believe that he had even one book in him. To her he didn't look like a writer, and he didn't look like a person to whom anything interesting had ever happened. He certainly didn't have the physique of an explorer or adventurer. He was pale. Had he been in prison? He had a Brooklyn accent, but was life in Brooklyn worth eleven books? She stared at him and wondered. He was bald with a fringe of gray hair, well past middle age, and rather frail. She tried to imagine what he had been like in earlier years when life was one book after the other.

When they got ready to leave, Yanko said, "Come have dinner with us the next time you're in Monterey. You'll be shopping in town soon, won't you?"

Lynda giggled. "I never shop in Monterey. All my charge accounts are in Carmel."

It was nearly a month later when she arrived at the barn. There she found Henry in a solemn mood. He explained that he was broke and that he was waiting to hear from two or three friends from whom he expected loans. He intended to return to New York as soon as the money arrived. He had been at the barn nearly two months. He hadn't worked on his books. There was no hope of getting to Mexico.

They discussed these problems while sitting around Yanko's homemade fireplace. The men were keeping their bare feet warm by resting them on the circular platform that extended from the coals. Virginia was not there. She was visiting friends in San Francisco.

After a while Yanko said, "Well, let's eat." He got up to put the water on to boil for the spaghetti and to prepare his Armenian-Arabic version of meatballs. Lynda followed him to make the salad. She filled a bowl with torn lettuce and was slicing onions, the tears running down her cheeks, when Henry joined them to start setting the table. Yanko was telling Lynda a way to avoid onion tears when the spaghetti boiled over.

"You can have my maid's room, Henry, if you want. I'm not expecting anyone soon. No one has answered my last ad." She opened the jar of pimiento-stuffed green olives which she had brought and emptied the drained contents into the salad. "Henry?" she called.

"Yes, I heard. I'm thinking it over. Thanks."

"Here, cut the bread." She handed him a knife and one of the two warm loaves of Italian round that she had also brought.

"Won't I be in the way?" he asked.

"Of what?"

"Yanko tells me you have a boyfriend who comes down on weekends."

"Red's back with an old girlfriend. She's a whore over in town and to hell with him."

A week later, on a day of pouring rain, Lynda heard a knock at her door at about two in the afternoon. She opened it to see Henry standing there, the water dripping off the brim of his hat, a wet bundle of belongings under one arm and the collar of his coat turned up. He had come from Monterey in the mail truck and had been dropped off at the highway.

It was not long before I received a note from Lynda. "Yanko had a rare bird that flew the coop. I have taken him in. You must come and meet Henry Miller."

11

During the time I was her guest she showed me stories and novelettes, some finished, some unfinished, which were altogether remarkable. They were largely about New England characters whom she had known as a girl. It was a New England more like the legendary Big Sur: full of violence, horror, incest, broken dreams, despair, loneliness, insanity and frustration of every sort. Lynda related these stories with a granite-like indifference to the reader's emotions. Her language was rich, heavily brocaded, tumultuous and torrential. She had command of the whole keyboard.

Big Sur and the Oranges of Hieronymus Bosch

I had known Lynda six years, ever since we both worked on W. K. Bassett's *Carmel Cymbal*. She had been writing the column "Clanging Cymbals" for two years then. I was taken on as the paper's only paid reporter, and I also sold most of the ads. At first I was in awe of Lynda, not only because I liked what she wrote and wished I could do as well but also because of her vivacious personality. All that merriness, all that laughter—I never saw her when she was not in high spirits. I was young, socially insecure, and hesitant about talking with strangers. I took the job on the paper to force myself to get over these drawbacks.

Lynda knew everybody in Carmel by their first names. Rushing about the village, on Ocean Avenue, Dolores or San Carlos streets, or running in and out of the post office, she hailed one person after the other and was greeted as warmly in return. If she came into the office when I was working, she would come over and sit beside my desk to confide in me current bits of news and gossip, including some amusing gaffe of her own. Giggling and guffawing, she was always brimming over with news or, if not news, then with presumptions and predictions. Bassett's desk was only a few feet away in the tiny office, and when he was there he would listen in, snorting and whistling at Lynda's gab.

We called him W. K., as everyone did except his wife Dorothea, who called him Willard. He was a perky little man with a

Vandyke beard. He usually had a cigarette in a holder sticking out of his mouth.

Later, when Lynda and I were better acquainted, she would entertain us with outrageous tidbits of information about one or another of her lovers. One of her best stories was about the time one of them had given her a vaginal infection, which, she said, her doctor diagnosed as hoof-and-mouth disease. She laughed so much in the telling of that story that she could hardly get the words out. Bassett's whoop and cackle brought the printers in the back room to the door to ask what was going on. One of W. K.'s remarks was that nobody could gossip about Lynda because she had already told everything to everybody.

She was in her early forties and while not pretty she was very attractive. Her thick brown hair was cut in a curly bob, and the fullness and bounce of it gave her a gamine look. Her eyes were blue. Invariably she covered them with sunglasses. She had great style, and she showed off her clothes best in the way she walked. It was a stride, really, for her steps were long for so slight a person. There was rhythm to her walk, a lightness and an occasional skip. She walked with complete self-confidence. She was always in a hurry.

Her taste in clothes was expensive, and she knew what looked best on her. Understated, beautifully cut, lightweight wool suits in muted patterns and colors. She wore with them only the loveliest of pastel silk or georgette blouses. Everything was purchased in Carmel's elite shops, where her credit was unlimited.

I never saw her in a dress. At home, on the days when she did not have an assignment, she stayed in her nightgown all day, wearing a frilly bed jacket with it and her usual high heels. She had many pairs of plain black kid or brown calfskin pumps with three-inch heels. She never wore hose. Nor jewelry, except for a plain watch on a leather strap. Nor makeup, except lipstick. She did not paint her nails, and she disliked perfume. She almost always wore short leather gloves to protect her hands, the skin of which she said was oversensitive.

What people noticed first about Lynda was her New England accent, which she came by naturally having been born in Henniker, New Hampshire. Her voice was warm, and she could hold the attention of people for as long as she liked, telling them one yarn after the other.

It was impossible to learn anything about her immediate background before she arrived in Carmel in 1934 from somewhere on the East Coast. She would sometimes casually mention something that had happened in her past, if the radio or daily papers brought it to her attention. Sometimes she was the wife of a very rich man she called Sidney, who was "close to FDR" and an insider on government affairs. She was then a part of the Washington social scene. At another time she and Sidney were New Yorkers, and again he had important government connections, and she led the glamorous life of a society hostess. She said that she had once been mistaken for Katharine Hepburn. This was during a train trip to the West Coast. She was invited to the cab of the locomotive where she sat in the engineer's seat with the engineer's cap on her head. They let her blow the whistle. Then, again, in the twenties, "when she was in Victoria, Canada," the Prince of Wales was there on a visit, and at the ball that was given in his honor he danced with her. I always wished the stories were true. They suited her so well.

She also told many stories that were surely true, about her childhood on a farm in Henniker, family incidents about Mother and Father, Aunt Fanny and Aunt Nell, Big Ed and the dog, and others. These were wistful, beautiful stories, many of which she put in her columns. Her readers looked forward to them, but they appeared only occasionally when she said she had run out of copy. She said they were stories from a book of fiction that she was writing.

She wanted people to think of her as "well off." If you happened to run into her in the snack shop, she insisted that you join her, and she always charged the tab to her account. If there was a drive on of any kind she contributed a large bill when others gave dimes. If she learned of some person in need, she sent a box of groceries, and often flowers as well, "from a friend." She was known as a Lady Bountiful and she liked it. She had charge accounts all over town, at the drugstores, laundry, beauty salon, gas station, apparel shops, the butcher, grocer, and fruit market, at all the gift shops. The truth was that she lived on a two-hundred-dollar-a-month alimony check that she spent as soon as it came. She never saved a dollar. She was always in debt to her creditors, although she gave them something on account every month.

Her maid at that time was Mary, a large woman of "pagan breasts and thighs," as Lynda described her, who was of Spanish and Indian descent. She looked to be about fifty, but it was impossible to tell her age. What amused me about Mary was her absent-minded way of "straightening up" Lynda's cottage. After she had shuffled the furniture around in order to sweep under it, the place was in more disarray than before because she never put anything back where she found it. Not the furniture, not the dishes she washed, not the food she took out of the pantry. She accompanied whatever she did with a Spanish song.

Lynda's columns often came from first drafts that she wrote in pencil while propped up in bed. It was Mary's duty to bring her breakfast on a tray, and perhaps lunch later. While Lynda was eating, Mary would rest herself at the foot of the bed, sharing whatever was on her mind. Lynda could easily lead her into reminiscences, many of which she used in her columns, for Mary had lived all her life in the area between Monterey and Big Sur, and she had many stories to tell. What fascinated Lynda more than anything else was the fact that Mary, when a young girl, was the "California" of Robinson Jeffers's tragic poem, "Roan Stallion."

The story that Mary told about herself and the stallion was that one night, during a bad storm, she was riding him across the soft mouth of the Carmel River when he floundered and fell. She struggled until daylight to get him to his feet, and, when she saw that she could not save him and that he was about to die there in the mud, she lifted her rifle and shot him. And then she lay down beside him and sobbed out her grief. From this one dark thread, Jeffers wove a many-colored tapestry.

I admired Jeffers's poetry very much. Whenever I would see him and Una walking up Ocean Avenue to the post office, I would stop to watch them and would wait until they had come out of the building and had walked back downhill to Scenic Road, where they turned left out of sight on their way home to Carmel Point.

Everyone who lived in Carmel could be seen on Ocean Avenue at one time or another, and there were always visitors, especially movie stars. One evening about dusk, at a discreet distance I followed Charlie Chaplin and Paulette Goddard who were window-shopping hand in hand. I never saw Orson Welles on the avenue, but I did see him in the audience at some of the little-theater productions. He was interested in one of the actresses, an exquisite young redhead, Dorothy Comingore. Later he chose her for the role of Marion Davies in his movie *Citizen Kane.*

A burly fellow I noticed at the post office, who always wore a sailor's watch cap and a dark turtleneck sweater, turned out to be Don Blanding, whose books of verse about the tropical charms of the Hawaiian Islands were popular at the time. When we became acquainted, he invited me to drop by the cottage where he was spending a few months with Carmel friends. We would all sit around the kitchen table talking, drinking coffee, and remembering the Islands. I had lived in Honolulu before I came to Carmel, and I knew his poems about hula moons, ginger blossoms, banyan trees, and little jade fishes—sentimental jingles, but, to anyone who had lived in the Islands they did not seem superficial. He would ask me to recite something and then say that I remembered it better than he did.

As it always did in July, the *Cymbal* brought out its handsome *Bach Festival Edition,* and, since W. K. had a tin ear for music, he always left the editing and some of the features to Lynda. When he gave me his two complimentary tickets, I invited my friend in Monterey, Ed Ricketts, to attend the concerts with me. Ed had been giving me a sort of musical appreciation course with phonograph records. I am not musical, but he was doing his best.

Ed lived near the beginning of Monterey's mile-long Cannery Row, where the fishing fleet came in and the canneries were lined up. The road was noisy, smelly, and, except at night, swarming with people. He lived there because he was a marine biologist and it was a convenient place to keep floating tanks of sea creatures out in back. The place he lived in was a small clapboard building with a basement entered from below street level. The incoming tide slapped against the wooden floor, and with a careless step out the back door you fell into Monterey Bay.

Most of Ed's friends called him "Doc." His work was with the creatures that inhabit the tide pools—starfish, anemones, sea slugs, limpets, tiny crabs, and small octopi among them. His laboratory was divided between the basement, where he kept the specimens, and upstairs behind the kitchen and bathroom, where he kept his microscopes, slides, drugs, chemicals, and other paraphernalia.

His sandy hair was always neatly trimmed, and to avoid the bother of shaving every day he grew a full beard. Of average build, he didn't look like a man who could wrestle a small shark or grapple with the tentacles of an octopus, but he was as tough and sinewy as an athlete, and his arms and long-fingered hands were very strong.

There was one room at the front of the house where he kept the phonograph, the records, and his many books. He also slept there. He was immune to the odors of his profession. For me, the fugues and rondos, sonatas and tone poems that filled the air shared with it the salty fragrances of sardine and sponge, barnacles, mussels, kelp, and, not infrequently, embalming fluid. In Carmel the Bach was odorless.

Soon after the highway opened to Big Sur, Lynda found a cabin and moved from Carmel. The coast became her beat for the paper, and her columns about homesteaders, ranchers, lighthouse keepers, cattlemen, and a self-styled hermit or two greatly interested many readers. Until then they had known almost nothing about the families who lived beyond the end of the old wagon road. She was acquainted with everyone—old-timers, newcomers who came to open motor inns and set up gas pumps, road maintenance crews, park wardens, forest rangers, the new postmistress. Lynda seldom lacked for copy.

She often wrote about Big Sur itself, personifying a favorite row of hills as "the Old Woman of Mule Canyon" resting on an elbow and looking out to sea. She saw the sharp coastal palisades "stamping their giant paws in the Pacific." The road lay on the breast of the Santa Lucias "like an old gopher snake, sunning." She wrote about the birds and animals of the forests and sea, and when the wildflowers came into bloom she described the scene.

Her prose was sometimes too rhapsodic for the taste of rival Carmel writers, who said she overdid it with such passages as: "Here on the left is the most beautiful display of bloom I have ever seen. Mingled poppy, golden and riant, and the ground lupin sassing it back. Rising on a distant hill to a mat of yellow and lavender, more than half a hundred different flowers woven unreally, so that you felt you could lift up the shawl the little hills were wearing and find their bare breasts underneath." But W. K. loved it and printed every word she brought in.

Now she rarely came to Carmel except on the day her column was due. I missed her, and I was glad whenever she invited me to go home with her for a few days. We had become good friends. Driving down the coast in her convertible, tearing along as far above the speed limit as she dared, soaring up the steep grades, her foot on the gas pedal, the tires screaming on the curves, and the road ahead invisible beyond the approaching bend, I wondered if we would make it to her place alive.

During my visits, we might take a long hike into one of the canyons, with Lynda naming every flower, shrub, vine, and fern along the way. Once she took me up to a homesteader's ranch where we ate supper by the light of a coal-oil lamp and then came home by flashlight and the pale shine of a full moon. She knew the way. She often hiked up these canyons to reach the high meadows where the ranch families lived near their livestock. If she wanted a story from a wife, she got it while helping with the chores, whether it was washing clothes or killing chickens. Lynda could kill, draw, and pluck a chicken as well as anyone because she had done it on the family farm. It was a side of her that no one in Carmel ever saw.

Usually each visit included a trip to Slate's hot springs, a popular place for taking a bath. It was not far from Anderson Creek, but there was no sign on the road to indicate where it was. You had to know the location to find it. Down on the side of a cliff were two claw-footed white enamel tubs sitting on a wooden platform. The water was slightly sulfurous and very hot. To fill a tub, you opened a spigot on a trough connected to the springs, and, as the tub filled, you cooled it down with cold water from a container that the last bathers had filled for that purpose.

Lying in our tubs with water to our chins, we could look up into the sky where hawks might be gliding, or we could listen to the barking of seals far below us on the rocks. Afterward, we released the water and let it splash downhill. Then we filled the containers with water to cool for the next bathers.

The tubs had been there for many years. People said they had been salvaged from a shipwreck.

The winter passed slowly. The only excitement around the *Cymbal* was when W. K. was "missing." If this happened when anything came up that required his immediate attention—when a bill collector appeared and threatened action, or when Dorothea was looking for him and he could not be located in town—the only conclusion was that he must be over in Monterey at Flora's. I was always the one who had to go after him. One of the men would let me use his car for the trip over the hill to Monterey.

Flora Woods ran a small establishment on Cannery Row, with no more than half a dozen girls. Until the cannery workers came off their shifts in the late afternoon and business picked up, there wasn't much to do, and Flora's friends were welcome to drop by for a few beers and some conversation. They kept her well informed about what was going on in and around town, especially if it took place behind closed doors. She always liked to see W. K. He had a sharp and witty tongue and was at his best when castigating the local moguls and politicians. Nothing of importance happened on the Monterey Peninsula that escaped his opinion. Flora was among his most understanding listeners.

Her place happened to be just across the street from Ed's laboratory. After I had made sure that W. K.'s brown Packard sedan was there, I would continue on out of sight and park beyond the laboratory. I knew better than to ask the bouncer at Flora's if W. K. was inside. I just told him "to tell W. K., if he should see him," whatever the message was that I had for him. During these brief moments at the door, I always tried to get a glimpse inside, but I never could. I had never seen Flora either. All I knew about her looks was that she dyed her hair red.

I would cross the street to Ed's—the door was never locked —and watch through the window until I saw W. K. leave. If Ed wasn't busy, we usually had a cup of coffee together before I drove back to Carmel.

When the spring of 1940 came, I decided to go to New York, where I had contacts with magazines that had taken my free-lance work. I hoped to find a job with one of them, and I did get editorial work. In my spare time I wrote articles on assignment for an advertising agency.

When I later returned to California I continued working as a magazine editor. In 1942 I was hired as the assistant director of publicity for the Extension Division of the University of California, and in 1944 I was made director of both publicity and public relations. My headquarters were in Berkeley.

Lynda and I had never lost touch, and when I was living again in California we saw each other often. She was no longer writing for the *Cymbal*. Through indebtedness incurred when he had bought a printing press that he could not afford, W. K. had been unable to stall his creditors and had to sell the paper in 1941. The *Carmel Pine Cone* eventually acquired it.

Lynda wrote for the *Pine Cone*, covering Big Sur, but she would never give them a column. She continued to work on her Henniker book. In 1943 the cabin she lived in burned down, and her manuscript burned with it. She then moved to The Log House, which she was able to rent because she was a friend of the owners. I was there many weekends, and it was through Lynda that I came to know the Vardas and to visit their barn in Monterey.

The afternoon that I arrived in Monterey on the Southern Pacific's Del Monte Special, she met the train as usual. We shopped in the markets in Carmel before driving down the coast. After she had given me the news of our mutual friends, she described in detail the day that Yanko had appeared at the house with Henry, and how she later had offered Henry the guest cabin. "He needed help and I thought, 'Well, why not?' " She giggled. "I expected him to be a big bore, but he's turned out to be very good company." Another giggle. "Of course, he talks about himself all the time, but I don't mind. It's all interesting. He lived in Paris for ten years."

She gave her attention to the curves ahead in the road, swinging us around each one as recklessly as ever.

"I haven't read any of his books yet. Some came the other day in a lot of cartons of stuff. It scares me to think he's sending for his things. My God! I hope he doesn't plan to stay forever. I thought maybe a month or two would help him get on his feet. He says his publishers owe him money."

"Are you getting any writing done?" I asked her.

She hooted. "How? He's using the typewriter! That's another thing he says will be coming along soon." With a shriek she added, "He also wants to send for his phonograph!"

I said that I owned one of his books, *The Colossus of Maroussi*, and that I had brought it with me to ask him to autograph it.

"What's the book about?"

"About a trip he made to Greece a few years ago."

"A travel book?"

"Not exactly."

"Well, is it any good?"

"Yes, it's a marvelous book."

For a second I saw the surprise on her face, and then it was gone, for we were already coming to the house and she had turned off the highway to climb the knoll. When she stopped the car, we could hear the muffled pound of a typewriter.

"Well, there he is," she said.

12

*Money has been the one thing I have never had, and
yet I have led a rich life and in the main a happy one.*
The Colossus of Maroussi

When Lynda took me in to meet Henry Miller, the sound
of the typewriter stopped the moment she rapped on the door, and
he immediately opened it to welcome us. We had interrupted him
at work, but he showed no sign of annoyance. He seemed delighted
to see us.

"I've been expecting you for an hour. Where have you
been?"

"We stopped in Carmel to do some shopping. We're having
lamb chops for dinner. And cherry pie!" Lynda said.

He clasped my offered hand. "So this is Kathryn! Lynda has
been talking about you for a week. I feel I already know you."

I wanted to say that I'd been looking forward to meeting
him ever since I had read his book on Greece, but it seemed such
a rehearsed thing to say that I couldn't get the words out. I smiled
instead and sat down on the bed beside Lynda.

She had described Henry's general appearance to me, mentioning especially the baldness, the Mongolian look of high cheek-
bones on a narrow face, and the heavily lidded eyes. She had
neglected to mention that his eyes were blue and that he wore
glasses. His vigor astonished me for "the old man," as Lynda called
him, was quick and full of bounce, moving about the room, adjust-
ing the curtains against the glare of the late afternoon sun, hunting
for a matchbook, offering Lynda a cigarette and lighting it, then

lighting one for himself, and finally sitting down in front of us. Being a non-smoker I had declined a cigarette.

He was wearing a gray sweater over a faded checked flannel shirt, old pants that had once belonged to a suit, and canvas shoes. I always look at hands. His were rather small but long-fingered, clean, with the nails cut short. He wore no jewelry, not even a wristwatch.

In the room where we sat, the bed was carefully made, and beside it on a table were a kerosene lamp, some magazines, a pile of typed manuscript pages, and a plate full of cigarette stubs and ashes. Through an open doorway I could see into a second, smaller room with two tables, one for the typewriter and a longer one behind it stacked with small packages, books, papers, and other articles.

There were pictures on all the walls. They appeared to be prints taken from magazines. I got up to look at one, a reproduction of a Man Ray photograph. It was a photograph of a painting of a metronome with a large human eye superimposed upon it. Miller was now standing beside me.

"I like that eye," he said. "Man Ray was one of the first surrealists working in Paris. He was a painter before he took up photography. That's his painting in the photograph."

I looked at it for a moment or two, finding it mysterious and secretive. I moved to three color prints, which were all of paintings by Marc Chagall.

"Chagall is a favorite painter of mine," Miller said. "Thirty years ago, when he was just getting started, he had the courage to paint in his own way, to get away from what the others were doing."

The prints were of *Girl on Horseback*, *Midsummer Night's Dream*, and *Bride and Groom of the Eiffel Tower*. I took my time looking at them.

"He has said that he paints from visions, a kind of supranatural second sight, and I believe him," Miller said. "The roosters, flying birds, fans, bouquets of flowers, the clocks, the Russian churches with their domes and crucifixes, all of which he uses over and over, have a special meaning for him. Like the violins. They're in many of his paintings. I've heard that he loves music, but I don't know if he plays the violin or not. Anyway, he likes to paint men playing the violin."

"I think the people he paints are interesting," I said. "Circus acrobats, peasants, little children. And the animals, especially the donkeys. Some of the figures are flying in the air or upside down. I wonder why he paints them that way."

"Why rationalize a painting? Just look at it and enjoy the vibrations you get from it. Chagall paints magic, and there's no magic in realism. If you ever get a chance to see the originals, don't miss them. The colors are beautiful. Deep, cool, shining, raging. They're extraordinary!"

I was intrigued by Miller's Brooklyn voice. It was low in pitch, with a repetitive cadence, a soft, flowing rhythm that swept the words along. As he spoke he flung his arms about, letting the cigarette ash fall where it may.

He said that he himself had been painting since he was in his early twenties.

"I don't call myself a painter, but I love to paint. But there's so much that I don't know, can't get the hang of, you know, but I learn something from every one of my paintings, especially from the failures. No matter how badly I fail, even when the results are cockeyed, I am pleased with them in one way or another. I never know how it happens when they're successful, when the colors are just right. It comes about like a miracle. It's fantastic! And though I try again and again I can never repeat the miracle at will. I really do not know how the best ones happen. Writing is hard work, but painting gives me pleasure, a marvelous feeling of happiness. Now today I've been writing all day and I'm tired. I'm exhausted. If I had been painting all day, I'd be refreshed, I wouldn't be tired at all. I'd be full of joy. I'd be in high spirits. I'd be crowing!"

Lynda interrupted. "It's almost dark. Let's go over to the house and have some sherry before supper." On the way to the house Lynda said, "Henry, I didn't know you liked to paint."

"My paints and brushes are somewhere in the packages that came yesterday. But I'm out of paper."

"We'll go to Carmel and get some," she said.

While Henry and I got a fire started with redwood kindling

and oak logs, Lynda went to her bedroom to change from her suit and high heels. When she returned she was wearing old jeans, red sneakers, and the same exquisite blouse of shell pink chiffon with a yoke and collar of handmade lace in a matching shade of pink. She had pushed the delicate sleeves up above her elbows.

We drank our sherry while sitting before the fire, with Sir Thomas on Lynda's lap and Frigga at our feet. Lynda talked about taking Henry to meet "the neighbors" who lived farther down the coast, saying that she had put it off long enough. She described each person enthusiastically, making them more interesting than they really were, I thought, but Henry showed little interest. I wondered if he was listening. If the fire died down, he put on another stick of driftwood.

Behind us on the table, the chimney of the kerosene lamp sent a pale shaft of light to the ceiling, otherwise the only other light in the room came from the fire. From the phosphorescence in the driftwood, tiny blue tongues occasionally came out to lick the charred logs back to life. I asked Henry what he was writing.

"It's called *Sunday After the War*. It'll be another New Directions book."

"I've read *The Colossus of Maroussi,*" I said and was finally able to tell him how much I admired it.

"Have you been to Greece?"

"I was on a cruise once, going up the Adriatic. We sailed past part of Greece and stopped in the Gulf of Corinth for a few hours. It was late afternoon. We took a launch to the quay. The town was Patras. I remember that you didn't think much of Patras."

"Did you?"

"Well, the town square was shabby, the shops were poor, and there was so much stone, no trees or flowers, and it made everything so drab. I want to go back to Greece someday and see the places you wrote about—Thebes, Mycenae, Epidaurus, Delphi."

"You will. But why Thebes?"

"Because you wrote that when you saw it you burst into tears. I can't remember ever reading anything as moving as your description of the plain of Thebes."

"No other place, and there have been many that left memorable impressions on me, affected me the way Thebes did. Maybe it was the mood I was in that day."

Lynda had already gone to the kitchen to start dinner. Henry and I went in to help. She was frying the chops. "Get some more wood, Henry," she said, handing me a can of creamed corn to open. When Henry returned with an armload of wood, she opened a lid on the stove and pushed in one of the chunks. She took the rolls out of the oven where they had been warming up. When the corn was bubbling, she handed Henry a bottle of wine to take to the table in the other room.

Between mouthfuls, as we sat around the table eating, Lynda, for Henry's benefit, began talking about the early days on the coast, stressing the loneliness and isolation, the hardships endured by the women especially. "The life was too hard for women not bred to it," she said. "There weren't too many women, not enough to go around. And if a man brought a woman in from outside she soon began to hate the life and to hate him." Her hair-raising exaggerations of rivalries, snatched wives, stranglings, agonizing childbirth, women gone mad, and the suicidal leaps into the sea by some of them had Henry's full attention. He watched her lamp-lit face, eerily bright in the near-dark room with only occasional flashes from the flames of the fitful fire.

"How do you know all this?" he asked her at last.

"When you live on the coast, you know these stories."

I got up to put wood on the fire, to brighten the room a bit.

"Henry, you are going to meet Shanagolden," Lynda said. "She and Harrydick live down the coast a ways. She's been collecting these stories for years. She's already published one book, a novel that Morrow published two years ago. It's about Big Sur in the 1870s. Now she's writing another book about the country."

Shanagolden was the name that Harrydick had given her long ago and by which we all knew her. We never called her Lillian, which was her real name. She and Harrydick Ross met when he was an art student at the University of Oregon and she was the buyer for a Portland bookstore. They fell in love but, because she was so much older than he, she would not marry him. When she took a job in San Francisco, he followed her, and they lived together for several years, until they married at last in 1924.

That same year they took a walking trip up the coast from San Simeon to Monterey and were so attracted to the country that they would have moved there had they had the money to sustain themselves. In the early thirties they moved to Salinas, where Harrydick opened a commercial art shop and Shanagolden contributed articles to the local newspaper. When, through a friend, they were offered a cabin to live in on Big Sur's Livermore Ledge, they closed the shop and came at once. Harrydick turned to sculpture, working in wood, stone, and metal. He took any carpentry jobs that came his way. People were coming into the country, opened now by the road, and they were building houses. Otherwise, the Rosses mainly lived off the country's game and fish, and they grew a garden.

Shanagolden was a born storyteller, as everyone who spent an hour or two with her found out. Dramatic narration was normal speech to her. Most of the time the stories were those she had heard from the descendants of the coast's original settlers; which she repeated in her own highly effective way to those who asked to hear them. She could also move people by her stories of native animals and birds. We all loved listening to Shanagolden. Everyone urged her to put her words in writing, and sometimes she did. She had written poetry since girlhood; still, she had never thought seriously of writing a book until Carl Sandburg happened to visit Big Sur and his friends took him to meet the Rosses. With her first words and the sound of her voice, Shanagolden captured Sandburg. He was impressed by her knowledge of local history, but it was her skill in bringing to life characters out of a distant past that so surprised and pleased him. She talked about these people as if they were her neighbors and he was about to meet them.

Before he left he insisted that she start work on a book. His praise helped her dispel any doubts she may have had about her ability to sustain a novel through to conclusion. She began to write the book that was published as *The Stranger*.

Lynda was cutting and serving the pie. "You know, Henry," she said, "there are no graveyards in Big Sur. Nobody dies here. They go out to Monterey to die." She paused. "Well, some go to Salinas."

Henry put down his forkful of cherry pie. "How do they know they're going to die? Sometimes it happens suddenly."

Lynda asked me, "Kathryn, do you know of anyone who has died in Big Sur?"

I had to admit that I did not.

Henry said, "What about those old-timers, before the road? They had to bury their dead somewhere."

"I have walked all over these mountains," Lynda answered, "and I have never seen a grave. Not one, anywhere."

Dinner was over and she and I were clearing the table. "Well, I'm going to bed," Henry said. He took one of the flashlights and went out, saying, "I'll see you two in the morning."

We started the dishes, and as I was drying I said, "I don't think you can bury anybody in a state park."

"There were people here long before any of this was a state park. Where are the graves? I've never seen one."

"Maybe the graves weren't deep enough, and wild animals dug them up and scattered the bones."

"Animals don't disturb old bones."

Lynda put more wood in the stove so that it wouldn't be cold in the morning when she started breakfast. "Take the other lamp to go to your bedroom," she said. "I'll take this one."

We got our nightclothes and undressed before the fire. She took the five-foot iron poker from the fireplace and, holding a lamp in the other hand, returned to the kitchen. I knew what she was going to do. We called good night to each other, and I took my lamp and went to bed.

Then I heard the stamping. It was always the last thing she did before going to bed. She went from room to room stamping on the floor with the poker to scare away any rattlesnakes under the house. There certainly were rattlers around. Big Sur was full of them. But I doubted if the stamping did any good. The snakes liked it under the house where it was dry. I could see no place on the floor of my room where they could get into the house, and I doubted if there were holes in other floors. However, I knew that some mornings Lynda found one in the woodbox on the porch.

I always believed that the reason she couldn't keep help was the snakes. I had heard that one woman had left in hysterics after discovering one outside the back door. She had thrown a pan of boiling water on it, or rather after it, for the snake had already escaped into the grass.

My thoughts as I fell asleep were not on the snakes but on knowing that I was lying on the last crumbs of a continent. America stopped outside the windows of the house. Big Sur is but a small part of the California coastline, but there I could sense the awesome end of cities, mountain chains, rivers and valleys, plains and deserts—all stopped by an ocean more vast than America itself. Although I could scarcely hear the quiet booming of the surf, I imagined that I felt the throbbing of that enormous body of water that had sucked and surged its way across half a hemisphere. I let it lull me to sleep.

13

When [the obscene] is recognized and accepted, whether as a figment of the imagination or as an integral part of human reality, it inspires no more dread or revulsion than can be ascribed to the flowering lotus which sends its roots down into the mud of the stream on which it is borne.

Obscenity and the Law of Reflection

I was up at daybreak the next morning. Coffee boiling in the kitchen told me that Henry was also up. I knew it wasn't Lynda. She never got out of bed before eight o'clock, if that early.

While we were drinking our coffee, I asked him if he'd like to join me for a walk on the beach. He said that he and Frigga walked on the beach every morning and that the tide would be out now, leaving room for us to walk around the bluffs.

We made our way easily down the side of the cliff. The sandy path was not difficult. It swung between clumps of grasses and mosses with no steep drops before reaching the bottom. The air was misty and cool, saturated with the bitterness of brine. Henry was a fast walker and was soon far ahead of me, with Frigga capering at his quick step. I lagged behind, stopping to look over the seashells that the rippling surf brought into view. My pockets were full of shells by the time I caught up with Henry. Noticing that I was far behind, he had stopped to wait for me.

"Do you like Big Sur?" I asked him.

"You mean do I like the scenery? Yes. It's overpowering. Beautiful. It's very beautiful, but it's lifeless. If this were anyplace else in the world, the whole mountainside would be covered with houses, orchards, gardens. People would be all over the place. In Greece there'd be shepherds with their flocks. Some of the mountainsides there are as rocky and barren as this. But the flocks find nourishment somehow. And there'd be fishing boats tied up along here."

"You can't have boats here on this beach. The ocean would crush them to pieces. And there are people here. Not swarming all over the place, of course. Most of this land belongs to ranchers, and they want to keep it open for the cattle. It's not for sale. People can only build in certain places. And in the state park they can't build either. I'm glad. I like it this way. I never tire of looking at it."

"That's because you live in a city. You're not here all the time. At night especially, when there's nothing to see, you feel you've dropped out of civilization."

"If I had the money I'd live here all the time."

He had picked up a few pieces of driftwood to take back to the house. "I'll be here until the war ends. Then I'll be off."

"Where to?"

"I really don't know. Mexico perhaps. I have a friend living in Mexico. Michael Fraenkel. We wrote a book together. All letters to each other. It's in two volumes. When we get back to the house I'll give you the first volume. I have no copies on hand of volume two."

"Thank you. I'd like to read the book."

"Would you care to read some of my manuscript of *Sunday After the War*?"

"Yes, I would."

We had reached a spur of a rampart of spikes and scarps confronting the approaching sea. The contest between tide and stone was lined up ahead as far as we could see, and the combers were coming in ever closer. We turned back.

I asked him if he had ever heard of the poet Robinson Jeffers. "He has written more about Big Sur than anyone else," I said. "He put the austerity and grandeur of the coast into his poems. They also have a lot of violence and tragedy in them, but that fits perfectly into a landscape like this."

"Yes, I know who he is. I read something of his in Paris a long time ago. Lynda was talking about him the other day. She read me one of his poems. For me the poem would have been more interesting written as a play."

Back at the house we went to his quarters, where he looked

over the pages of manuscript that he had finished for *Sunday After the War* and selected chapter three for me to read. It was titled "The Gigantic Sunrise" and was about the Greek poet Anghelos Sikelianos, none of whose books had been translated into English. I found it wordy, discursive, and difficult to follow. Henry wrote nothing about the poetic quality of the work—how could he? He could not read Greek. The piece lauded the poet as "an awakener" to the Promethean role of his countrymen in the destiny of the world. I could only say when I had finished the six pages that I hoped to read Sikelianos in an English translation someday.

"New Directions is planning to publish a book of his poems," he said. "I don't know who the translator is." He handed me the *Hamlet* book. On the flyleaf he had written: "Dear Kathryn —Volume 2 will follow in due course, but will reveal no more of the mystery surrounding Hamlet. Henry Miller, Big Sur."

I read the inscription and thanked him. "I have my copy of the *Colossus* with me. Would you autograph it?"

"Sure. Where is it?"

"In Lynda's bedroom. I'm leaving it for her to read."

"There's no need to do that. I'll give her a copy."

During lunch it was decided that Lynda and Henry would come to Oakland in two weeks and spend a weekend with me. I lived in a large old house on the edge of the business district of the city. It was a convenient twenty minutes by streetcar to my office in Berkeley.

When it was time for Lynda to drive me to Monterey to catch the afternoon train, Henry decided to come along. They would visit the Vardas before coming home. Henry handed me my copy of *The Colossus of Maroussi*. On the way to the station I read what he had written in it: "To Kathryn (like Catherine the Great) Winslow, who came as a surprise and disappeared like a meteor. *On se verra à* Oakland. Henry Miller, Big Sur, 4/8/44. From his 'Lodge.' "

The day after I returned home, I phoned my friend in San Francisco, Bobby Ferro, to tell her about my visit with Lynda and Henry. It was she who had given me *The Colossus of Maroussi* when it had come out three years before. Her sister Marjorie was married to Ed Grabhorn, and Bobby had heard all the stories about Henry's visits with the Grabhorns during the preparation of that book. She had never met him, but her impression of Miller, based on what she had heard from the Grabhorns, was that he was "a character." She was eager to hear what I had to say.

I assured her that he was not "a character" but a very nice person and rather quiet. I told her that he and Lynda were coming to visit me in two weeks.

"Be sure to come over before that. I'll have two books for you to read. They're Marjorie's but she'll lend them to me. You take them home and read them. He doesn't write like a nice old man. There's some pretty raw stuff. The books were published in Paris, where, I guess, you can get away with it. Anyhow, some of it is terribly funny. Whatever you think of the clowning and the Casanova stuff, you'll never forget the books."

The books were *Tropic of Cancer* and *Tropic of Capricorn.*

Not knowing anything about either of the *Tropics*, the book I opened first was *Tropic of Capricorn.* The callous self-denunciation with which he begins the book surprised me: "I had need of nobody because I wanted to be free, free to do and to give only as my whims dictated. The moment anything was expected or demanded of me I balked. That was the form my independence took. I was corrupt, in other words, corrupt from the start. It's as though my mother fed me a poison, and though I was weaned young, the poison never left my system."

I read on about his life from boyhood until he was nearly forty years old. It was a merciless, blasphemous, delirious recitation, a chaotic confession, and it stunned me. The style was hyperbolic, intoxicated, and lashed with obscenities. The ugly scenes of sex that he described were offensive to me. For that I would have thrown a lesser book aside. But *Tropic of Capricorn* has such force that I felt compelled to follow Henry's experiences to a conclusion. The book has no conclusion. It left me exhausted, wrenched by Miller's pain and anger, his frustrations and despairs.

This Miller was not the one I had met and talked with. I had found a kindly, soft-spoken, "oldish" man whose exceptional command of the English language had produced a joyous book about a visit to Greece. He was not the twenty- and thirty-year-old

Miller of Brooklyn and Manhattan who, by comparison, seemed wholly fictional.

Tropic of Cancer was also autobiographical, I found, but in a blithe, clowning way. These were the early Paris years of his forties, and, though he was usually penniless, often not knowing from day to day where he would sleep, he wrote about that time with a mischievous humor that was entirely missing from *Tropic of Capricorn*. I did not know that the books were not written in chronological order but that *Tropic of Cancer* was his first book and *Tropic of Capricorn* his sixth. The rough language and ribaldry still disturbed me, but I accepted the details as an honest part of the writing.

When I had finished reading both books, I wondered if I would ever again recognize the traveler who was so inspired by the spirit and beauty of Greece. I opened *The Colossus of Maroussi* to one of my favorite passages, the one about Crete's magnificent plain of Messara: "At the very gates of Paradise the descendants of Zeus halted here on their way to eternity to cast a last look earthward and saw with the eyes of innocents that the earth is indeed what they had always dreamed it to be: a place of beauty and joy and peace."

Then I read again what he had written about his friend Katsimbalis, the "colossus" of the book, a man who was a teller of "endless and seemingly fabulous stories." Of those stories Miller wrote that "there must have been a good element of fancy and distortion, yet if truth was occasionally sacrificed to reality the man behind the story only succeeded thereby in revealing more faithfully and thoroughly his human image." Was he also describing himself? I wondered.

14

When I am true to myself I find, by some strange
logic, that I am usually untrue to others. The reason is,
no doubt, that I am out of step. And when I am
thoroughly out of step I usually arrive at some
passionate truths.

Hamlet, Vol. 1

Lynda and Henry arrived on a Friday evening. I turned the library with its daybed over to Henry and settled Lynda in my bedroom.

The house had many rooms honeycombed here and there under a peaked roof. Seven were on the first floor, and there were three unfinished rooms in the attic. The kitchen, with its ten-foot-high ceiling, was the heart of the house, stretching across it from side to side, and a porch had been added on beside it. In addition to the usual appliances, there was a six-foot-long table with its chairs, and a sofa alongside one of the windows. In one corner of the room, a door opened to a staircase leading to the attic.

It was a seventy-year-old house located in a neighborhood that was awaiting certain demolition when the land was needed for business construction, parking lots, or whatever. A streetcar line was a block away.

After dinner, when Henry was stretched out on the kitchen sofa, I mentioned that George Leite was anxious to meet him and that we had all been invited to his home the next day for lunch, if that was agreeable.

"George Leite! Where did you run into him?" Henry asked.

"I see him all the time. He works in a bookstore near the campus. Last week when I went in there, I picked up a copy of a new publication called *Circle,* and as I was looking it over George walked up and told me that he was its editor and publisher. It's not a real magazine with covers, it's just some mimeographed pages folded together. There was a letter in it from you."

"I know. He sent me a copy. A few months ago he wrote me asking me to send him something for it. He offered to pay me five dollars. I turned him down, but he published the letter."

"He wants to meet you. He said he was going down to Monterey to look you up the first chance he got."

"I hope you told him that I'm not in Monterey. I don't want him pestering Yanko."

"I told him that if he wanted to meet you he might be able to this weekend. I told him you were coming here."

"Why did you tell him that? I don't want to see him."

"He's just a young guy. In his mid twenties. He's very nice. Why don't you want to meet him? He's so anxious to meet you."

"I didn't like the way he approached me about contributing to the magazine. Like he was doing me a favor. And offering me five dollars! The letter he published sums up the way I feel about him."

"Well, I doubt if he can pay you more than five dollars. He's on a shoestring, although he said he's expecting to have a backer soon, and if so the following issues will be printed, not mimeographed."

"That's what they all say."

"He's got a wife and little baby, and to make ends meet he drives a Yellow Cab in the evenings and on weekends."

Henry smoked another cigarette. Lynda had taken off her pumps and rolled up the sleeves of her blouse. She was shelling walnuts for me. I had planned a buffet supper for the next night and had invited some friends in to meet Henry. I had written him about it, and, when he replied that it was all right, I had invited nine members of the university faculty to dinner. Lynda was helping me get things ready. I had two cakes to bake. I had saved up enough ration stamps to buy a ham, which was already in the oven. I would only need to reheat it the next night.

"Well," Henry said, "what time does he want us to come?"

"About noon. They live in Berkeley."

I phoned his wife to let her know that we were coming.

The next morning Lynda decided to wash her hair, which made it inconvenient for her to drive us to the Leites, so we took the streetcar and walked a block. There was a Yellow Cab parked in front of a house, but we discovered that the Leites lived in back of the house in a small cottage.

George greeted us warmly and ushered us inside to meet his wife Nancy, and then we all went to the kitchen where lunch was on the table. There were cold cuts and cheese, a round loaf of sweet Portuguese bread still warm from the bakery, and a bottle of red wine. The wine was enough for each of us to have a small glass.

Everything went well. Henry was all smiles and charm as he listened to George's ambitious plans for *Circle*, which was to be a quarterly. Henry had a way of giving his full attention that was very flattering. When George mentioned his backer, Henry asked who it was.

"He's a young guy, a nuclear physicist working for the government on something called the Manhattan Project. Sometimes he works in Oak Ridge, Tennessee, and sometimes he's here in Berkeley at the radiation lab the university has up on the hill."

"Is his name Bern Porter?"

"Yes. You know him?"

"He's having a small booklet of mine reprinted next month. *What Are You Going to Do About Alf?* it's called. I had it printed in Paris some years ago. Porter looked me up in Beverly Glen last year and wanted to publish my work. If he wants to put money into *Circle*, let him. He's a scientist, but what he really wants to do is get away from science and into publishing books. He writes, too, you know."

"That's what he told me."

While they continued to talk about Porter's interest in *Circle*, Nancy and I went to the bedroom where the baby had awakened and was fussing. When we returned to the kitchen, George was about to write down the names of people Henry believed would be willing to send their work to the magazine: "Anaïs Nin, Kenneth Patchen, Lawrence Durrell, Michael Fraenkel, Man Ray, Nicholas Moore, Harry Herschkowitz . . ."

"Who's Harry Herschkowitz?"

"A merchant seaman friend of mine in New York. He's got

his heart set on becoming a writer. So far nothing published, but he's making the effort. Never discouraged. He's helped me out with a few dollars now and then. I'd like to do him a favor."

Henry said he would write all these people and urge them to send him something. He also promised to send something himself for the next issue. No mention was made of payment. It was three o'clock before we left the Leites. George drove us home in the taxi with the meter off.

In planning the party for that night, I had chosen people I thought Henry and Lynda would enjoy. They were all good company, friends I'd had to the house before. I was acquainted with many faculty members through my job with the Extension Division. When I had invited them, I had said that I would be having as one of my houseguests that weekend an author they were sure to like. They had wanted to know his name. "Not *the* Henry Miller?" they had asked—all except Bernie, professor of "the Age of Goethe," who had never heard of Henry Miller.

I had invited Mac by note. He was an assistant professor of modern American poetry and a distinguished poet himself, but he was not teaching that year. He had mailed my note back with "YES" scrawled across it.

Besides Bernie, his wife Helga, and Mac, I had also invited Blake, professor of contemporary American fiction, and his wife Gazella; Luis, a young Spaniard who had earned his doctorate from Columbia the year before and was a newcomer to Berkeley and an instructor in the Spanish Renaissance; Josephine, a Frenchwoman and my good friend, who was an assistant professor of French literature; Theo, an instructor in short-story writing; and Harley, professor of East Asian civilization.

They began arriving around six-thirty. Lynda was the first to be introduced. Her chic suit, three-inch heels, and bare legs set her apart at once. Josephine was a very quiet dresser. Plump Helga unfortunately had a taste for jabots and pleated skirts. Gazella dyed her hose to match whatever outfit she might be wearing, and that night the color was what was then called "electric blue." Tall and bony-thin, she imagined that her long, dangling earrings drew attention from the stalk of her neck. She was devoted to the little theater off campus and worked tirelessly on its behalf, raising money, painting scenery, sewing costumes, typing—and occasionally pinch-hitting in a minor role. She was very bright and had graduated magna cum laude from Smith College.

Smiling, shaking hands, and laughing in that giggly way of hers, Lynda was quickly getting acquainted when Henry sauntered into the living room. He was wearing the same sweater, shirt, and pants in which he had arrived the night before, and, except for the corduroy jacket, they were about what he been wearing when I had met him two weeks earlier in Big Sur. Clean, of course. He looked like the impoverished writer that he was. I introduced him without giving academic titles.

I had set up a bar for martinis, and I asked Bernie, who made excellent ones, to take over. Henry immediately declined to drink a martini, asking if he couldn't have wine instead. There were several bottles open in the kitchen ready to be served with dinner. He went to get one.

When he returned Helga asked, while passing him the cheese crisps, "Are you making your home now in Big Sur, Mr. Miller?"

Catching her accent and not replying to her question, he asked, "What part of Germany are you from, Elsa?"

"I am Helga, and I am not German. I am Czech. And I am in America now sixteen years with my husband." She passed the crackers to Theo, who was waiting to speak with Henry.

"Mr. Miller, when you were living in Paris, I suppose you knew Gertrude Stein," said Theo.

"No, I never met her."

"That surprises me, Mr. Miller, she was friendly with so many American writers. I've read about it. They came to her studio . . ."

"She never invited me to her studio."

Theo helped himself to the salted almonds that were going around and let Bernie refill his glass. He was a young man, not much older than Luis.

"However," Henry said, "I was told that she read my books. She knew of me all right. I had no desire to meet her anyway. I never met Hemingway either. Or Fitzgerald, or Thornton Wilder, or Ford Madox Ford. That was her crowd, not mine. You see, I had my own friends who came to the Villa Seurat. That's where I had *my* studio."

Gazella joined them.

"Mr. Miller, I owned a first edition of the *Tropic of Cancer* once."

"You did? Where did you get it?"

"Well, it's a long story. My sister, who was still in college at the time, acquired a roommate who had been studying at the Sorbonne the year before, and she had brought the book back with her. After everybody at Smith had read it, she gave the book to my sister, but my sister wanted to get rid of it—oh, excuse me, Mr. Miller . . ."

"That's all right. Go on."

"So she gave it to me. I was living in New York at the time."

"And what did you do with it? Burn it?"

"No! I had it for years, and then Blake probably lent it to somebody and, of course, I never saw it again. My husband is always lending books to people and never getting them back."

Blake was listening to their conversation while he was taking sides with Mac in an argument with Bernie over the university's action in dismissing Mac from the English Department. The question was, Did they have the right to do so? Mac was appealing the decision. Blake called out to Gazella, "The book's in my office." He joined her and Miller.

"You keep books in your office?" asked Henry.

"I'm a teacher. My students study contemporary fiction written by our leading American authors—Steinbeck, Hemingway, Faulkner, Katherine Anne Porter, and the others. The university would never allow me to discuss your books in class, I'm sorry to say, but I keep the *Tropics* and the New Directions books in my office and I let the students borrow them. I want them to be acquainted with your work as well as that of the others we study in the course. I had the Colt book, too, but, as my wife says, somebody borrowed it and hasn't brought it back yet."

"That's very interesting." Henry would have said more, but just then the last guest arrived. When Lynda caught sight of him, she screamed, "Harley!" and rushed to his arms to be hugged and kissed. This reunion, a surprise to me, appeared to be mutually enjoyable.

Bernie looked into the pitcher of martinis. "There's just enough left for one for you, Harley."

"None for me, thank you."

Bernie asked me, "Shall I make more?"

Several said "No more for me," and Bernie sat down. I said that I had better be looking after dinner and excused myself. As I left the room, I noticed that Mac helped himself to what was left of the martinis. Lynda came with me to help.

In the kitchen she said, "He's the one from Pacific Grove. 1937—remember? He's a kind of guru."

I was adding the asparagus tips to the boiling water; I said that I couldn't remember. Together we lifted the ham from the oven and put it onto a platter on the tea cart. She took the scalloped potatoes and the corn bread from the oven and put them on the tea cart, too.

"You *must* remember! I told you all about it: how I went to their retreat—I was just curious, I wanted to see what they did— and there he was, in his kimono, with nothing under it as I found out while he was showing me over the building and courtyard."

"How in the world did you find that out?"

"He took me to his room—his cell, he called it."

Helga came to help us. I gave her the salad to toss. "When you've mixed the greens, you can add the vegetables." I finished the sauce for the asparagus.

"You know," Helga said, "Mac had a few before we picked him up. I could smell it on him when he got into the car." Mac was their neighbor, and they had come together in Bernie's car. "Too bad, too bad," she said as she set off for the dining room with her arms around the huge salad bowl. Lynda continued her story.

"That night on the beach the chiggers bit us. Our behinds swelled up and the next day mine hurt so much I couldn't sit down, and he came to the cottage to dope me up with calamine and I don't know what else, and he stayed for the rest of the summer."

"Well, now I remember."

"At the end of the summer he went to Cambodia, and I never saw him again. How did you meet him?"

"He teaches at Cal."

"I wonder why he never looked me up."

"You haven't been living in Carmel for the last seven years."

While she was lighting the candles on the buffet table, I asked the others to come in. Card tables had been set up in the library for seating.

I saw to it that Henry sat with Josephine, but while they were seating themselves Mac and Luis slipped into the other two chairs. I had told Josephine about *Sunday After the War*, and now she asked Henry what it was about. "About the war?" she asked.

"Not at all. It's a collection of essays that I've done on a variety of subjects, my travels around the country since I returned from France, about a book of Anaïs Nin, the work of D. H. Lawrence, my experiences as a psychoanalyst . . ."

"A *what*?" cried Mac, putting down his fork and staring at Henry.

"Anyone can become an analyst. All you have to do is listen and speak only when necessary and then in a soothing voice. People heal themselves as soon as they let go of their egos, when they cease to be egomaniacs."

"Have you had any professional training along those lines?" Mac asked.

"No, of course not." Heads were turned in Henry's direction. He changed the subject by telling Josephine that writing books was no way to make a living, that in spite of all the books he had written he could barely survive on the royalties. And that led him to the subject of Guggenheim Fellowships. He said that he had applied three years before and had been turned down. He mentioned the names of the prominent American writers who had endorsed his application. "Useless," he said. Then, making up cockamamie names and projects, he rattled off what to him typified the undeserving awards. "It's useless to apply unless you can write *Professor* before your name," he concluded.

Mac said, "It may interest you to know that I got a Guggenheim in 1938."

The look on Henry's face was of both surprise and disbelief. "For what?" he asked.

"For a translation of *Faust*."

"There are already several translations. They paid you to do another?"

The dishes had been cleared, and dessert was being served. Mac brushed his piece of pineapple upside-down cake aside. "Say, Kate," he called to me, "got any more wine?"

Henry said, as Helga was putting a dish of whipped cream on the table, "I had to read Goethe when I was in high school, in my German class. I hated him then and I have never read him since, in German or English!"

"How can you say such a thing!" said Helga, with a ferocious look at Henry.

"What about Rilke? Or Schiller?" asked Mac. "What do you say about ol' Schopenhauer? Don't tell me." He was leaving the table to walk unsteadily toward the kitchen.

To Josephine and Luis, and to anyone else who might be listening, Henry said, "Why didn't he mention Spengler and Keyserling? And Nietzsche? I have read about everything they've written—in English, naturally. I long ago lost whatever high school German I ever knew."

I said, "Why don't we go into the living room for our coffee? I'll be right in with a tray." Luis offered to carry it for me and followed me to the kitchen. While I was transferring the coffee to the silver pot, I caught sight of Mac in the pantry. When Luis left with the tray, I went to Mac. "What are you doing?" He had been gulping gin from a bottle. "That'll kill you," I said.

"Jus' a li'l pick-me-up," he said and then made his way toward the kitchen sofa, where he lay down and closed his eyes.

Mac was one of the most brilliant men on the faculty. He had been teaching at the university for the past fifteen years, ten of them on the West Los Angeles campus. After he had returned from Europe with his *Faust*, he had been appointed to the faculty at Berkeley. Four of his books of poetry had been published, and he had written two textbooks. His translation of fifty selected poems of Rilke had been as well received as his *Faust*. He was working on a translation of Baudelaire. But last summer he had not been reappointed and had been given severance pay. He had appealed to the Committee on Privileges and Tenure, whose seven members were professors from various departments. They had unanimously recommended that Mac be appointed a professor-at-large and not be attached to any department. No action had been taken, and several months had passed. I wondered if he was drinking because of the situation, or if he had been dismissed because of his drinking. I felt sorry for him and sat beside him on the coffee table. I tried to get him to take a sip of coffee. He refused.

Blake and Theo came to the kitchen and turned on the radio. "It's time for the news. We want to find out if the marines have landed in New Guinea yet," said Blake.

Returning to the living room, I passed the library and saw that the card tables had been folded and put away and that Lynda and Harley were snuggled together against the cushions on the daybed.

In the living room, the rest of the guests were listening to Henry's outcry against the government's censorship of his books. He pointed out that there was no statute defining obscenity. He asked them if they could define it.

"It's certainly not a question of language," Gazella said.

"That's right," said Josephine. "Words alone are not obscene because people use all sorts of words and, while some of them are vulgar and offensive to others, they are not to the people who use them. If you are writing about these people in a book, you use their language, if you are being honest. You don't put your words into their mouths."

"When you come right down to it," added Gazella, "there aren't any dirty words, only dirty minds."

Helga asked, "Do you write obscene books, Mr. Miller?"

"If you mean pornography, no, I do not."

Luis said, "Art—paintings and sculpture and those things—they are not censored even when they are certainly erotic. In the Cloisters in New York, for instance—everybody looks at the erotic sculpture there, and nothing is said about it."

Helga interrupted. "Why do people have to make that kind of sculpture? Who needs to see it? And who needs to be shocked by books?"

Luis said, "Ah, Helga, have you read the Bible?"

Gazella left to see what was keeping Blake in the kitchen.

"He and Theo wanted to hear how the war is going," I told her.

"The war!" cried Henry. "That's what disgusts me; that's the real obscenity! People killing each other without mercy, inventing the most ferocious forms of massacre—and they've been at it since the beginning of time, starting wars and killing themselves. And they have the indecency to call themselves heroes."

Bernie said, "I was in the last war. I was only a boy. It took me many years to get over what I saw and what I felt—the terror, the insanity of it all. And now it is happening all over again, and other boys, if they are not blown to hell, will live with the bitterness."

"This won't be the last war," Henry said. "They won't stop until the whole planet is swimming in blood."

Helga noticed the time and said that they had better be going.

"Mac's completely out," I said. "Do you think you can get him on his feet?"

"Let's see what we can do about that poor fellow," said Bernie.

While helping the others get their coats from the hall closet, I noticed Henry and Luis together in the dining room. Luis was saying, "I'm not Mexican, Mr. Miller. I'm Spanish. I have never been to Mexico. I know nothing about that country."

Mac came through the hall, supported on either side by Bernie and Blake. I hurried to open the front door and watched them start down the eight steps to the sidewalk. The others were shaking my hand, thanking me, and saying good night when we heard Mac tumble down the steps. Blake was swearing.

"What happened?"

"Is he hurt?"

"Gimme a hand."

"For crissakes!"

"He dropped on his ass and began to slide, and I couldn't stop him."

"You okay, Mac?"

Mac was pulled to his feet. There were still several yards to go between the two trees in the front yard. They got him through the gate and the few steps to Bernie's car. Then the cars took off, and the street was quiet.

I had not seen Harley leave, nor had I seen Lynda during all the commotion. Henry had walked back into the house as soon as they had gotten Mac to his feet. I walked back up the steps, locked the front door behind me, and turned off the lights in the hall and living room. The library door was closed. I saw a light under it and under my bedroom door. Guessing that Lynda was getting ready for bed, I tapped on the door. There was no answer. Perhaps she's in the bathroom, I thought. It was a private bath connecting with the bedroom. I opened the door a crack to call her name and saw that Harley was in bed with her.

I went to the kitchen, turned off all the lights except the lamp on the table, sat down, and poured myself a cup of cold coffee. The table was stacked with unwashed dishes, cups, saucers, platters, glasses. I took a sip of coffee and shut my eyes. There were footsteps behind me—Henry. He had put on his cap.

"Do you want to go for a walk?"

"At this hour!"

I found my purse and a coat and followed him out the front door.

It was only a short distance to Broadway, and there we turned left toward the center of town, ten blocks away. The street was deserted. Ahead the two- and three-story buildings crouched on each side of the street, and their roof lines notched a pattern against the dark sky. Where there were shops, the lights in the windows had been switched off. Except for the lamplight on the street corners and the flicker of headlights and taillights from the few cars that passed us, the city was hushed and dark. The streetcars had stopped running. Oakland had closed down for the night.

Henry was always a step or two ahead of me, and, when I got out of breath trying to keep up, I asked him to slow down. He did for a while. He said he liked to walk in cities early in the morning or late at night, that it was an old habit of his.

"There's not much to see in this town," I said, "it's more of a residential city. You can walk all over the downtown area in ten minutes."

After a few blocks the buildings were taller and the street-lamps brighter. There were some parked cars. At Fourteenth Street I pointed out the city's cherished landmark, its City Hall. It was off to one side behind a patch of park, a rectangular column of white stone with architectural frills and a wedding-cake cupola. On a corner, a block east on Thirteenth Street, the upper floors of the Tribune Tower were ablaze with lights, and on the street below the racket of men shouting and of trucks being loaded and taking off with the Sunday paper cracked the stillness of the night. Nearby, a hamburger place was doing business, puffing out hot smells of grease and frying onions. On Twelfth and Eleventh streets, the two downtown movie theaters had darkened their marquees.

From there on, Henry's interest picked up. After Tenth Street we were in the old section of town, where the wooden buildings had been standing for half a century or longer. Now their street floors were pawnshops, counter cafés, bars, second-hand clothing stores, or lobbies of cheap hotels. Chinatown was crowded into the blocks to the east.

Broadway was not empty. There were people walking about, most of them shabbily dressed men, although there were some women, and everyone was alone. I felt uneasy, out of place, but no one gave us more than a passing glance, if that. Henry stopped to look into the lighted window of a pawnshop. I noticed that he was taking in everything on the street, from the faces of the men in the dingy lobbies to the posters in the windows of a vacant store. We stopped at a corner where we could look into Chinatown. It was dark.

"This might be an interesting place in the daytime," he said.

I knew that Oakland's Chinatown was a very uninteresting place day or night, but I said nothing.

At Seventh Street the door to a bar was partly open, and we could see men sitting on stools and hear a jukebox playing. I hoped that he would not want to go in. He didn't. We walked on.

"There's nothing farther on," I said, "except some empty old buildings." I knew that ahead there was an estuary, an inlet of San Francisco Bay that was used by small boats and the car ferry to San Francisco. I didn't want to go down there. Henry was not a person to count on in case of trouble. At no time during our walk had he taken my elbow, not at curbs or in crossing streets, and I was sure that he would not offer me a hand to cling to. To my immense relief he said, "Well, I guess we've seen enough." We turned back up Broadway.

When we were near the hamburger stand, I offered to treat if he cared to join me. He did. The buns, each wrapped in a paper napkin, were passed to us through an open window, and we ate as we walked along. I had tried to get him to talk about his books, but he had said little in reply to my questions. Now the good taste of the hamburgers had loosened his tongue.

"My books seem like someone else's work now. Sometimes I wonder, Did I write this or that? Was it I writing about myself, or was it somebody else writing about me?"

A few steps more and he said, "I have often said to myself, 'Why keep on writing? For whom?' I have wanted to quit, to never write another book. Yet there are things I want to say, whether my books are read or not."

Walking on he said, "Once I foolishly thought that everybody would read my books. There was so much attention paid to the first two, *Cancer* and *Black Spring*. I can understand it about *Black Spring*. I think it's my best book."

His voice was hard as he named the writers whose books did sell. "They don't write any better than I do. In fact, I out-write them. Yet I'm out in the cold, while the American public rushes to the bookstores to grab up their output ad nauseam."

We had reached my front gate. To my surprise he stepped ahead and held it open for me to walk in first.

15

During the first months on Partington Ridge I toyed
with the idea of going to Mexico to finish The
Air-Conditioned Nightmare. *I drew up an "appeal*
for funds"—sufficient to last me a year. I specified—
and begged Frances Steloff, of the Gotham Book Mart,
N.Y., to post it on her bulletin board. I had little
expectation of getting results from this appeal. It was
worded rather flippantly, I thought, probably because
at the bottom of my heart I really did not want to go
to Mexico. All I wanted, truly, was a little hard cash.
  Big Sur and the Oranges of Hieronymus Bosch

In May Lynda was told that The Log House had been sold
and that she would have to give it up by July 1. The word got
around that the purchasers were Joseph Cotten and Orson Welles.
This startled everyone. Was Hollywood moving in? They need not
have worried; Welles bought the property but never lived there.

Lynda knew that she could move into the Big Sur Lodge
until she found someplace else to live, but she was concerned about
Henry. Was there an unoccupied, habitable cabin somewhere that
he could live in for a while? She could think of only one, the cabin
on Partington Ridge that belonged to Keith Evans. He had a build-
ing-supplies business in Carmel. She went to see him, only to learn
that he was in the service. She wrote him a letter, which he answered at once, saying he was glad to rent the place, to have it
occupied and looked after while he was away. It was a two-room,
comfortably furnished log cabin with indoor plumbing, the water
piped from a nearby spring, and he asked fifteen dollars a month
for it with the understanding that Henry would give it up when
Evans returned from the war. Lynda accepted on Henry's behalf
and mailed the first month's rent. Henry moved in.

Partington Ridge breaks away from the Santa Lucias in a
steep roll of hills tufted with live oak, pine, madrone, and syca-
more. The ocean is a thousand feet below. For as far as the eye can
follow the shoreline north and south, the view is one of steep coves

and headlands and of huge rocks that have tumbled into the water.

The forest belongs to wildcats and coyotes, bear, fox, and deer. Small creatures such as mice, wood rats, squirrels, lizards, and weasels abound in the chaparral, and there are quail skittering about in the lilac and sagebrush. Above, observing the scene, are circling eagles and golden-tailed hawks. Rattlesnakes hide in the stony outcroppings.

Henry was a city person. He had never been alone in a wilderness, left to look after himself. It was hard for him to get to sleep that first night. At daybreak, when he awoke and looked outdoors, everything below the ridge was hidden in fog. After a miserable breakfast, he wrote a few letters. Whenever he was in need of anything—clothes, paints, money, or whatever—he asked for them in letters. Now he had need of companionship, and he thought of Emil White.

He and Emil had kept up a correspondence ever since their meeting two years earlier in Chicago. The last address to which Henry had written was in the Yukon, where Emil was working on the Alcan Highway and saving his money so that he could go to Mexico, expecting to meet Henry there. Henry had been writing to him from Beverly Glen.

Early in 1944, Emil was ready for Mexico and had made his way to Beverly Glen. But Henry was in Monterey with the Vardas. When Emil had written him there, Henry was in Big Sur. Now that they were in touch again, Henry urged him to visit him and to send on the things he had left behind in Beverly Glen—his books, clothes, art supplies, the typewriter, phonograph, and records. Emil shipped the things but put off coming to Big Sur for a few more weeks while he visited with friends in Los Angeles.

Henry was working on *Sunday After the War*, which was long overdue at New Directions. James Laughlin had written him that he was coming to California and would make a special trip to Big Sur to pick up the manuscript. To find enough material to fill the book, Henry had added some of what he had written for *The Rosy Crucifixion* and his rewrite of *The Air-Conditioned Nightmare*, but it was not enough. He added a letter he had written to his longtime friend Emil Schnellock a few years before. Very little of the writing was new.

It did not bother him that he was stuffing the book in this way. He had made up his mind that whatever he wrote should be published several times and that what had appeared in magazines should be repeated in books. He thought this was not too self-serving because he would be reaching different readers. He was sending "fragments" of one work or another to *The Quarterly Review of Literature, The Leaves Fall, Dartmouth Alumni Magazine, Interim, Tricolor, Chimera, The Harvard Advocate, Artists and Writers Chap Book,* and to a few magazines in England. He sent a two-year-old poem to *Harper's Bazaar,* one he had written in Beverly Glen during a passionate interlude with a young Greek woman. The poem, "O Lake of Light," appeared in the magazine's August 1944 issue.

None of this writing was bringing in much money, and his ever-present need for cash kept him busy writing to people who could help him out. It was at this point that he sent Frances Steloff a letter along with a general appeal for funds that he asked her to post on the bulletin board at her Gotham Book Mart in New York. She had come to his rescue before, and she did not fail him now. He could also count on Lynda, who came to the cabin every few days to bring him food, wine, cigarettes, kerosene for the lamps, typing paper, stamps, and anything else she thought he might need. Besides, she was always good for a touch of a few dollars.

While he was waiting for Emil to arrive, Bern Porter came to see him, wanting more of his work to publish. Henry could not dismiss Bern's admiration for his work and his eagerness to become his publisher. The only drawback that Henry could see was that he wouldn't be paid, nor would Bern realize anything on his investment until the sale of books had exceeded the cost of producing them. Bern wanted to publish all of Henry's future books, paying the cost out of his salary, for he had no other income, and promising to bring out his new work at frequent intervals. This would keep Henry's name before the public. He was willing to take work that other publishers had turned down, work that Henry wanted to see in print.

Henry had recently finished a fierce denunciation of war that he entitled *Murder the Murderer.* He gave it to Bern, who took it back to Berkeley to publish at considerable personal risk. He would certainly have lost his job if his association with an antiwar tract had been discovered. Privately, Bern spoke of Henry's booklet as "one of the greatest antiwar satires ever written," yet the booklet would necessarily carry this statement: "Neither the publisher nor the printer is responsible for or subscribes to statements made herein by Henry Miller."

It was about this time that I planned to spend my vacation in Carmel with Bobby Ferro in her summer cottage. When I wrote Lynda about it, she asked me to come to Big Sur, too, for a last visit in The Log House. While I was with her, we made a trip to Partington Ridge to see Henry. The drive up from the road was so dusty that we parked the car and walked up, keeping away from the poison oak. I wondered if the scarlet weed, which was clustered in bushy splendor on either side of the road, was too dense for the rattlers, all the while dreading that one might slither across in front of us. As we neared the cabin a large white dog ran out to greet us. Someone had given Henry a dog.

Henry had been painting. The fresh sheets were drying here and there around the room, and after we finished lunch he asked me to choose one of the watercolors as his gift. While I was looking them over, he suddenly unpinned one from the wall and handed it to me.

"Never mind," he said. "Take this one. It's my best."

It was the "Echolalia" that he had painted in Beverly Glen and had not wanted to part with. It was a hauntingly beautiful "self-portrait" painted in a radiant blue veiled with smoky gray and sweeps of lime, violet, and yellow. While it did not resemble him at all, I was moved by the beauty of it and the composition, which seemed to me ethereal. I said that I could not accept it as a gift but that I would like to buy it. This he refused.

"That's why I want you to have it, because it's my best. I want you to take it as a gift."

He explained that the veils of smoke color at one side of the head represented his deafness in the left ear. That the dictionary's definition of *echolalia* does not convey this meaning didn't matter to him. He just liked the word.

Propped up on the ledge above the fireplace were a number

of snapshots of women, some of them posing in the nude. He had told us that women were writing him, enclosing their photos and begging him to let them come to him. Now he took the photos down one by one to point out this one's fleshy buttocks, that one's big breasts, another's heavy thighs. The women were all young and some had pretty faces, but he didn't mention their good looks.

He told us that one of the rangers had brought him the dog, which had either fallen from an open truck or been abandoned. He was glad to have it because it kept the snakes away. It was a very friendly animal, wanting to be petted. I gave him a lot of attention, stroking his head and back, and a few hours later I broke out with poison oak. Rummaging through the bushes was harmless to the dog, and apparently Henry was immune to the stuff.

Emil White arrived, near the end of May, after an all-night bus ride from Los Angeles. As Henry had instructed him, he phoned Yanko upon his arrival in Monterey and was invited to come to the barn at once. He would have to spend the night because the mail truck to Big Sur had already left, and it was the only transportation down the coast if one didn't have a car.

Emil said later that he knew he had come to the right place as soon as he saw the life masks that decorated the outside of the barn. At the door he lifted "a Rube Goldberg device" that set off a doleful monasterial clang, and soon "the Angel Gabriel himself appeared before me." It was Yanko, pink-cheeked, smiling like a cherub. His feet were bare, and he was in a faded blue shirt and old red pants that had been washed out to a strawberry-frappé pink.

By jumping and climbing over boxes, barrels, boards, bags of cement, cans of paint, piles of glass, and more, they reached the stairway to the upper realm, where Virginia was waiting to welcome Emil. "She saw at once that I was one of their kind—dirty corduroys and sweatshirt—and that I was badly in need of a haircut." To Emil, the upper part of the barn was "a fairyland, the setting for *A Midsummer Night's Dream.*"

In the morning Emil set out from Pacific Grove in the mail truck with Jake Hodges and his wife. Hodges was under special contract with the government to carry United States mail three times a week with his deliveries of meat and groceries, milk, newspapers, liquor, medicines, cigarettes, and whatever else the people along his route asked him to buy for them. Mrs. Hodges did the shopping.

After completing the Carmel Valley route, which took most of the morning, they returned to the coast and headed for Big Sur. They stopped at every mailbox or cluster of boxes on the highway, where there were people waiting for them, knowing what time the van was generally due. While they collected their mail and supplies, they exchanged the local news. In this way people kept in touch with each other. Emil was surprised to learn that his arrival had been expected for several weeks. Now everyone greeted him like one of the family.

At the Big Sur post office, Emil was handed a note from Henry that the postmistress had been holding for him. It told him to go on up to the cabin and if Henry wasn't there to wait for him.

When the van arrived at Henry's mailbox, it was midafternoon and he was not standing there. Emil looked inside the mailbox and found some fresh eggs that had been left for Henry, presumably from a neighbor. He took the eggs and the perishable foodstuffs that he had brought as gifts and started walking up to the ridge. It was a long, hot haul, and he often sat down on the road to rest. He saw no sign of life.

At the fork in the road he chose the direction that, as it turned out, led to a sign: PRIVATE PROPERTY—NO TRESPASSING. He tried the alternate direction, and this led him to a gate with a padlock on it. Back at the fork and not knowing what to do, he saw a slight trail leading downhill. When he followed it, he came to the Evans cabin. The door was not locked, and he went in. Henry was not there. After resting, Emil went back down for another load and was about to trudge uphill for the third time when he heard a car honk and stop. It was Lynda's car; Henry leapt out and rushed to Emil to throw his arms about him.

It was a happy week for both men. Emil took over the chores of the cabin and Henry followed him around, helping some while talking nonstop. Emil kept the cabin clean, cooked the meals, washed the dishes, made the beds, kept the kerosene lamps filled, and did anything else that was necessary. He and Henry went into the forest to find firewood, which Emil chopped.

Emil, a Viennese, was a gentle, warm, and trusting person. In stature he was slightly shorter than Henry. His dark curly hair grew in a bush about his head. He had come to the United States as a young man, changed his name from Wieselmann to White, taught himself English, educated himself, and become knowledgeable about writers and books. He was not talkative or self-assertive. He had a soft voice and a pleasing manner. He was exactly the kind of person Henry found easy to get along with.

The idyllic week suddenly came to an end when Henry learned that one of the letter-writing women had arrived from New York. She was June Lancaster, a young artist's model and dancer with a curvaceous figure, which she had shown Henry in a variety of nude poses. When Harry Herschkowitz had written him that she was a friend of his and that she was just what Henry needed, he had answered her letters. He hadn't been sure that she would show up, and he was pleasantly surprised when he heard from Yanko that she was at the barn, waiting for him.

Miserable with poison oak and in bandages, I had left for Oakland and missed what happened next. Lynda wrote me about it. She, Henry, and Emil went to the barn together, bringing with them all the wine she had on hand at the house. On the way they stopped to pick bouquets of wildflowers for June.

At the barn, the outdoor masks had been decorated with flowers, and there were more flowers inside in the entranceway. The junk had been cleared out, which must have been a Herculean task. Upstairs, in the big room, was "the pièce de résistance," as Lynda called June. Alerted to Henry's arrival, she had got up onto a barrel to pose with her hands raised above her head in a supplicating gesture. She was wearing a circus getup that had been put together by Yanko and Virginia, and her long black hair fell to her thighs. Henry was stunned at the sight. After staring for a moment, he rushed to her feet and knelt down. When he helped her off the barrel, they clung to each other in a long embrace, the signal for Yanko to fill the wineglasses for a toast to the happy couple.

In addition to the "wedding party," the Vardas had guests visiting them from Hollywood. Virginia had prepared lunch, and

along with the eating and drinking there was dancing to the phonograph. Yanko danced first, then Virginia, then Emil. "Yanko
made us all paper masks to wear. It was New Year's Eve, the
Fourth of July, and the Mardi Gras all rolled into one," said Lynda.

June was coaxed to dance. No leaps, kicks, or pirouettes for
her. When the others had finished, she slowly began to circle the
room, arms swaying dreamily and her torso bending, lifting, twist-
ing voluptuously. Henry was bewitched.

In the late afternoon Lynda drove the two of them to the
cabin on Partington Ridge and then joined the others who had
followed her from Monterey to The Log House. They had decided
to continue the party there. It lasted two days. On the second day
Lynda's Big Sur friends heard about it and joined what had now
become her sentimental farewell to the house.

Things were in full swing when James Laughlin drove up
looking for Henry and the manuscript of *Sunday After the War*.

16

Some people say: "Why don't you take a job in the
movies for a few months, then you can do as you please
for a year or two." My answer to that is: Why don't
you send your daughter into the streets for a little
while before marriage so that she can bring in a little
much needed change? Once she's married nobody will
know the difference.

The Plight of the Creative Artist in the
United States of America

In spite of the isolation of Big Sur and the living conditions
that in various ways were harsh and primitive, Henry began to
enjoy his life there. When he became restless, missing the places
where people get together, bars, restaurants, theaters, he went for
a walk in the forest above the cabin. He followed the trails that led
to the numerous springs in the area, and frequently ventured
farther into the hills. On the heights, the vastness and beauty of
the scene moved him deeply, more than he would have thought
possible a few months earlier. The rasp of his shoes on the hard
grass was softer than the lively twitter of the sparrows or the sharp
quacks of the jays that he heard on all sides, and in July the burnt
grass and dry chaparral smelled bittersweet. The poppies were
gone, but the yucca stalks were in bloom, each regal stem holding
up its candelabrum of cream-white petals.

Emil also began to enjoy life in Big Sur. He and Henry no
longer talked about going to Mexico. After he had moved to a
motor court, Emil heard that the former guardhouse at the Anderson Creek convicts' camp was available for rent for ten dollars a
month, and in August he moved in. The one-story, rambling
wooden building was on the highway at the northern end of the
Anderson Creek bridge.

Emil discovered that the battery-operated alarm system for
dealing with the possible escape of prisoners was still in working

order. He was told that it had never been used because no prisoner had tried to escape. Life in Big Sur was far better than the usual prison life. In the prisoners' spare time, when they were not working on the road, they were gambling and making hootch. A few of the men took up gardening, some growing flowers that took prizes in a Monterey Peninsula flower show.

Bern was spending the weekends with Henry, working on *Henry Miller: A Chronology and Bibliography*. It was Bern's idea, and Henry went along with it when Bern pointed out that a bibliography had never been compiled and that Henry had written fourteen books, four booklets, and hundreds of articles for magazines and newspapers in France, England, and the United States. Moreover, five more titles were to come out in the next few months, all of them to be published by Bern.

In addition to listing Henry's books, they would need to include the books to which he had contributed material, the newspapers and periodicals that had published his work, two magazines he had coedited, and the private collections of his letters. About three hundred articles, notices, and reviews had been written about Henry or his work, and all of these would have to be listed. The ghostwritten columns he did for the *Tribune* and some of his earliest writing, such as the Mezzotints, would be included. Everything had to be identified by its one or more publication dates, the number of pages, and whether it had been translated into French. The names of the publishers would be given. There were also works of art and poetry that had been inspired by Henry, and these, too, must be identified.

It was a huge undertaking that required tedious cooperation on both their parts in order to organize the countless details, and Bern could not do it without Henry's help. To keep the work moving, he never got off Henry's back. When he was not there working with him, he needled him to keep at it by himself. But Henry was bored with the drudgery involved, and, anyway, he wanted to get on with his own work. *The Air-Conditioned Nightmare* was not yet finished in its rewritten form, and New Directions was waiting for it. He also wanted to work on *The Rosy Crucifixion*, which he saw now was going to require at least three volumes. He gave them the titles of *Sexus, Plexus,* and *Nexus.*

Meanwhile, June's presence became a problem. She offered Henry no intellectual companionship. She bored him. He began asking her when she was going back to Harry. During the day, when he wrote steadily and wanted to be alone, she was in the way, distracting him. He would tell her to get out, to leave him alone. Emil had put up a sort of practice bar for her outside between two trees, and she used it for exercise. She often danced in the woods. She could not cook, and she had no housekeeping skills. Her use to Henry was purely sexual, and she willingly accommodated him.

Every day Emil walked the three miles between his place and the cabin to do the chores and gather firewood. He also did all the shopping, in either Pacific Grove or Monterey, whenever he got a ride with Lynda. She was living in a little house farther down the coast. Emil, Lynda, and Bern were usually the only ones who saw June at Henry's. If anyone else called, she fled outdoors to avoid the embarrassment of Henry scolding her for one thing or another.

Lynda came to the cabin most evenings when there was no longer enough daylight for Bern and Henry to continue working. They would be tired; the atmosphere might be a little bumpy between Henry and June. Lynda would break up the tension by getting supper ready while chattering, laughing, and clowning around. After they had eaten, she might persuade June to join her in dancing to the phonograph records, two chorines in panties and bras. Or they might do a striptease for a Minsky performance. Then Henry would liven up and join them, prancing around the room and flinging out his arms. Giggling and out of breath, someone would have to stop and wind up the phonograph.

One day June slipped quietly away, and Henry never heard from her again. Later Bern wrote me: "Somehow she got to Los Angeles, sent me her address there, and once when in L.A. I tried to call her and a man answered and said she was out. I have wondered what happened to her. She had talent, a fine figure, and so much ambition. A lost child, used by men . . ."

Bern noticed that the cabin was beginning to fill up with thermos bottles; at last count there were seventeen of them. They arrived from friends to whom Henry had written pleading to be sent one to keep his early-morning coffee hot while he continued to work through the day. To be sure of getting at least one or two, he wrote to twenty people. Now the bottles were in the way, everywhere, and, because he considered them tokens of friendship, he would not part with any of them.

Not only thermos bottles but other gifts arrived in the mail along with a heavy delivery of letters. Henry was a compulsive letter writer, especially of lengthy letters, and he kept up a correspondence with friends halfway around the world. Emil made a cart for him that rumbled behind him the mile downhill to the mailbox and that he then had to drag uphill filled with all that Hodges delivered.

Bern was preparing to publish more than the *Chronology and Bibliography*. He had a paperback ready of Henry's "open letters to all and sundry" on a number of subjects, especially on his inability to make a living as a writer. A few of his watercolors would be reproduced in the booklet, which he would call *The Plight of the Creative Artist in the United States of America*.

Another book that Bern had in mind was a small deluxe edition of some of Henry's earliest writings, including one of the Mezzotints, two pieces written for *The Booster*, a newspaper column written in Paris in 1931, and other little-known work. He would give it the title *Henry Miller Miscellanea*, and its cover would reproduce one of Henry's self-portrait drawings surrounded by several sentences in his handwriting.

Among these sentences would be the phrase "semblance of a devoted past," which happened to be the title of one of Bern's photographs. Henry liked the phrase so much that Bern let him have it. It also became the title for another forthcoming book, a collection of Henry's letters written to Emil Schnellock from France and Greece between 1930 and 1939. In general, the letters would be about Henry's trials, failures, and successes as a painter.

Bern planned to go to Virginia to spend a few weeks with Schnellock, go through the bundles of letters, and choose those he wanted to use in the book. When the folio-sized deluxe edition came out, it included reproductions of nine of Henry's watercolors, the "Echolalia" among them. Bern's photograph with its title, "Semblance of a Devoted Past," appeared at the end of the book.

Bern's considerable talents as an artist and literary editor contributed immensely to the beauty and quality of all of the books that he published for Henry, whether they were soft or hard cover, large books or small books. Henry's work had never before been given this kind of attention.

Because Henry liked to see his watercolors reproduced, Bern brought out a portfolio of twelve of them under the title *Echolalia.* The watercolor of that title was placed first in the collection.

Another book that Bern published at this time was *The Happy Rock,* the title taken from a phrase Henry wrote in *Tropic of Capricorn* describing the emergence of "the true rock of the self, the happy rock." Its purpose was to give a many-sided picture of Henry's life and work as seen through experiences he had shared with others. Henry had given Bern a list of names of people he thought might contribute to such a book. Bern went ahead with the idea and surprised Henry with the finished work. Abraham Rattner had drawn a portrait of Henry for the frontispiece, and Fernand Léger had made a drawing for the book's cover. Henry had met Léger in 1941, when the French painter was living in New York City for the duration of the war. After he returned to Paris, the two men had kept up a correspondence.

When Henry was not working with Bern or writing, he got out his paints and brushes and relaxed. Emil was often there watching him paint. Henry suggested that he take up the art, and to get him started he gave him tubes, brushes, and paper. Emil had never held a brush in his hand, but with Henry's help he began to pick up the watercolor technique.

What Emil produced was altogether different from Henry's work—no full-page faces, no furbelowed figures, no pulpy-pupiled eyes. Emil confined himself to a miniature scale, making every tiny brush stroke an exact part of a complicated design. The effect was a tight pattern, like threads in a tapestry, and yet the scene was in action. There was sway and rhythm to it. As he continued to learn, to experiment and improve, this became his style: When he painted boats they were bobbing. When he painted children they were dancing. The clouds in the sky were racing, the hills were tumbling, the sea was surging. Looking at a painting of Emil's made you think of joyful melodies, and the colors were crisp and sunny. There were no portraits. The people he painted were stick figures, or sometimes tiny paper dolls.

Through the summer of 1944, I visited Lynda at her new place, or I took a room in one of the inns in Carmel and she joined me there. I saw Henry several times. I took my copies of *Sunday After the War* and *The Wisdom of the Heart* to him to autograph. As was his way they were flourishes to *"amie de coeur, poète,"* and *"vagabonde."*

We took him with us when we visited Shanagolden and Harrydick. We took him to the hot springs, which had been expanded to more tubs and separated for men and women. We went to Monterey to visit Yanko and Virginia, and sometimes we stayed for supper. One day we took him to Salinas, where he wanted to see a movie starring one of his favorite actresses, Geraldine Fitzgerald.

In mid September Lynda wrote me that Henry had received a wire notifying him that his mother was on her deathbed and to come at once. She had been suffering with cancer for some time, so the news did not come as a surprise. As usual, the lack of money was the problem, and he was borrowing what he could from friends.

I was at Lynda's the weekend that Henry was ready to leave, and I went along on the drive to Monterey where he was to catch the train to San Francisco. He was in high spirits, telling us how glad he was to get away for a while, although he said that he would be back. He talked about his sister Lauretta, wondering how he would look after her when his mother died. There was no money for institutional care, and to bring her to Big Sur, we hastily agreed, was out of the question. We arrived in Monterey in plenty of time to have hamburgers and coffee at Herman's Café.

As Henry got ready to board the train, we slipped a few more bills into his overcoat pockets. He took a seat where he could wave to us as the train pulled out.

Neither of us heard anything from or about him until Christmas, when Lynda was spending the holidays with me. A Christmas card from Emil to me said: "Henry got married and will probably be here around New Year's. I'm busy fixing up his cabin and gathering wood for the newlyweds. All I know about her: 21, intelligent, and Polish."

17

*I have a certain amount of guilt about receiving
money as a painter when I know that there are
painters of real talent who are in an even more
unfortunate position than myself.*
                              The Plight of the Creative Artist in the
                                          United States of America

Henry's mother made a good recovery from surgery, and,
when he saw that she was being well cared for and that Lauretta
could continue to live at home, he took off to visit friends. He had
already seen Herschkowitz and through him had met a young
woman, Janina Martha Lepska, who had come from Poland with
her family some years before. She had graduated from Bryn Mawr
and gone on to Yale for a degree in philosophy, which she was
working on when Henry met her. Her brilliant mind made an
impression on him, but he was attracted even more to her blonde
Slavic good looks. When he went to New Haven to stay two weeks
with Wallace Fowlie of the French Department at Yale, he looked
her up.

    While he was there, Fowlie opened his apartment to small
groups of students who had asked to meet Miller. Henry enjoyed
these rap sessions. Talking about his books, his life-style, his ideas,
whatever was on his mind, and he was pleased when one of the
students asked to arrange an exhibit of his watercolors. He had
brought a few with him, intended as gifts to the friends he visited.
When Fowlie was teaching, Henry and Lepska had the apartment
to themselves. She called herself Lepska, not caring for her given
names.

    His stay at Dartmouth College, where he went next to visit
Herbert West, was altogether different. West was on the faculty of

Dartmouth and was a longtime admirer and champion of Miller's work; when he asked Henry to address the student body, it was hard to turn him down. Henry could easily hold the attention of a small group, but he was no public speaker, and it was only after much persuasion that he reluctantly agreed to do it.

His talk was ruined by a heckler in the audience who denounced him as an anti-American menace. The incident withered Henry, and, when the FBI came around the next day to question him and Professor West, he was genuinely alarmed. In spite of the garrulous passages that he had let fly in some of his books, he was not disloyal to the United States, and he was in no way guilty of treason.

In *The Air-Conditioned Nightmare* he had written:

Nowhere have I encountered such a dull, monotonous fabric of life as here in America. Here boredom reaches its peak. We are accustomed to think of ourselves as an emancipated people, we say that we are democratic, liberty-loving, free of prejudice and hatred. This is the melting-pot, the seat of a great human experiment. Beautiful words, full of noble, idealistic sentiment. Actually we are a vulgar pushing mob whose passions are easily mobilized by demagogues, newspaper men, religious quacks, agitators, and such like. To call this a society of free peoples is blasphemous.

About war, all wars, he wrote in *Murder the Murderer*:

No man, in my opinion, has the right to demand the sacrifice of human lives. We throw up our hands in horror when we read of the sacrificial rites of the Aztecs, but we see nothing ignoble in the periodic sacrifice of millions of lives in the name of country, God, democracy, or civilization. . . . I do not say that men who believe in war as a last resort are necessarily evil, necessarily worse than other men; I say they are stupid, they lack vision, magnanimity, wisdom. When they speak of war as being the last resort can we be certain that they have tried every other means of preserving peace? I am afraid not.

The FBI did not detain him, and he left Hanover for calmer surroundings. Lepska joined him to go to Washington, D.C., to visit Caresse Crosby and after that to go to Virginia to see Schnellock. On the train trip west to California, they stopped in Boulder Creek, Colorado, to stay awhile with Henry's friends from Beverly Glen, Margaret and Gilbert Neiman. On December 18, 1944, Henry and Lepska were married in Denver. It was February before they reached Big Sur.

Almost immediately Henry set to work on *The Rosy Crucifixion*. Although it was during the first honeymoon weeks of his marriage to Lepska, he felt compelled to continue with the anguished account of the tormented years he had known while married to his second wife, June. To write about it was like reliving that time, when he was possessed with a desperate, hungry love. He wrote of "studying her morsel by morsel, feet, hands, hair, lips, ears, breasts, traveling from navel to mouth and from mouth to eyes, the woman I fell upon, clawed, bit, suffocated with kisses."

It is unlikely that he let Lepska see any of this writing. He took the finished pages to Emil to have him read them aloud to him. He liked to hear his work read. If Emil had any criticisms to make, Henry usually dismissed them, although he did delete an entire chapter at Emil's insistence.

Lepska adjusted to life in the cabin, although she found the isolation hard to get used to. She longed to be with people, to socialize and to talk. When Emil came to the cabin, he and Henry seemed to leave her out of their conversations, and, when she talked her way into one, they ignored what she said. After the Leites took a shack at Anderson Creek for the summer, she spent much of her day with them.

When George drove to Berkeley to get out an issue of *Circle*, she went along to assist in whatever way she could. The final editing was done at Bern Porter's rented house on Durant Street. He was the assistant editor, and with his financial assistance the magazine was being printed instead of mimeographed. The covers and illustrations were the work of various artists, and the contents carried the names of well-known poets and writers. Leite's poetry and Bern's prose, photography, and artwork were also used. It was Henry's name, of course, that spurred the magazine's rapid rise as one of the best of the new little magazines.

He had given them an essay from *Sunday After the War* for

the second issue but nothing for the third. *Circle* 4, which came out in December while he was still away, used a piece that he had written about Varda when he was staying at the red barn. Now something was expected for *Circle* 5, and, since he had just finished writing a preface for a book coming out in London in 1946, he let *Circle* have it. The book's title was *The Power Within Us.*

This was a new edition of Haniel Long's translation, which was based on various other translations from the Spanish, of an account of a journey made between 1528 and 1536 by a small band of conquistadores led by Cabeza de Vaca. The men had been shipwrecked off the coast of what is now Florida, and, without provisions of any kind, they set out, naked and starving, to walk across the continent to Mexico. Along the way, the few who were still alive experienced a spiritual transformation that enabled them to work miraculous cures among the Indians. Multitudes came to be healed. Until then the only white men the Indians had encountered had burned their villages and enslaved them.

Henry readily agreed to write the preface because "even as a child I was impressed by the story of how the Indians greeted the first white comers as gods. Later . . . the shameful record of our relations with the Indians saddened me to a degree beyond anything I had ever felt in connection with man's inhumanity to man." Of Cabeza de Vaca he wrote that the miracles he accomplished for himself and others offered "the first bright spot I encountered in the bloody legend created by the conquistadores."

It was his habit to work on several pieces of writing at the same time, spending a few hours, or perhaps a few days, on one thing and then switching to something else. He did not forget the notebooks that he had filled with passages about justice and his hopes for altering the human heart, written three years earlier while he was working on the ill-fated movie script of *The Maurizius Case.* Now he decided to turn his notes into a book that he would call *Maurizius Forever.* He was able to interest Colt Press in bringing it out in 1946 in a deluxe edition that he would illustrate with his watercolors.

For several years he had been making notes on the life and works of Rimbaud and at one time attempted to translate *Une Saison en Enfer.* He was drawn to the poet, comparing his "season in hell" with his own trials and mortifications. Now he began writing what he envisioned as a book about Rimbaud and when the first chapter was finished he sent it to Laughlin, who took it for his 1946 New Directions annual. Excerpts from Henry's work had previously appeared in the 1936, 1937, and 1939 annuals.

During 1945, Ben Abramson brought out *Aller Retour New York* for private subscription.

Fragments and chapters from Henry's published work were appearing in more than a dozen magazines here and abroad. A new piece, "Obscenity and the Law of Reflection," came out first in the London magazine *Now* and later in New York's *Tricolor*, where Henry's friend Oscar Baradinsky saw it. He asked Henry to let him have it for the first issue of a projected series of Outcast Chapbooks that he planned to publish twice a year under the imprint of his Alicat Book Shop in Yonkers. Henry let him have it and also gave him, for the second issue, a piece he had written called "The Amazing and Invariable Beauford DeLaney."

DeLaney, a black painter, was another friend of Herschkowitz. He had taken Henry to meet DeLaney in his walk-up flat in lower Manhattan soon after Henry had arrived in New York in 1944. The visit was a memorable one for Henry, for he discovered that DeLaney was a remarkable painter and a more remarkable individual. He visited him several times and sat for a portrait.

All of the Bern Porter books and booklets had now been published. New Directions had issued a second printing of *Sunday After the War* and had also brought out *Why Abstract?*, a book of three essays by Henry, William Saroyan, and Hilaire Hiler in defense of modern art. *The Air-Conditioned Nightmare* in its rewritten form was due for publication soon. But, although so much of his work was in print, this did not mean that it was bringing him an adequate income. To have a little cash on hand, he continued to paint his watercolors. Selling them for five dollars apiece, he could expect a response from the people on his mailing lists.

He was also being asked for watercolors from England, for Bern had printed an order from *Poetry-London* for copies of the *Echolalia* portfolio, and it was bringing attention to his work there. *Circle* also advertised his paintings. Emil did the wrapping and mailing of these orders, a chore he undertook for the book orders as well. After Bern had published the books, there was the problem of distribution. They were advertised in *Circle*, giving Bern's home address for orders, and they were also available from Henry. To wrap the orders that came to Henry, Emil hoarded every scrap of paper, cardboard, and twine that came with the magazines, books, cigarettes, clothing, art supplies, and other gifts.

Almost every day Henry made the jaunt to the guard-house, for there was always something he wanted Emil to do for him, whether it was reading to him, translating from the German, or helping him with the mail. People wrote Henry asking for his autograph and picture. Some asked him to read their enclosed poetry and prose and give them his opinion of it, even edit it. Women were still sending their photographs. Strangers wrote him the unhappy details of their personal lives, seeking his counsel. Occasionally someone wrote him with advice on how to handle his own life. A few asked for money. All of this mail he turned over to Emil to answer in any way he chose. No envelope was left unopened in case it contained a check or a few dollars.

It was not necessary for Henry to walk all the way to Emil's for someone to visit with when he had nothing more to talk about at home. There were other people living on the Ridge, in houses separated by just a few hundred yards. Maud Oakes, a noted anthropologist, was one of his neighbors. The faith healer Jean Wharton was another. He was first curious and then overwhelmed by Wharton. He had no need of her healing services for any physical ailment, but after talking with her he always said that he felt better. For many years she had been a faithful follower of Mary Baker Eddy but had broken away from the teachings of Christian Science to formulate her own concept of "the Truth." Henry took it all in.

A letter from Lynda mentioned that Jean Wharton had gathered Henry into her fold: "Everyone's talking about it. Frankly, I never knew her really well and I never liked her too well, either. The feeling's mutual, I'm sure. Anyway, if it brings peace to the Miller household it ought to help. It's no love nest up there. Henry grouchy and clammed up and Lepska yelling at him. I never go there anymore. Red and I went once, and after the first hello

Henry acted like he'd never seen me before. Red doesn't like him at all."

I had met Red once at The Log House long before Henry came there to live. Not much taller than Lynda, he had a tough and sinewy look. Bear-paw hands, bristles of red hair showing under the brim of his soiled hat. Face too small, the features squeezed together. He worked for the county with a predator-control group that tracked down and killed the wild animals that the Big Sur ranchers wanted exterminated because they killed their cattle. I could never understand Lynda's attachment to him.

In the same letter Lynda said that Emil had bought an old car and that "they don't need me anymore." In closing she wrote, "By the way, she's pregnant."

I would not see Lynda again for several years, for after the bomb was dropped on Hiroshima on August 6, 1945, I moved to New Mexico. At the Los Alamos National Laboratory near Santa Fe, the government was in need of public-relations personnel to deal with information regarding the new weapon, and the university was under contract to supply scientific and other personnel.

In her Christmas letter to me, Lynda wrote that Lepska had delivered a girl in a Berkeley hospital on November 19 and that they had named her Valentine after Henry's middle name. Another piece of news was that Keith Evans was out of the army and home in Carmel. "He'll be wanting his cabin back. It looks like Anderson Creek for Henry et al. There's no other place."

18

My earnings were just about sufficient to keep a goat alive.
Big Sur and the Oranges of Hieronymus Bosch

When Henry and Lepska returned from Berkeley with baby Val, they began getting their things together for the move to Anderson Creek. As Henry had promised a year and a half earlier, he was returning Keith Evans's cabin to its owner. They would be out by the first of the year. He had already arranged to rent the place where the Leites had lived during the past summer, a small shack on the edge of a promontory with an obstructed view of the Pacific Ocean.

Henry's fifty-fourth birthday was on December 26, 1945. That day a stranger came to the cabin door, the thirty-three-year-old Palestinian artist, Bezalel Schatz, who lived in Berkeley with his mother and sister. The women had become acquainted with Bern Porter and George Leite. Mother Schatz had written a book on the history of art and had offered it to the University of California Press and others without success. Then it was suggested to her that an introduction by Henry Miller might sell the book. She and her daughter Zahara drove down to Big Sur to seek his cooperation. The book did not interest Henry, but the voluptuous daughter did, and while he put off the mother he carried on a furtive, fantasized pursuit of the young woman during the trips he made to Berkeley that October and November. Nothing came of either the proposed preface or Henry's intentions. And now the brother, whom he had not met, was at the door. Because Schatz arrived on his birthday, Henry thought he might be bringing him good luck —or at least a sign that better things were in store for the coming year.

Schatz wanted to work with Henry on a special kind of book, one that had never been done before. It would be a parallel production of writer and artist working together from the same creative roots. Schatz would reveal in his art what Henry was developing with words. He would expose the inner feelings that came to Henry at the very time that he was writing. For this purpose, Henry would need to write the text by hand.

Schatz had been thinking of such a book for a long time and had considered myths, legends, even the Bible's Song of Songs for his subject, but in them something was missing. At last he realized what it was. Life! He needed to work with a living writer for the experience to be spontaneous and vigorous. He had read some of Henry's work and it seemed to be what he was looking for. To acquaint Henry with his art, he had brought along some of his paintings.

Henry was intrigued and agreed at once to do such a book. He invited Schatz to stay on and look through his writing to find exactly what he wanted. Schatz stayed with the Millers a week. When he read "Into the Night Life" in *Black Spring*, he chose it for the subject and title of the book. The shock and frenzy of the nightmare episodes offered all the inspiration he needed to do what he wanted with the illustrations.

Schatz had been painting since the age of six, when he started out as a student in Jerusalem's College of Arts and Crafts, founded by his artist father. When he was sixteen, the originality and high quality of his work had been judged so exceptional that he was invited to exhibit it in the United States during a two-year exhibition tour of his father's work. Boris Schatz brought the boy with him to America.

When Bezalel Schatz was twenty-one he was living in Paris, where he had broken away from the classical tradition taught him by his father and had begun painting in a freer, highly personal style. Exhibitions followed in London, Paris, and again in the United States. In 1943 the San Francisco Museum of Art had given him a show. A local art critic wrote that his paintings were joyous and ablaze with color.

He did not plan to illustrate *Into the Night Life* with paintings, choosing instead to work in silk screen. He felt that only through this medium could he become wholly involved in the book's creation. Paintings would have to be used as reproductions, while the silk screens could be done one at a time to give each copy of the book its own artwork. To perfect the silk-screen technique, he said he would go at once to Santa Fe, New Mexico, in order to study with the master, Louis Ewing.

Meanwhile, at Anderson Creek Henry went about choosing the contents for his next New Directions book, *Remember to Remember*, which was to be volume two of *The Air-Conditioned Nightmare*. The preface would introduce the theme that a person's memories should be cherished and that one should always remember to remember. He begins by paying "homage" to men he remembered with great affection, Attilio Bowinkel, Jean Varda, Herbert West, and Jasper Deeter, director of the Hedgerow Theatre in Moylan, Pennsylvania. He included others from casual encounters, among them a man who had a candy store in Boulder, Colorado; a lavatory attendant in a New York hotel; a bootblack in a Hollywood barbershop; an *Encyclopaedia Britannica* salesman; and two saloon keepers, one of them a Sunday artist. From these memories he moved on to Main Street in Los Angeles, which he described as "about the worst street in America," frequented by lonely, miserable, empty souls.

It was his habit to sit at the typewriter for hours at a time, referring neither to notes nor a first draft, just letting his thoughts spill pell-mell onto the page. He rarely paused as one sentence after the other flew by beneath his fingertips.

Main Street was as far as he got that first day. The next morning he had other things on his mind, in particular the likelihood of a continuing war. He wrote: "The atomic bomb is only the first little Christmas present, so to speak, from the blind forces which are shaping the new era. Does anyone suppose that we are going to be content with just this one dazzling toy?"

From here on the preface became an antiwar tract with Henry begging people everywhere, Americans especially, to put an end to war and refuse to surrender their lives to political propaganda:

> We are told about the oil wells in some distant region of the earth, and how important it is that this country or that should not get hold of them. . . . We are warned that the next war will probably be started over the possession of these foreign oil fields. . . . We will be told that "we" need them, that our very lives are dependent on the possession of these natural resources. By that time it is quite possible that one of these nations will have found the way to the moon, possibly other planets. It is altogether conceivable, in view of the unrestricted fear, distrust, panic, and alarm, that these neighboring planets will be used as hide-outs for the monstrous new engines of war which will be invented. . . . to satisfy our lust for destruction we are ready to invade the stars, exploit the very heavens.

Continuing on the subject of inventions and pointing out that every new one is appraised for its usefulness in war, Henry predicted that what was coming would be beyond anything then imagined, that nothing was impossible considering how long ago sound, light, and heat had been made to issue from the end of a wire. Perhaps as a solace, he added, "When we get ready to destroy the earth we shall doubtless have invented the means of migrating to another planet."

He prophesied further that the United States and Russia, each jealous of the other's influence upon the rest of the world, would ultimately destroy each other while Japan watched and waited, biding her time to make herself strong again, invade Europe, and take over the world: "Nonsense! Ridiculous! The critics will scream. And, burying their heads in the sand, they will whistle from their rear ends."

He had more to say about war, but, rather than repeat much of what he had already written in *Murder the Murderer*, he simply included that booklet's contents as one of the chapters. Then, to relieve the doomsday tone, he included his lighthearted piece,

"Varda, the Master Builder," which Circle Editions, Leite's new
venture, had brought out as a booklet following its appearance in
Circle 4. The amazing and invariable Beauford DeLaney was someone else Henry wanted people to read about, so he added that essay
as well.

The banning of his Obelisk books by the United States and
England was a subject that gnawed at him almost as much as the
immorality of war. He believed that what he had to say about the
freedom of expression could not be repeated often enough, and
so he made *Obscenity and the Law of Reflection* a chapter of the
book. Two more chapters came from writing that he had done
earlier, a piece about Jasper Deeter and another about Abraham
Rattner.

He was writing the title chapter, "Remember to Remember," which was about his "glorious" years in France, when he
received his first copies of *Maurizius Forever* from Colt. The book
was beautiful. The hard cover was teal blue, and on its face the title
had been written in a facsimile of Henry's handwriting. The
book's design, the printing, the quality of the paper, were all he
could ask for. Best of all, his watercolors and drawings used as
chapter headings were the best color reproductions of his work
that he had ever seen.

Just five hundred copies had been printed for Colt by the
Grabhorn Press, and the price was ten dollars. He could not deny
that the book was worth the price, yet he wondered how many
people would part with the money to buy it. Work of his that sold
for far less was hard enough to move. Nevertheless, he was immensely pleased with the book and glad that he had dedicated it
to Keith Evans and his wife Virginia.

Henry was acquainted with Jack Stauffacher, a San Francisco printer whose Greenwood Press had printed some of the
issues of *Circle* and, later, two of the Miller books published by
Bern Porter. When Stauffacher and his friend, James Ladd Delkin,
decided to bring out a deluxe edition of three of Henry Thoreau's
essays under the title of one of them, *Life Without Principle,* they
asked Henry to write the preface. He readily agreed, not only

because he admired Thoreau but also because it offered another opportunity to speak out against the atomic bomb.

Henry wrote:

> The important thing about Thoreau, in my mind, is that he appeared at a time when we had, so to speak, a choice as to the direction we, the American people, would take. Like Emerson and Whitman, he pointed out the right road—the hard road . . .

Henry saw Americans at the crossroads again. He wrote:

> With the creation of the atomic bomb, the whole world suddenly realizes that man is faced with a dilemma whose gravity is incommensurable. . . .

Bringing Thoreau into it, he wrote further:

> . . . . I feel certain that, had he been told of the atomic bomb, of the good and bad that it was capable of producing, he would have had something memorable to say about its use. And he would have said it in defiance of the prevalent attitude. He would not have rejoiced that the secret of its manufacture was in the hands of the righteous ones. He would have asked immediately: 'Who is righteous enough to employ such a diabolical instrument destructively?' Thoreau would have been the first to say that no government on earth is good enough or wise enough to be entrusted with such power for good and evil.

Henry continued: "Some blissfully imagine that the threat of extinction—cosmic suicide—will rout us out of our lethargy," but he believed that this was not the way, that the fear of extinction was not the way to face the problem. "The deeds which move the world," he explained, "which sustain life, and give life, have a different motivation entirely."

In writing of Thoreau's life at Walden Pond, he noted that "he lost nothing by not mingling with the crowd, by not devouring the newspapers, by not enjoying the radio or the movies, by not having an automobile, a refrigerator, a vacuum cleaner." Henry thought that young people should profit from Thoreau's example, especially "the budding American poets, sages, and artists because they appear so appallingly helpless in this present-day American world. . . . They never think anymore of going into the desert or the wilderness, of wresting a living from the soil, of doing odd jobs, of living on as little as possible. They remain in the cities, flitting from one thing to another, restless, miserable, frustrated, searching in vain for a way out."

Henry did not follow his own advice. In Big Sur he had a vast Walden, and yet he longed for the sights and sounds and distractions of the city, the crowded streets, the busy traffic, the shops, bars, and places to drop in for a meal. He would have liked to see a few movies. He desperately wanted a car.

Henry hated war and the atom bomb, and yet he knew that, without Bern's salary, much of his recent work would not have been published. Bern had been with the Manhattan Project as an experimental physicist since its beginning in 1941. In the Physics Department at Princeton University, he had worked on applying Einstein's theory to the molecular structure of uranium. He had trained and supervised other scientists there and at Oak Ridge. Henry knew all of this, but neither he nor Bern, nor almost anyone else, had foreseen such a weapon as the atomic bomb.

The Millers were struggling along on the fifty dollars a month that Laughlin sent whether or not Henry was earning it in royalties. The rent was only five dollars, but the outlay for food, household staples, oil for the lamps, cigarettes, Henry's writing supplies, and stamps came to much more than forty-five dollars. He borrowed from Emil and wrote letters begging people to take his books and watercolors for any amount they could spare. He could pay Hodges for only part of what he delivered, and Hodges carried him on credit for months.

He walked the three miles to Slate's hot springs where he washed the baby's diapers and did other laundry. All Big Sur people took advantage of the unlimited supply of hot water; at most any time of day people were there washing clothes or taking baths. The San Francisco sculptor Beniamino Bufano and Henry often met there. Bufano was doing redwood sculpture and living in one of the shacks at the former Free Camp nearby. The two men got along well; they had much in common.

They were both against war and hopeful of peace, goodwill, and brotherhood among people everywhere. They were champions of lost causes. They were antiestablishment and against what they saw as the shortsightedness and often selfish goals of politicians, bureaucrats, and others in positions of authority.

While words were Henry's tools of expression, stainless steel, granite, marble, stone, and mosaics were Bufano's. His statues were usually very large, deliberately intended to attract attention. They were never sentimental or decorative, to be half-seen and soon forgotten. A sculpture of his could not be dismissed by anyone looking at it. It either fascinated the beholder, or it was scoffed at for its misshapen ugliness and missing details. To some it was obvious that the sculptor had no talent. On the other hand, those who were receptive to the purity of the lines, the powerful abstract forms, and the harmony and serenity of the work saw that Bufano was far ahead of his contemporaries.

Few communities or organizations would accept his work for display. He wanted it placed out of doors, preferably in public parks where everyone could see it. He refused to confine it to the "dead space" of art galleries and insisted that it rest upon the earth and be open to the sky. Unfortunately, the pieces that were displayed in this manner were usually vandalized, even destroyed. One exception was the statue of Sun Yat-sen, the founder of the Republic of China, which had been set up in a tiny square in the Chinese community of San Francisco, where it was revered and cared for.

San Francisco's city officials had hurt Bufano the most. After they had accepted his offer of a statue of Saint Francis of Assisi, the saint after whom the bay and later the city had been named, they turned upon him in scorn when the colossal black granite statue was completed. "Hideous, grotesque, unseemly, and without merit as a work of art," they cried. Although a site had been purchased on which the statue was to stand overlooking the city, the officials refused to allow it to be erected, and it was hauled away and hidden in a warehouse.

Henry had an opportunity to see Bufano's work when a friend drove them to San Francisco. After that there was no doubt in Henry's mind that Bufano was the greatest sculptor that America had produced. He included an essay about his work in *Remember to Remember.*

Strangers were finding their way to Henry's door. They were usually people with whom he had had some correspondence or who had bought his watercolors, were in the area, and wanted to meet him. Judson Crews was one of these people.

When Crews was a private in the army and stationed at Indio, California, he had discovered *Circle* and offered Leite a selection of his poems. Crews was one of the country's gifted young poets whose work had been published by the leading literary magazines as well as by Chicago's greatly admired *Poetry: A Magazine of Verse.* Leite had accepted one of the poems for the third issue of *Circle.*

As soon as Crews was demobilized, he had made his way to Big Sur to look up Henry, and he stayed around for several months, living at Emil's place on the highway. There was plenty of room in the old guardhouse, and it cost Emil nothing to feed Crews. He subsisted on wild mustard greens and peanut butter, a diet that so horrified Henry that he offered to buy him some groceries. Crews refused Henry's help, as he had Emil's.

Before Crews returned to his home in Waco, Texas, where he had a small printing press, Henry gave him *Maurizius Forever,* asking him to bring out an edition that would sell for under a dollar. The first thing Crews did when he got home was to print it as a sixty-four-page booklet issued by the Motive Press. A friend, Delia Kinzinger, made a woodcut for the cover. The price was sixty-five cents.

Bern Porter was no longer coming to Big Sur. He had resigned his job the day after the bomb had fallen on Hiroshima, and he had begun what he called a guilt trip that would last the rest of his life. He moved to Sausalito, a small city on San Francisco Bay, and opened a gallery of contemporary art. He was no longer with *Circle.*

Bern had promised Henry that he would bring out an American edition of *Money and How It Gets That Way,* and he did. It was far more attractive than the somber, black-paper-covered booklet published in Paris as a Booster Broadside. Bern's booklet was white, tall and narrow with pen-and-ink drawings on the cover and inside. The artist was Jack Wright, a local young man whom Bern had come to know through the gallery.

In the summer of 1946, Bezalel Schatz returned from Santa Fe after several months of study with Louis Ewing. He had acquired considerable skill in the silk-screen process and was ready to work with Henry on *Into the Night Life*. One day there he was at Henry's door, ready to begin.

19

*Out of whalebone and gunnysack this mad thing called
sleep that runs like an eight-day clock.*

Black Spring

The planning and preparation of *Into the Night Life* began
with determining the book's size and appearance. Schatz suggested
that it be folio size, twelve by fifteen inches, in order best to
present his single- and double-page illustrations. Also, large pages
would leave enough room for any artwork to be added to the
handwriting. The total number of pages could not be determined
until they saw how many would be needed for the text, and they
could not use the twenty-eight pages of the published work as a
guide because in manuscript the contents would differ considerably from the printed version. Henry started writing, following his
own text.

He began in his usual easy-to-read style of writing—steady
strokes, straight lines, and normally spaced sentences. The first
few pages are filled from top to bottom, written in India ink with
a medium-sized pen point. Then the nightmares take over. In
describing a scene of writhing, hissing cobras, his words slide
across the page in thick, black loops: He winds a pair of cobras
around his arms and attacks an old hag. Their bodies come undone.
Suddenly he is walking on a beach where the sand is strewn with
human clams. "In a blinding surge of grief the sand slowly fills my
bones." The ink splatters.

Streets buckle and snap, the stars are rusting, wolves are
howling, the clock is running down. "Girl of my dreams, what a

splendid cage you make." The sentences begin to slip downward toward the bottom of the page.

He is gouging out a man's eyes, bursting his eardrums, slitting his tongue, breaking his windpipe, burning his chest "until it smokes" and then pouring nitric acid into the raw flesh. He can hear the man's heart and lungs "sizzling." The pen stabs and twists, leaving blots.

In an open field that was once a cemetery, he lies against a broken fence, scalped by an Indian's tomahawk, "the grey meat hangs over my ears. . . . I lie with my bowels beside me. . . . the tent of the world collapses like a gasbag." He pinches the words together.

The dreams are not always terrifying. He lingers on the curve of a Japanese bridge that is decorated with paper lanterns, and he is "lost in a boundless security, lulled and forever rapt by the lapping murmur of a stream." He hears a carousel in the distance. When he walks "in golden leisure" on the street of his youth, he writes in loose, swinging sentences to describe his happiness.

But then he remembers when "along the mountain ridges I howled with pain, when in the sweltering white valleys I was choked with alkali, when fording the sluggish streams my feet were splintered by rock and shell, when I licked the salty sweat of the lemon fields or lay in the burning kilns to be baked, when was all this that I never forgot what is now no more?" The words swell, grow immense, and scratch the paper in escaping to another page.

To achieve the variety of handwriting, he used pens of different-sized points and also paintbrushes, twigs, quills, and bird feathers.

While Henry wrote, Schatz sketched and painted, working to make visible in his way what Henry was evoking with words. None of the artwork would be illustrative in the usual descriptive sense, merely providing scenes taken from the text. Schatz wanted to unlock the rage, shock, despair, and other repressions that were concealed in the dreams.

He used color to give strength to his work; he might use twenty or more in an orgy of slashing and sweeping. A great bleeding jaw. An enormous screeching bird. A miasmal mist. The paper absorbed pools of vermilion, cobalt, black, green, purple, orange, yellow. When the text relented, the illustrations also subsided, some into a labyrinth of threadlike human shapes, some into pastel space. Through an imaginary grid, he squeezed tiny line drawings of city roofs, railroad cars, a cemetery, a Ferris wheel, a grandfather clock, a carousel, animals, waves on a beach. These were the subconscious clues that Schatz saw seeping through the sieve of Henry's dream disguise.

He frequently came to Anderson Creek to work with Henry on the designs for the pages. They went over and over each one, judging it for its calligraphic style, general appearance, and whether or not the illustrations were successful in interpreting the nightmare. They arranged and rearranged details. Henry varied his handwriting for new versions of some of the pages. Schatz changed the illustrations. They would agree on a page and later discard it. Before they had decided on the final fifty-one pages, Schatz had designed hundreds of layouts.

Schatz then worked alone in Berkeley on the enormous production job ahead. He converted a bedroom in the family home to this use. His first problem was in reproducing the handwriting for which stencils could not be cut. There was a photographic process being used commercially for the reproduction of similar work, and he set about learning how to apply it.

Meanwhile at Anderson Creek, Henry was trying to finish the chapter he most wanted to write for *Remember to Remember*. It was the one about his happy memories of France. But there were many interruptions. The summer people were arriving, some to open their cabins, others to look for cabins to rent. Emil put up a succession of single young women. The campground at the state park facilities was full. All the shacks had been taken. Margaret and Gilbert Neiman and their infant daughter Ariane were living in one of the shacks. Henry had been urging them to leave Colorado and join him and Lepska at Anderson Creek, and they had come and were now his next-door neighbors.

Gilbert's first novel had been taken by Harcourt, Brace and

was due to come out soon, and he had started a new book. He was also drinking, which slowed down the book's progress and stirred up his behavior, which tended to be boisterous when he was among companions who came out of the corners of his mind.

The Neimans discovered that they had an acquaintance living on the outskirts of Monterey, a tall redhead whom they had known in Boulder Creek. This was Walker Winslow, and he, too, was writing his second book. His first, a successful novel set in Hawaii, called attention to the growing dominance of the Islands' resident Japanese in territorial affairs. It was a coincidence that the book had come out just a few days before the attack on Pearl Harbor. He had not been writing for the past few years but was now working on *If a Man Be Mad* for Doubleday. The new book was a case history of an alcoholic—his recoveries and relapses, hopes and despairs while in and out of jails and institutions in Hawaii, California, and New York. His purpose in writing the book was to call attention to the ignorance of the medical profession, and of psychiatrists in particular, in the treatment of the disease of alcoholism and to the apathy of facilities that take in alcoholics but do nothing to help them. The book was a plea for reform. It was his own story, which he was writing under the name of Harold Maine.

He drove the forty miles to Anderson Creek in a pickup truck that he had the use of and stayed a week with the Neimans. He got to know Henry, who liked him so much that he offered him a smaller shack in back of the one that the Millers lived in as a place to stay for a while and work on his book. Walker couldn't see depriving Henry of "the studio," as Henry called it, where he did his own writing and where there was a cot for his daily afternoon naps. Instead, Walker moved into the guardhouse with Emil.

Henry happened to write to me at that time and mentioned that Walker was at Anderson Creek; Walker had told him that I had once been his wife. Henry and I had kept up a correspondence, and I had bought his watercolors and books. When he asked me to look for a gallery in Santa Fe where he could exhibit and sell his paintings, I looked around but had to report back that the only art they wanted was of regional subjects: Indian faces; Indians weaving blankets, tending sheep, making pottery, dancing in the pueblos; old adobe churches; any adobe house with a string of red chilies hanging beside the front door.

Walker was writing me with every outgoing mail:

> Here's my situation at the moment. I just today rented Emil's studio from him for $25 a month and will stay here until the rewriting is finished. Santa Fe and you, my sweet, lure me and I would catch a bus in that direction if this book did not have to be finished and damn well soon. . . . Henry says it's the most dispassionate autobiography he has ever read. He is taking more interest in it than in his own work. He claims it makes him howl, suffer, cry, and quiver. I'm strangely unmoved by it.

In all of his letters he told me about the progress of the book:

> Here I am at 6 in the morning and as busy as a little bee. Actually, I have a desk made out of 3 beehives. . . . My typist is a washout. She is one of Emil's girls, has a clubfoot and though a nice person wouldn't make a suitable bedmate either. . . . She types very slowly. I wish you were here to help me with the editing. I'm on page 440 wondering where the hell to stop.

He had received an advance of a thousand dollars from Doubleday:

> After Lieber [his agent in New York] took his $100 cut he sent me $900. Henry's broke but he is expecting $3,000 from his Paris publishers. I lent him $400. It was my suggestion, not his. He is a best seller in France. They have had the *Tropics* translated into French and running them off in printings of 10,000.

In his letters there were usually bits of news about friends of mine:

> Bobby Ferro dropped by yesterday with a gal from Carmel. They'd been bathing at Slate's. She looks great and asked to be remembered to you. . . . Shanagolden was here this morning with a pan of biscuits. . . . Henry keeps telling me I should read her book *The Stranger* but I can't spare the time. . . . I haven't met Lynda yet. Nobody has seen her around but her ex-cowboy has been in to bum a cup of coffee. He says they broke up months ago. . . . Yanko

is away, teaching at Black Mountain for the summer. . . . Re: G.
Leite. He has no literary judgment. Henry has no respect for him
as an editor. He is simply sorry for him. Leite is only interested
in one thing as far as I can see and that is spreading his name
around. He is a fairly nice guy I guess. . . . I saw Emil off for
Chicago today. His mother is terminally ill in a hospital there. He
may be gone for a month or more.

Walker did not know whether or not he liked Emil:

He has been swell to me but I probably irritate the pants off him.
He is very afraid that I'll get his women and pulls phony tales of
prowess that only tend to egg me on though I haven't egged yet,
nor spermed for that matter. I find I become asexual when I am
really creative. . . . I don't know if you remember Emil's joint or
not. There are three buildings, one big place which he lets the girl
have, and two studios. He has one and I have the other. Mine has
a porch. I eat in the house with the girl who is doing my typing
but who is too slow and who paints. I have to cook in self-defense.
Since Henry is in Monterey today she has just gone to see if Lepska
will join us for supper. Henry's wife is very nice, only much
younger and so on. Bryn Mawr and graduate work at Yale, Polish,
attractive, pleasant, and very likable. In some ways she is hardly
suitable as the wife of a genius. About the typist, she and I have
a companionable arrangement, which you could understand if you
were here, and I wish you were.

He sent me carbons of some of the chapters but never those
in which I appeared as "Virginia." I did not know until later, when
I read the published book, that he had written in a role for me of
a wife whom I only partly recognized. He had told me all along
that he was "synthesizing" some of the characters in order to
disguise their real counterparts and to develop the story line. I had
never asked him if I was in the book, and he had never let me think
that I was.

The chapters that I did read tore my heart out. He had told
me that Henry and Lepska wept when they read parts of the book,
and so did I.

Henry is reading each chapter as it comes off the typewriter. He
has been acting as a sort of advisor but if you can find one sentence

written under his influence I will eat it sprinkled with arsenic. He has helped me but he has not altered my conception of it or the contents of it in any way. . . . I'm working 9 or 10 hours a day correcting and rewriting. Right now I'd like to be lying on the bed dictating to you and you could interrupt me by getting onto the bed with me.

On another day:

I'm being nursemaid to Gilbert today. He's coming out of a bad one and still trying to break up the furniture. When he's hallucinating he's scary. His book has been delayed again because of the paper shortage. I heard that Saroyan's publication date was also set back because of it. . . . I'm helping Henry put up a small fence. . . . Little Benny Bufano is also helping. He's quite a guy! . . . Between Gilbert, two babies that get in the way of the fence building, and the fact that I have to cook supper tonight for everybody (Lepska's ill) I'm going nuts. By the way Lepska's a very good cook. She often invites me to join her and Henry for a meal.

Nearly every evening Walker and Henry took long walks together, usually on the highway. They relaxed in each other's company, talked some, but mostly just enjoyed the great natural beauty around them. Henry was interested in the breaking point between the sane and the insane, and because Walker had worked with mental patients as an attendant in a private sanatorium and also in a Veterans Administration hospital he sometimes discussed the subject with him. Henry had no interest in diagnosis or the treatment of the insane but only in surmising how one person's imagined reality differed from another person's so-called true reality. Were they not both real? Is an insane mind ever "reasonable"?

During a time when Walker had feared that alcohol was finally driving him mad, he had thought that if he could work with the truly insane it might help him to find his own mental peace. He had begun what he described as a journey through darkness, and the journey had become part of his book.

Near the end of August he wrote me:

Today I am sending the book to N.Y. I wonder what the editors will think of it. They may decide it's the dullest book ever

written. I've long since learned that in N.Y. people think differ-
ently from other people. Anyway, I wanted to please you more
than anyone else and from what you've written me I guess I have.
. . . Now I'm thinking of taking a cabin 12 miles down the road
at Lucia. It's $12.50 a month, has four rooms, hot and cold water,
a toilet and shower. What do you think? Could you come for a
month anyway? The view? Redwoods all around and watercress
in the front yard. No view of the ocean but it's out there. Bobby
promises to lend me a bed and blankets and Virginia Varda will
give me two chairs. I'll have to make a couple of tables. Oh, yes,
there's a kerosene stove and I have an Aladdin lamp that's as good
as electricity. We'd be a whole colony to ourselves. We could drive
up to see Henry and Lepska once in a while.

He told me that the editor of *What's Doing*, a magazine that
featured stories about the Monterey Peninsula and a variety of
local activities, had offered him a job writing features on a straight
salary of two hundred dollars a month. He had been doing an
occasional piece for the magazine for fifty dollars an article under
the name of Gerald Henderson.

I turned him down. I prefer to stay on my own. At one time, my
love, $200 a month would have been a godsend for us, or have you
forgotten those days? If the book sells it ought to bring me about
$7,500 and there'll be more when Lieber sells separate chapters to
magazines. I have good connections in Europe through Henry. I
wonder what the people who told you I was a no-good bastard
headed for the gutter would say to that? Well sometimes I listen
to myself and wonder, is it me?"

Walker and I were not legally married. We had lived together for nearly four years in Honolulu before I learned that he
had not been divorced from a previous wife. In defending himself,
and not admitting deliberate concealment from me, he explained
that he had been drunk during what he called "the alleged marriage." He had deserted her, and assumed that she had had the
marriage annulled or had divorced him, but he did not want to
contact her to find out.

I knew that he could be very drunk and not show it. I had
taken care of him through many a bad drunk, and I knew that later
he would remember nothing about it.

Not long afterward, I went to San Francisco, leaving him to untangle his marital affairs. He followed me. Later he went to Southern California, to the county where the marriage had taken place, in order somehow to set things straight. His parents lived nearby, and once when he was visiting them he met "a sort of cousin" who had also come to visit. When two weeks had passed and I had not heard from him, I called his mother, who was surprised to learn that I did not know he was in Las Vegas getting a divorce.

When he got it, he married the "cousin," and I did not hear from him for two years. He was then single again and living in New York, where he was writing the Hawaii book.

I had continued to use his name because I expected him to untangle his marital status and set things right between us, and because I was already being published under the name of Winslow. Later, when I asked him about it he begged me not to drop it. "You are the only one to whom it means anything," he said.

In New York there had been bad spells with drink; he had been in and out of Bellevue Hospital; he had joined Alcoholics Anonymous, worked with the organization for a while, and left it. There had been women. His long letters to me were confessional and sometimes contrite. He wanted to come back to California and to me, he said, if I would have him. "It would be ideal if we could live in the same town for a while, getting used to each other again. You wouldn't have to live with me but we could be together most of the time."

He did return and worked in the San Francisco area in institutions for the insane. He came to me in Oakland on his days off and once just missed meeting Henry there. Henry and Yanko had driven up to Berkeley and dropped by the house to see me.

When Walker quit his job to write *If a Man Be Mad,* a doctor friend of his arranged for him to stay in the cabin near Monterey. He kept begging me to spend weekends there with him, and when I didn't he found that the girl who was doing his typing would. I didn't expect to hear from him for a while, and I was surprised when he began writing me from Anderson Creek. When I didn't hear any more about the cabin at Lucia, I guessed that he had already found a companion to occupy it with him. I was surprised to receive a telegram from him: "Arriving Santa Fe 2:30 Friday afternoon. Sober, solvent, and full of explanations. Reserve room." I met the bus.

Los Alamos, where I lived and worked, and Santa Fe were an hour's drive apart on buses operated at specific times of the day for the convenience of personnel at the installation. Los Alamos was a restricted area in the mountains, reached by climbing through Bandelier National Monument, a government reservation. There was no way that I could give Walker a place to stay with me. I spent Saturday and Sunday with him in Santa Fe. He said that he was on his way to New York to consult with his publishers, and he wanted me to quit my job and go with him. In his heart he knew that I would not do it.

He had brought with him a bundle of gifts from Henry, magazines that had something of his in them and a watercolor. The day after Walker left, I received a letter from Henry, who assumed that Walker was with me in Santa Fe. (Los Alamos had a Santa Fe post office box for all of its mail.) After Henry's letter, I wondered if Walker had really planned on going to New York or if it was just a way to save face.

A long time afterward, Emil wrote me that at first he had liked Walker very much "until he became very difficult and troublesome. He was either drinking or on drugs, and sometimes he took both. Shortly after he moved in, he fell asleep and left the kerosene heater on. Not only was it an extreme fire hazard but everything in that room, the walls, the ceiling, the books on the shelves were covered with a thick layer of oily soot. It took him and a number of volunteer helpers many weeks to clean it. Some items remained black forever."

20

Without the enthusiastic reader, who is really the author's counterpart and very often his most secret rival, a book would die. The man who spreads the good word augments not only the life of the book in question but the act of creation itself.

The Books in My Life

When Bezalel Schatz finished reproducing the pages of Henry's script for *Into the Night Life*, he set to work on the silk-screen illustrations. He made just five screens and cleaned each one after it was used, and prepared it for the next stencil. The book required 250 stencils, some of the multicolored pages requiring as many as twenty-four. The silk screens were made on a fine grade of watercolor stock of prewar manufacture.

Since they had decided to make eight hundred books it meant that each silk screen was repeated eight hundred times. Schatz also made many extra pages to loan to museums and galleries for their exhibition of the book. Generally Schatz worked on a schedule that began at eight one morning and continued through two the next morning. When the work became too much for him, he hired an assistant. Friends volunteered to hang the pages to dry and to sort and arrange them in their proper sequence.

Henry did none of this work but he did try to raise money for the expenses involved by selling manuscripts to dealers and his books and watercolors to whomever would buy them. Schatz had exhausted what capital he had, and the situation was critical, until, much to their surprise and relief, someone they scarcely knew made them a loan of a thousand dollars.

Remember to Remember had been completed and sent off to New Directions, and Henry was looking through his writings for pieces to send to little magazines, anthologies, and collections of short stories whose editors had asked him for contributions. He was paid very little, often only in copies of the publications, but he was getting his wish to be known to an ever-widening circle of readers. He was being published not only in the United States but also in England, France, Canada, Scotland, Australia, and Greece.

One day the mail brought him a copy of a new magazine called *Death*. He had been expecting it ever since Harry Herschkowitz surprised him with the news that he was bringing it out as its editor and publisher and asked him to write something for it.

Sometime before that Michael Fraenkel had returned from Mexico to live again in New York, and Henry had put him in touch with Harry. As it turned out, Fraenkel's philosophy of "the bastard death," his metaphysical arguments and analyses, and his pedantic style had overwhelmed Harry. He had a little money set aside and offered to finance a magazine devoted entirely to Fraenkel's ideas. *Death* had but one purpose and that was to extend Fraenkel's influence. The magazine was dedicated to him with a suitable foreword of praise and appreciation. Beauford DeLaney had drawn a portrait of Fraenkel that served as a frontispiece.

Henry leafed through the first issue, noting that indeed all of the articles were addressed to the death-in-life theme. Fraenkel had written an article and collaborated with Walter Lowenfels on another. There were excerpts from his Mexican journals. The *Hamlet* books were mentioned along with Henry's part in them as coauthor. Remarks about Fraenkel's work that had appeared in book reviews and articles from as far away as China filled up two pages. Henry's contribution was not the eulogy that Harry had expected. It was a reprint of a letter he had sent a friend in London expressing his thoughts about the end of the war, and it was placed at the back of the magazine.

There was no reason for Henry's stubbornness. He and Fraenkel had been friends and he owed him a lot, both as a benefactor and as a leading influence in the direction his writing took after Fraenkel told him to throw out "the tripe" he had written for twenty years and attempt the kind of writing that became *Tropic of Cancer*. The tension between them was present from as far back as the second volume of the *Hamlet* letters, which had very often included clouts and jabs, snarls and slurs that had shoved the Hamlet theme aside temporarily.

In one of the *Hamlet* letters, Henry criticized a bookseller friend of Fraenkel, calling him a cunning liar and a cheat. The man had recently died. Henry wrote: "My one fear is that he might even rob the worms."

Fraenkel answered back:

> If he did any scheming and wiggling to sell books . . . I know of one in Paris who at about the same time did some fancy wiggling and scheming to get a free dinner, or a free bed, or a free fuck. Wiggling is wiggling whether it's . . . selling books or praising the ass off some rich bitch to get a few sous out of her."

In another letter he wrote:

> You sit down at your machine and begin rolling all those big words on your tongue, it becomes a vast and horrible distortion, a horribly twisted and tortuous and endless gob, a nightmare born of fear and hatred and words, words, and more words. There's no stopping Henry Miller then. He'll be going places and seeing things, by Jesus! He'll twist, distort, deform, beg, borrow, steal, cheat, lie, hoodwink, do anything and everything . . . he is absolutely irresponsible, in the grip of a mania over which he has no control whatsoever.

Henry wrote:

> When I say I am hungry you talk about my soul or about my lack of loyalty. Whereas all I ask is a little food, *real* food. . . . It is a common failing not to hear rightly when a man asks for simple things like bread and money. People get strangely metaphysical then, you may have noticed . . .

Going further, Henry said:

> I smell a rat. . . . if I were to feed this rat which is lodged in your intestines I would be to you what Lowenfels has been, or may still be, for all I know. Lowenfels would keep the rat alive, rather than Michael Fraenkel . . . because in truth Lowenfels is more interested in rats than in human beings. I am more interested in the one

and only Michael Fraenkel, in the self behind the facade which he has erected and which he insists on asking me to take for the real thing. . . . You are very close to me and a vital part of my inner bookkeeping. While you live you are on my books as a human entity, a flesh and blood creature, say a friend, if you like, and withal a damned queer specimen of a man, but a man, by Jesus, and not an ideological rat in the entrails.

From Fraenkel:

Am I sorry we ever met? But I am also glad. For if, as I have always known, you are the last person on God's earth to whom I should have entrusted so much of myself and my ideas, as you are the most irresponsible artist I have ever met, and so, the most irresponsible friend I have ever had, you are in another sense, in the sense that you can still be a man and human being—sometimes!—my staunchest support and most understanding audience.

The *Hamlet* letters were exchanged during the time Henry lived in Paris and Fraenkel was moving about the world, living in a number of countries. They had corresponded, but they had not seen each other in seven years.

It was now about time for copy to be sent to Leite for *Circle* 7. Henry knew that he was expecting another essay in the series on contemporary American painters that had begun with "Varda, the Master Builder" in *Circle* 4, but he did not want to send him what he had written about Abraham Rattner before it appeared in *Remember to Remember*. In *Circle* 6 he had written about Knud Merrild, a painter he had come to know in Beverly Glen through their mutual friend, Man Ray.

It was Merrild's technique that attracted Henry to his work. Merrild called it "flux" since the paints were applied to the paper in such a way that they moved in three dimensions. They could flow, run, merge, drown, and reemerge as the forms continued to change during the next twelve to forty-eight hours. After the painting had "stiffened" there was a period of from six months to a year to wait for it to harden to its permanent state.

Henry kept a photograph of a Merrild painting on his

kitchen wall. "I gaze into it frequently," he wrote. "I lose myself in it with abandon. . . . The fluidity of the composition makes it as much mine . . . as it does the artist's. . . . There is music as well as color in this strange phantasmal setting."

Certain books had been on Henry's mind, and he decided to write reviews of them for *Circle* 7. Two years earlier Lawrence Durrell had sent him *Men God Forgot,* a first book by a young Egyptian living in France, Albert Cossery. The book was fiction and written in French, and the forgotten people were the wretched poor who live in misery and hopelessness in the native quarters of large cities in the Middle East. Henry saw them as forgotten people everywhere, "lodged in the heart of civilization, like a chancre." He felt that Cossery had revealed a despair beyond anything that he had read in the work of Gorky or Dostoyevski. At Henry's insistence, Leite's Circle Editions had brought out an English translation. Bern Porter had done the cover for the book. Now Henry wanted to review it.

Another book, published more than a hundred years before, was *Life After Death* by Gustav Theodor Fechner, a German physicist and experimental psychologist. His message was that what we do with our lives on this plane of existence will directly affect our experiences in the next life. Henry seized upon this idea to point out the mistake men make in applying themselves to the invention of ever more devastating engines of destruction for the purpose of war. There had been a recent reprinting of the book by Pantheon. It was " a flop," as Henry wrote, while blaming the critics who had refused to review it and the bookstores that had returned their copies to the publisher.

A third book review dealt with *Quest* by George Dibbern, which had been published in 1941 by W. W. Norton. The book is a well-told sea adventure shared by two men in a thirty-two-foot sailboat on a voyage that left Kiel, Germany, in 1930. Dibbern, the owner of the boat, was its captain, and his young nephew Gunter was the mate.

They had left behind them a Germany torn by Communist and Nazi politics and propaganda. More than six million men were out of work and the future offered no hope of better times. Dibbern had been unemployed for several years, and his family was destitute. A wife and three young daughters had been left behind at the mercy of friends. The only way out of such a discouraging situation was to sail his boat, his last possession of any value, to a country that promised a better life, where he could find work and send for his family. The country he wanted to reach was New Zealand, where he had lived as a young man and had friends who would help him. He expected to get there in two years.

Instead, they were at sea five years, and as the years passed Dibbern's moral and spiritual values changed. The people he had met in the ports of many countries had helped him to become "a citizen of the world" who was free of national prejudices, a man who did not belong to one country but to all countries. He lowered the German flag, which the boat had always flown, and raised one of his own design. He printed a passport for himself as a citizen of the world. It was this courage in breaking away from political barriers that made Dibbern and his book important to Henry.

Quest ends during happy times, when the boat competed in, and won, sailing races in Australia. Dibbern does not reveal what occurred soon after when, because of his German origin, he was put in a concentration camp and kept there for five years, until the Nazis were defeated. When he was released, his hope was to get his boat ready to sail again. He was penniless.

Henry learned of Dibbern's internment and wrote to him, and when he was released in 1945 Henry let him know that financial help was on the way. He had Emil locate and start buying up all the remaindered copies of *Quest*, some of which he could buy for as little as nineteen cents apiece. Since it was Emil who first brought the book to Henry's attention, he was as much concerned with Dibbern's plight as Henry was.

As they obtained the books, Henry began writing to everyone on his mailing lists urging them to buy a copy, for which he asked its original price of three dollars, plus an additional ten cents for postage. He reminded them: "In all this wide world there could be no more innocent victim of man's stupid injustice than George Dibbern. If there was just a little love, just a little imagination, George Dibbern would be given another boat, the best boat afloat, and his flag and his passport too, and we would urge him with all our hearts and soul to continue sailing the four seas in the name of freedom." The orders came in.

He asked Leite to advertise the book in *Circle* and to take orders for it but insisted that all of the money go to Dibbern. He saw to it that Emil handled the Dibbern fund. Money reached New Zealand a few hundred dollars at a time.

Leite was in a financial bind that held up *Circle* 7 until the printer was paid. Then a combined *Circle* 7 and 8 reached subscribers. In the meantime Dibbern had sent Henry a photograph of his passport, which ran with Henry's review.

Max Padell, the publisher of Kenneth Patchen's books, asked Henry to write a few pages for a publicity brochure that was coming out soon to promote the poet's books abroad. Henry admired Patchen, whom he had met in 1941. Like himself, Patchen rebelled against social injustices and intolerance, and he abhorred war. He put his protests into his writing, for not all of Patchen's books were poetry.

When he wrote prose, in regular size or greatly enlarged letters, using red ink as well as black, some of the sentences were like billboards. There were explanatory boxes and marginal asides. The paragraphs were often interrupted with shouts and howls. Patchen made his readers experience what he was telling them.

When he wrote poems they did not always look like poems, for rhyme, meter, and form had no hold on him. He had mastered their uses and now he could reject them at will. He did not need to confine himself to sonnets or quatrains, or free verse, or blank verse, or lyrics. He simply wrote poetry, allowing the thoughts that leapt from his heart to find their own place on a sheet of paper. He wrote love poems, and they were all addressed to his wife Miriam.

Patchen had a mischievous wit and could make words chuckle for him even when a laugh was least expected. The illustrations that he did for his books unmasked a prankish taste for jokes and puns. Most of his writing was done in bed, where he had been confined for several years because of a severe spinal injury incurred when he was younger. He was now thirty-four.

When Henry first read Patchen's book, *The Journal of Albion Moonlight*, which Patchen had published himself in 1941 by private subscription, he wrote him a letter to tell him that his book was "a work of unmistakable genius. Nothing like it has been written since the inception of our literature. . . . in all English literature it stands alone. I say earnestly that I know of no other American writer capable of giving us such a naked, fearless and harrowing account. Albion Moonlight is the most naked figure of a man I have encountered in all literature."

Henry permitted Padell to use the letter along with a post-script referring to another of Patchen's books, *Sleepers Awake*. He described that book as "a startlingly beautiful and gargantuan piece of work . . . a veritable cyclone of imaginative originality and vision." Still not satisfied with his praise of Patchen, Henry wrote an article for Padell's brochure, calling it "Patchen: Man of Anger and Light." Padell used the title for the brochure, which had now become a thirty-two-page booklet. Patchen's poem "A Letter to God" was included.

In November 1946, Schatz let Henry know that *Into the Night Life* had gone to the binders and that the slipcases were being made. He planned to come to Anderson Creek to take Henry back to Berkeley as soon as the books were delivered to him. Henry and Schatz had to begin cosigning each of the eight hundred books, a chore that was spread over the next few months.

21

> *To have money in the pocket is one of the small but
> inestimable pleasures of life. To have money in the
> bank is not quite the same thing, but to take money
> out of the bank is indisputably a great joy.*
>
> Money and How It Gets That Way

Lynda had written me that she was thinking of going home
to Henniker for a visit, and then three months passed without a
word from her. I wondered if she was back in Big Sur and wrote
Henry for news of her. His answer was that he had not seen her,
that she had "disappeared." I hoped Shanagolden would know
where she was, and I wrote her. She answered immediately:

Lynda has been and gone, here only long enough to pick up
her old car and take it to Monterey to sell. She's broke. Absolutely.
Her ex died while she was east. You know she went east this
summer? To see her family. Well, that was a big mistake. She never
in her life got along with her sister and when she left the farm and
struck out for herself and took up city ways and made a catch with
a man who gave her fine clothes, a car, and all, her sister, so Lynda
said, just hated her. It was plain old envy. The sister was trapped
in a bad marriage to a man she never loved. Another thing, she was
hard on Lynda because she had been her mother's favorite. Well,
her mother has been gone for many years, her father too. Lynda
wanted to go home and make peace with Marion. It didn't work
out. It hurt her so much to find the old enmity still there. The tears
ran down Lynda's face when she told me how it was, the accusals,
the spite. You know the way Lynda puts things into words. She
said, "She took me apart and lay my blood and ganglia on the floor
and stamped her feet in it." She said she never answered back a
word, just got her things and left. You know Lynda would never

be able to keep her mouth shut in a situation like that. But that's the way she told it. Anyway she looked a wreck when she was here. She admits to fifty but she looks sixty. (Wish I could say the same. Ha Ha.) Not having money like she used to has changed her. She doesn't know how to cope like the rest of us. When she tried to see her ex in New York they told her he was too ill to see anyone. He was already in the hospital, dying. His wife wrote out Lynda's last alimony check.

While she was away her dog died. Janet Tolerton had been keeping her. Lynda took it very hard. She carried on in the same way last year when that old tom cat of hers died. I tell you she was a wreck. We couldn't take her in because Harrydick and I are building on Partington Ridge. We bought the land just below Jean Wharton's place. We're camping out while we do the work. Expect to be weather-tight by November.

Lynda hiked up to Jaime d'Angulo's. The old wizard is still up there on the mountain. He always liked her. He took her in for a month or more but the latest is that she's in Carmel looking for work. Wilma's still putting out the *Pine Cone* and Lynda could always work for her, but the pay wouldn't keep a bird alive. If I see her I'll get after her to drop you a line.

Here's some other news! Lolly and Bill Fassett bought the Log House property. Couldn't have paid much for it. They say they're going to put up a restaurant. I can't believe it but Harrydick says they've already hired a fancy architect. If anything comes of it Harrydick will get work when they start building. Can you imagine anybody coming all this way down the coast to eat dinner? What we need around here is a hamburger stand for the tourists. There are a lot of cars on the road now.

Has Henry told you that he has come into a lot of money? His books have been selling well in Paris, earning him thousands of dollars in royalties. He found out about it. They might move to Paris. That will be a change all right, from Anderson Creek to the Rue de la la-de-da. Well, I guess I've told you all the news from here.

The windfall that Henry was expecting from Paris was an accumulation of royalties due him from the Obelisk Press. During the German occupation of the city, business had been at a standstill but afterward, when American soldiers discovered the *Tropics*, Obelisk could scarcely keep up with the demand with huge printings rolling off the press. Henry was waiting for his money.

Henry had heard that Maurice Girodias was living beyond

his means and was also frequenting the racetrack where he was usually unlucky. It appeared that he was not the businessman that his father had been, nor as astute an editor. Other Obelisk books were not selling, and it was Henry's account that was keeping the business alive.

When Girodias wrote Henry to let him know that there were 410,000 francs in his account, he explained that postwar government regulations forbade him to send such a large sum out of the country. In American money it was about forty thousand dollars. For Henry to collect it he would have to go to Paris, and, since he could not bring the money back to the United States, he would have to live in France to spend it. He was against moving the family to France. Instead, he urged his Paris agent to get some of the money to him. He also asked people he knew who were going to Paris to pay him in dollars for what he would authorize Girodias to reimburse them in francs. Caresse Crosby helped him in this way. He also asked Albert Cossery to exchange his dollars in American royalties for francs.

Lepska argued that it would be more practical to go to Paris and spend the money in living well. She thought of the conveniences, comforts, and luxuries, and most of all, of the financial security. Henry was stubborn. He would not go.

In the meantime the value of the franc continued to fall, and although his account kept growing, especially when the *Tropics* were sold to other publishers for translations, the devaluation on the exchange reduced it daily. While the news of his fortune traveled quickly up and down the coast, he despaired of ever seeing any of it.

Jean Wharton kept assuring him that the money would come to him "at the right time." She was about to leave Big Sur for two years and asked the Millers to move into her house. The property had been on the market for some time for six thousand dollars, and she had not found a buyer. Now she wanted the Millers to have it. Henry explained that it was not likely that he would ever have the six thousand dollars to pay for it, but she convinced him that the matter was out of his hands, that the money would come, and that in the meantime he was to move the family to Partington Ridge. "It's your house now," she said.

He made a bargain with her. He would take the house if she would let him build her another one on other property that she owned on the Ridge—that is, if his ship came in as she said it would. This was the agreement when the family moved into the house in February 1947. The next change for the better came soon after, when his agent managed to send him a few thousand dollars.

While Henry never hesitated to ask for loans he was also conscientious about repaying his benefactors. He kept their names and the sums he owed them on a large sheet of paper tacked to the wall above his desk. Now he gave everyone something, if not all, of what he owed them. Then he bought a car, a 1941 Cadillac for which he paid a hundred dollars. The car held up long enough for him to drive it home. When Emil looked under the hood he was furious. "It's junk!" he told Henry, and he was right. For as long as Henry had the car it was in and out of the garage for repairs and temporary restoration.

The Millers and Rosses were not the only recent newcomers to Partington Ridge. Nicholas and Tirzah Roosevelt had just finished building on their four acres. He was an Oyster Bay Roosevelt, a cousin of Theodore, and had served three presidents as a distinguished diplomat. He had been an editorial writer and special correspondent for two New York newspapers, and had written five books on world affairs. When he retired in 1946, he gave up the post of assistant to the publisher of the *New York Times.* Now he just wanted to grow roses, play the cello, and perhaps write more books, among them cookbooks, for as busy as he had been he had found time to become a cordon bleu chef.

While the Roosevelts were building, Shanagolden got acquainted with them and was the first to see their finished kitchen. She could talk of nothing else for days. They had a sink with hot and cold running water and a gas range and refrigerator. The electrical appliances included a toaster and an iron, and when she looked into the music room, where she expected to see a piano and cello, there was also an electric phonograph.

The stove, refrigerator, and hot-water tank ran on bottled gas, and a generator supplied the electric power. It would not be long before other homes on the coast had similar conveniences, but the Roosevelts had them first.

Now that *Into the Night Life* was finished, Henry and Schatz had to decide what to charge for it. In the beginning they had expected to put together a book that would sell for fifteen or twenty dollars, but, as the work progressed, they saw that if they wanted to meet their standards the price would have to be much higher. Schatz figured that each copy cost them seventy-three dollars, including materials, the salaries that had been necessary, the binding, which was done by hand, and the slipcases. Perhaps one hundred dollars would not be too much to ask. It would be necessary to handle the book themselves, for if they turned it over to dealers there would be nothing left for them. Henry took out a license to engage in business.

Leon Shamroy, the head cameraman at Fox Films, was a friend of Henry's. He had bought his books and dozens of his watercolors and had given him cash and many gifts. He was the first person whom Henry let know that the book was finished and that a copy would cost a hundred dollars. Shamroy answered that he would take half a dozen copies and invited Henry and Schatz to come to his house with a load of books and make his billiard room their headquarters. He would invite people in to view the book, people who were likely to buy copies.

Schatz loaded books into the trunk of his car and drove to Big Sur to pick up Henry. Bufano wanted to go along, and they took him with them. At Shamroy's house everything went ahead as planned. They sold three dozen books. Henry insisted that Schatz take all of the money because he had done the real work on the book. Henry said he could wait for his share.

Since they were in the south, they showed the book to W. R. Valentiner, director of the Los Angeles County Museum of Art, who enthusiastically agreed to give them an exhibition in the very near future. When they returned north, Schatz contacted Grace L. McCann Morley, director of the San Francisco Museum of Art, who set a date in June for an elaborate exhibition that would present the book page by page through its production.

Schatz sent books to art galleries and museums in Paris, London, Berlin, Munich, Brussels, Tel Aviv, Jerusalem, Rome, Geneva, Stockholm, Amsterdam, and New York. Orders were taken at all of them.

Into the Night Life created a sensation among art critics. It was described as the most original undertaking in modern book publishing, "a work of art comparable to a Chinese painting or an illuminated manuscript of the Middle Ages." It was extolled as a unique creation "without precedent in the art and métier of bookmaking." It was "magnificent," "superb," "a lavish feast for the senses."

Schatz thought of other ways to bring in money. It was not necessary to buy the bound book; it could be purchased page by page at five dollars each for the script and ten dollars each for the double-page illustrations. If the entire book was bought in loose leaf, the price was eighty dollars. Fourteen books had been bound of the script alone, and these could be had for seventy-five dollars. Two trial runs had been silk-screened over newsprint, and these were offered at fifty dollars each.

The bonanza offer was a complete record of the book's creation. It included everything from all of the preliminary designs and sketches, the calligraphic experiments, silk-screen tryouts, the films used in the reproduction of the script, and the evolutionary sketches in oil, to the final stage of all the graphic material, and every finished silk-screened page as it appeared in the book. There were more than a thousand items in all, indexed, classified, and assembled in six linen-bound portfolios. The price was fifteen hundred dollars.

The book could never be reproduced because, when it was completed, no art remained, only the five empty screens.

Henry kept busy checking the proofs of *Remember to Remember*, which had an August 1947 publication date. He had sent Laughlin another chapter of the Rimbaud book in progress but did not tell him that he had also given it to Leite for *Circle 9*, which would be issued with four different covers designed by Schatz.

As soon as the proofs were out of the way Henry began a short piece about circus clowns that Fernand Léger had asked him to write. Translated into French, it was to accompany a limited edition of Léger's paintings of circus subjects. He had sent Henry several sketches to give him an idea of what he expected.

Clowns had always fascinated Henry. When he was a schoolboy he had said he wanted to grow up to be one. For years he had admired the clowns of Chagall, Rouault, Miró, Max Jacob, Seurat, and others. He was pleased to do this writing for his friend. However, as he wrote he felt drawn to one of Miró's paintings, that of a full moon and a clown with a ladder. A story began to grow in his mind. Fablelike, mystical, it was about a clown's desire to find true happiness. The pleasure he knew when he heard the delighted laughter and, finally, the applause of an audience at the end of his performance of trying to climb a ladder to the moon was not true happiness.

The clown's act opened with him sitting at the foot of the ladder, smiling in what appeared to be a trance until he was awakened by a white horse nuzzling his neck. The audience liked this. But once when the trance went on too long, when the clown had lapsed into unconsciousness, they jeered him off the circus stage. He was fired. After months of wandering about the countryside, never wishing to resume his life as a clown, he came to a circus that hired him as a handyman to move props, feed the animals, and so on. To serve others, he found, made him truly happy.

One day the circus's clown fell ill, and Henry's clown takes his place pretending to be the other one, who was not much of a performer, certainly second-rate. The performance of Henry's clown was so dazzling and brought so much applause that the other clown, coming to see what it was all about, dropped dead "of a broken heart," knowing that he could never follow such an act when he recovered. In remorse, Henry's clown takes again to the countryside as a vagabond.

The story then comes to a wrenching and bizarre conclusion. It was not what Léger was waiting for.

Henry titled his story *The Smile at the Foot of the Ladder* and sold it to Duell, Sloan, and Pearce. When the book came out in March 1948, it was dedicated to Léger.

22

Moricand was not only an astrologer and a scholar steeped in the hermetic philosophies, but an occultist. In appearance there was something of the mage about him. Rather tall, well built, broad shouldered, heavy and slow in his movements, he might have been taken for a descendant of the American Indian family.

Big Sur and the Oranges of Hieronymus Bosch

By the summer of 1948 Miller had recovered from the three-month visit of his Paris friend, the astrologer Conrad Moricand. The visit came about when Henry learned that his old friend was living in Switzerland in miserable circumstances, half-starved and penniless. Taking pity on him, and ignoring Lepska's advice, he begged him to come and live with them and be taken care of for the rest of his life. Moricand accepted, and, when Henry had raised the money for the rail, ocean-liner, and air fares, he came, arriving a few days before Henry's fifty-sixth birthday and his own sixty-first.

It was the beginning of a debacle. First, Henry was dumb-founded by his guest's whimpering pleas for French cigarettes and Yardley's talcum powder. Next, he was demanding a certain size of stationery common in France but unavailable in the United States. And always he was offended because Henry worked for hours at a time instead of keeping him company. Pouting, he would then remain in the tiny quarters that had been given him, sitting behind a closed door and darkened window. The place was the former garage, which Henry had looked forward to having as his own nook to work in. Emil had just finished fixing it up.

Moricand did not speak English and had a way of taking over conversations, particularly at mealtimes. Lepska knew some

French, but even Henry was unable to follow Moricand's lengthy monologues. He disapproved of the hours at which meals were served. He carped continually about the American custom of eating a light lunch and having dinner the main meal, in the evening.

Henry asked Moricand to do him the special favor of teaching French to his little daughter. But Moricand disliked children and especially two-year-old Val, whom Henry adored and spoiled outrageously. Much of the wrangling between Henry and Lepska was over this indulgence of the child. During these arguments, if they were in Moricand's presence, he took Lepska's side.

He was continually scratching himself on the legs, which he showed Henry one day. They were covered with running sores. He begged Henry to get him some codeine to ease the torment, and Henry tried but was unable to procure a prescription for the drug. Moricand then wrote a druggist in Paris to send it to him, and when the crumbled tablets arrived illegally in the mail Henry exploded.

The isolation of Big Sur depressed Moricand. "If there were only a café I could walk to, or a library, or a cinema. I'm a prisoner here," he complained to Henry.

When the discomfort from his sores became unbearable and doctors in Salinas gave him no relief, he insisted that Henry find him a hotel room in Monterey. He said he wanted to return to France.

Henry took him to San Francisco and settled him in a hotel while he consulted the Swiss consul. To his immense relief, the consul arranged free passage for Moricand on a French freighter leaving San Francisco soon. At sailing time Moricand was not there. In a harsh letter to Henry, he explained that he did not care for long sea voyages and that he would be bored to death. The consul then found a plane that would take him to Paris free of charge, but again Moricand failed to show up.

Now Yanko Varda came to Henry's aid. The Vardas had been divorced, and Yanko was living on an old ferryboat moored in Sausalito, a discarded hulk that was his houseboat, "dance palace," and studio. He knew a wealthy, aging "countess" who collected odd characters, and he said she would be sure to take to

Moricand. He arranged a "soirée" so that they could meet, but
Moricand took one look at her, insulted her, and left.

The consul arranged another flight to Paris. This time Moricand refused to leave the United States until Henry had deposited
a thousand dollars in his account in a Paris bank. When Henry said
that he would not do it, Moricand went to the *San Francisco Chronicle* to give them the story of how he had been deceived by Henry
Miller in being brought to the United States and then abandoned.
The paper played it up with photographs. Moricand also demanded that the consul force Miller to support him, since he had
signed an affidavit that made him responsible for his upkeep. But
the consul cleared Henry of further responsibility.

Moricand's last resort was to bombard Henry with letters.
After the first few, Henry stopped opening them. When Moricand
dropped out of sight Henry did not know what had happened to
him and he did not care.

Moricand did not accuse Henry of licentious living, but the
newspaper story about his falling out with Miller attracted attention, and other papers and some news magazines picked up the
story. Anything the least bit derisive about "Henry Miller, the sex
guru," as he had been labeled by the press, was worth a paragraph
or more to some editors. Writers who had never met Henry nor
seen Big Sur wrote about its colony of followers of "the Henry
Miller sex cult."

The people closest to Henry were still Emil, Schatz, Bufano,
and Gilbert Neiman. Schatz was staying at Free Camp near
Bufano's studio shack. Emil had married. Certainly there were
some eccentric people living in Big Sur, but this had nothing to
do with Henry's presence on Partington Ridge. Any oddballs who
filtered into the area to join "the cult" soon learned that they had
been deceived. Other strangers who came to Henry's door were
like those who had pestered him before, asking for his autograph,
wanting to "interview" him, or just there to take a look at a famous
writer. He sold watercolors to some of them.

Two of Emil's acquaintances from Los Angeles, Dan and
Gertrude Harris, had been in Big Sur for more than a year. Dan
was a painter and sculptor who called himself Zev and signed his
work that way. Henry came to know the couple well. Zev's flam-

Miller's cabin and studio at Anderson Creek, 1946.

BERN PORTER

Miller painting in The Green House, Beverly Glen, 1943.

June Mansfield, Miller's second wife and "Mona" of the *Tropics, circa* 1927. *Courtesy of Capra Press.*

RAYMOND SZYMANOWITZ

Bern Porter when he was Miller's publisher, *circa* 1944.

Dream of Jan. 25th, 1933 (circa)   *Death Decatur St. Osman*)

Recorded a week later from bare notes made following morning.
This occurred during profound sleep in afternoon during very
cold spell. Aside from vividness of dream I recall awaking and
lying in trance--awake, but in a reverie, chained to bed by delirious expectancy of continuing dream, dreaming while awake.
Observed that the shadow of window bars threw a cross on the
wall over xx the foot of my bed and was much impressed by that,
as if by an omen of death. Think I was engaged on a revision
of "Tropic of Cancer" and finding it difficult, because drawing
from so many xxxxxx sources for new insertions. So much material on my desk it overwhemlmed me and made me despair. So perhaps I went to sleep as an escape from all that cloying, un-
formulated mass of data and facts that I was trying to synthe-
size, poetize.

Am in bed, hall bedroom in Decatur Street , where I xxxxx
slept so many years and heard such terrible things (mother
groaning and threateneing to kill father for his drunkenness--
taking away my revolver, waking me up in middle of night and
asking me to telephone police to find father, etc. me sullen
and indifferent, knowing damned well he is out with his cronies
having a good fling, etc. Thinking it would be better for all
if he killed himself and left mother his insurance money.)

I realize, in my dream, where I am. Then, to my astonish-
ment, I find I am in bed with Osman the deaf psychologist (who
was said to be a homo and who liked me very much.) And He's
saying to me, with that big, silly grin of his (so full of as-
surance) "Isn't this fine, Henry?" (one of his habitual phrases)
And then I get twisted in the sheets and I am strangling.

Page, with Miller's notations, from his unpublished manuscript of "The Dream Book."
Author's collection.

Jean Varda and Geraldine Fitzgerald at a showing of his paintings, Los Angeles, 1944. *Courtesy of Virginia Varda Goldstein.*

Lynda Sargent (l.), Harrydick Ross, Lillian Bos Ross, Big Sur, 1943. *Courtesy of Richard French.*

WILLA PERCIVAL

Virginia Varda at a window of the Red Barn, 1945. *Courtesy of Virginia Varda Goldstein.*

Miller (l.) and Emil White at gateway to Miller's home atop Partington Ridge, Big Sur, 1958.

Untitled watercolor by Miller. *Author's collection.*

Miller at his desk, Anderson Creek, 1947. His portrait on the wall is by Beauford DeLaney.

Emil White at work on a watercolor, *circa* 1945. *Courtesy of Emil White.*

"Big Creek Bridge on the Big Sur Highway," a painting by Emil White. *Courtesy of Emil White.*

To Kathryn — for this Xmas and the next. Pax Vobiscum!

Henry Miller

Miller's self-portrait Christmas greeting, 1945. *Author's collection.*

"Tony and Val," watercolor of his children by Miller, 1951. *Author's collection.*

Anaïs Nin in her New York apartment with engravings by Ian Hugo, *circa* 1950. *Courtesy of Gunther Stuhlmann.*

boyant way with paint and his wit and charm made him someone special to Henry. A year or so later he wrote about Zev for the *Paris Review*, and soon after that the essay was published as a small book. During the months of 1946 and 1947, when the Fassetts were building their restaurant, Zev worked there, and it may be that he suggested the restaurant's name, for he had made the remark that in *The Odyssey* Homer described a drug called nepenthe that induced forgetfulness of sorrow and woe. This coastal Nepenthe was expected to charm its visitors and help them forget their cares.

The architect for the restaurant was a brilliant young student of Frank Lloyd Wright, Rowan Maiden. He created an aerie of glass, redwood, adobe, and stone poised on the brink of a precipice above the Pacific. Since an aerie suggests a birdlike occupant, the legendary phoenix was chosen as Nepenthe's logo. Zev did a sculpture of a phoenix for the courtyard.

Nepenthe was an immediate success. People drove the many miles for the pleasure of sipping drinks there and eating steaks and ambrosiaburgers—and to look up at the grassy spill of little round hills that had tumbled off the Santa Lucias. After the sun went down and the stars came out, a bonfire was lit and the five Fassett children danced in folk dress for their guests. Rowan Maiden would never be one of those happy guests. Soon after Nepenthe was completed he committed suicide.

Henry and I wrote to each other occasionally, sometimes just a postcard from him written in green or purple ink, his favorite colors for correspondence. He sent me *Of, By, and About Henry Miller*, a folio-sized paperback that Baradinsky published in 1947. It was made up of excerpts from laudatory reviews of *Tropic of Cancer* that had been published years before; reprints of five articles in praise of his writing; and four essays reprinted from work of his published between 1942 and 1946.

I had seen New Direction's *Spearhead*, a gleaning from "the best" of the writing published in the New Directions annuals since 1936. The first eighty-one pages of *Tropic of Capricorn* had been courageously included. As Henry usually did when something of his was published, he called my attention to it. If his work came out in a magazine and was written in English, he often sent me a copy. When I wrote him that *Town and Country* magazine was unavailable where I lived and that I had not been able to read his review of Walker's now-published book, *If a Man Be Mad*, he sent me a carbon to read and return.

Now that *The Smile at the Foot of the Ladder* was out, he wrote me the usual card, saying that it was the book he had most enjoyed writing. I had already seen the advertisement and bought a copy, but I did not write him to say that I found the book disappointing. To me most of it was a child's tale, and a wispy one at that. I couldn't understand the ending at all. It surprised me that such a handsome and expensive book had been devoted to it.

I had been in Chicago since the spring of 1948, married now to Bill Mecham, whom I had met at Los Alamos. He was at the University of Chicago, which was under contract to the Atomic Energy Commission, and doing much the same kind of scientific work that he had done in New Mexico. The laboratory facilities at the university were in the area adjoining the former football field, and our apartment was only a few blocks away.

When Henry learned where I was living, he asked us to look up his friend Wallace Fowlie, who was teaching at the university. Also, there were two Chicagoans he wanted us to meet, Clark Cosby and Joseph Flagg. They were among his most reliable benefactors, and he wanted me to tell him something about them.

Apartment life had never appealed to me and I escaped the confinement of ours by taking walks about the neighborhood, which was called Hyde Park, and by going to the university library to read. Our social life centered on university activities, the lecture programs at Mandel Hall, campus showings of classic and avant-garde films, and concerts in the vast Gothic nave of Rockefeller Memorial Chapel. The university favored Gothic architecture. Its older dark stone buildings with their arches and turrets stood in quadrangular embraces.

The small community of Hyde Park was there long before the university was founded, but now it was crowded out and its ramble of old homes, lawns, and gardens was being further encroached upon by newly built apartment houses. Bookshops, a few stores, a pharmacy, a small bar, were on East Fifty-seventh Street.

A larger business district was confined to East Fifty-third Street.

Now that it was summer, in the warm evenings Bill and I often walked to Jackson Park, three blocks away on the lakefront. We might go in our swimsuits and sandals, towels flung over our shoulders, as everyone did in those days, to join the crowd swimming in Lake Michigan.

As Henry had asked me to do, we got in touch with Wallace Fowlie and liked him a lot. We had him over to dinner, and after that he cooked dinner for us at his place. We also got acquainted with Clark Cosby, a soft-spoken Kentuckian who was very friendly and warm. He owned a supplies-and-maintenance business that serviced office buildings, hospitals, stores, garages, and so on. We didn't meet Joseph Flagg until later, and he was always a man of mystery.

Part Three

Big Sur

Chicago and M, THE STUDIO FOR HENRY MILLER

23

*I love old ramshackle buildings, dilapidated buildings,
buildings that are good to draw or paint, that have
atmosphere about them and tragedies inside them, or
misery, or starvation, or just bleak nothingness.
Buildings, at any rate, that permit one to dream . . .
that are like dreams themselves, in a way, because they
seem pathless, often absurd, always mysterious,
frequently awesome.*

The "Dream Book" manuscript

One day I took a new route for one of my walks, going over
to East Fifty-seventh Street where I planned to turn toward the
lake. At Fifty-seventh I came to an underpass below a high railroad
embankment, and when I walked through it I faced a short block
lined with trees on both sides; just beyond it there was an entrance
to the park. Lined up on each side of the little street, like a scene
in a fairy tale, stood eight odd one-story buildings strung together
at their rooftops with a curlicue garland of pickets and scrolls.
They had glass doors and tall glass windows and were separated
from each other by pillars meant to be Greek columns. Rising from
the roof over each door was a tall, heavily decorated triangle that
suggested an Indian tepee, and at the peak of each of these there
was a rusty golden metal balloon. At some time in the past all of
this, except the balloon, had been painted barn red, but time and
the seasons had dulled the color. The buildings appeared to have
been standing there a very long time.

I chose one side of the street and walked along looking into
the windows. Behind the first two there was a magnificent coro-
mandel screen arranged in such a way that I could not see further
into the room. On a small table in one of the windows there was
a neat card that read: NAN RICE, PORTRAIT PAINTER.

Next door, ten feet of the space behind the windows were
crowded with large, gilt-framed oil paintings that were resting on

easels or leaning against the legs of easels or propped against the walls. They were all paintings of forests ablaze in autumn colors. And pushed out from the black cloth divider that closed off the back of the studio was an aluminum canoe. A small American flag hung from its stern.

The next four sets of windows were hung with concealing curtains of white or unbleached muslin. Geraniums grew in one. On down the street an open window revealed a sculptor's studio. There were rough benches, stands, tables, and a few folding chairs. Bags of what I supposed was plaster from the spill around them were leaning against one wall. A long wooden table held a variety of heads and a torso. Two near-life-size female nudes were standing nearby. The sculptor was not present, but his smock and hat hung on a peg. There were coffee cups on a small table and an aluminum coffeepot on an electric plate.

The studios at the corner faced Stony Island Avenue, the busy cross-city thoroughfare that along here followed the park. They were being used to store secondhand furniture, which was piled to the ceiling, and the doors were padlocked. The remaining studios facing the park contained a hobby shop featuring miniature car construction sets, an antique shop, and a final studio with curtains in the windows.

On the opposite corner of the street, several studios had been converted into a counter-and-tables eating place that advertised BREAKFAST, LUNCH, DINNER, GRILLED STEAKS, written in white paint on its windows. Next door, on the avenue side, was a bait shop, and its windows had MINNOWS, FROGS, WORMS painted in white on them.

I walked back to East Fifty-seventh Street and passed a bicycle shop next to the café and then a studio that had been turned into a shop selling tropical fish and aquarium supplies. Just then it was thronged with customers, many of them strolling along in the green gloom between the shelves of lighted fish tanks.

Between the fish shop and the next occupied studio, there was a vacancy. A FOR RENT sign was in one of the windows. Looking into the place, the thought crossed my mind that this might be a lively change from the apartment, a place where I could get to work on the book I was thinking about doing, one based on diaries that I had inherited. They had been kept by a writer who had lived in San Francisco during the eighties and nineties.

I looked into the long narrow studio and saw that the ceiling was high, that there was a kitchen sink on one wall and a huge round iron stove on a steel slab sitting in the center of the room toward the rear. A dirty window and a bolted door were on a back wall, and I guessed that the cubicle in one back corner was a water closet. The ceiling and walls were dingy, dirty, and stained. The floor was warped, scuffed, and dusty.

Walking to the next studio, I saw that its windows were painted with the words BELLE ISLE STUDIO in gold paint. As I stood there I heard the scream and whine of machinery coming from behind heavy screens. The last three studios on that side of the block had curtains in their windows.

That evening I showed Bill the street and the place that was for rent. He was not as taken as I was by the whimsy of leftovers —from what, I could hardly guess—and the bare room made him groan. I had not decided whether or not I wanted the place, but I knew that if I did I could talk him into renting it for me. I planned to come back the next afternoon and knock on one of the doors where the windows were curtained. I thought there might be someone behind them who could tell me about this odd little neighborhood.

The door I knocked on was just across the street from the vacant studio. A tall, handsome, white-haired woman wearing a pretty blue summer dress and pearl jewelry opened it. After I had introduced myself and explained why I was there, she smiled and graciously invited me to come in. We sat in a small front parlor that was separated from the back of the studio by wallboard partitions. I noted how tastefully the room was furnished, mostly with antiques. A silk Chinese embroidery was on one wall, and four watercolors of flowers were on the other. There was a well-worn Chinese blue and gold rug on the floor. She was telling me that her name was Mary Webster when a calico cat entered and leapt onto her lap.

"And this is Mittee," she said.

I asked her if she was the artist who had done the water-colors.

"Oh, no! I do sculpture. I don't do much anymore, just something now and then."

When she asked me what I did, I told her that I was thinking of writing a book.

"Oh, another writer! That will make two of you in the colony. Cyril Kornbluth writes mysteries." She smiled. "What kind of books do you write?"

I told her as little as possible, since I didn't know myself what my book, if I wrote one, would be about. I changed the subject. "Colony?"

"Yes, this is the Jackson Park art colony. It's been here since the Columbian Exposition. It was where Jackson Park is now. These buildings were put up in the spring of 1893 when they were getting the exposition ready. They weren't meant to last; they were just to be used to sell souvenirs and refreshments. Then when the fair closed and it was being torn down, they didn't touch this block because it was outside the fairgrounds, on private property. They were taken over right away by writers and artists for studios. They were young people who didn't have much money. The rent was five dollars, and some didn't pay at all. Even though they weren't meant to be lived in, people did live in them and that's how the colony got started."

"How long have you lived here?"

"I've been here twelve years, but I've known the colony since the early twenties, when I came to Lorado Taft's studio over on Sixtieth Street. He was teaching at the university and had his main studio there. Do you know his work?"

I had to admit that I did not.

"His work is all around Chicago, in parks mostly. And, of course, in other cities, too. Many of his sculptures have a theme represented by a group of figures. The pieces are huge. Some of them are fountains. I have his books if you want to look at them sometime."

I thanked her and said that I would sometime soon, but today I just wanted to hear more about the colony.

"Well, it was a very popular place right from the start—

especially with those who were trying to be writers. They would come to Chicago to get jobs to earn a living and then write on the side. Theodore Dreiser was one who lived here. Of course, he wasn't famous then. And Ben Hecht. He's supposed to have had the studio across the street, the one you're interested in. Sherwood Anderson and Maxwell Bodenheim. Around the twenties Chicago had a lot of writers and poets, and the colony was a sort of rendezvous for them. They didn't live here, but they came to the parties. Oh, there were so many parties and get-togethers! I was lucky to get invited to them when I came to visit my sculptress friend. This was her studio then. You're too young to have listened to Harry Hansen on the radio. He used to be on CBS, but he started his book-review program here in Chicago. He was here a lot."

"Did you ever meet Carl Sandburg? I think he was in Chicago in the twenties."

"Oh, yes! He didn't live here, but he came here to recite his poems. He sang them, really, in that singsong voice of his, playing the guitar at the same time. There was another poet who came here, Vachel Lindsay. When he was in Chicago he came out here to stay with his friends. But I always missed him. I wish I had heard him recite. Everyone liked to hear him recite his poems, especially the one he called 'The Congo.' They said it was a real scary performance."

"Please tell me about the people living here now. Who is Nan Rice?"

"She's one of the best portrait painters we have in Chicago. She's a lovely woman. She and her husband Hugh—he's a biology professor—are away just now or I'd take you in to meet her. One of the recent portraits she did was of Joe E. Brown."

"The comedian?"

"Yes, but it was a serious portrait. He's not making that funny grinning face of his like he does in the movies."

"Tell me about the artist next door, who has all the paintings in the windows."

"That's Mr. Rodowicz. When you see a man wearing a beret and an artist's smock, that's him. He thinks that's the way an artist ought to look. He's European, from Poland, where he says he was

one of Warsaw's leading artists when he was young. When he first
came to America he lived in the East. He says the War Department
bought his paintings to hang in some of their offices. Then he was
a maritime painter."

"What's the canoe doing in the window?"

Miss Webster grinned and shook her head. "He paddles it
down the Mississippi River. He started out someplace up north
where the river has its source, and now he's making his way on
down to the Gulf of Mexico. Every year he takes the canoe to the
place he reached the year before and continues the trip from there.
He's got a friend who takes him and his canoe there and follows
along on the road. When he completes the trip, he expects to get
some kind of recognition for being the first person to make a solo
trip in a canoe the entire length of the Mississippi."

"The way he's doing it doesn't seem quite honest."

"Oh, well."

"What do think of his paintings?"

Miss Webster raised her eyebrows. "He sells every one of
them. He's very popular. On Sundays, when people stroll by the
colony, they all look in his windows. Maybe that's because he's the
only artist showing on the block. Anyway, he sells to them."

The thought of my two windows full of Henry Miller's
watercolors flashed through my mind. Suddenly I had a good
reason for taking the studio. Whether I wrote anything or not, I
could open a gallery for Henry. I thought how much I would
like doing that. And it would help him because I would turn over
to him whatever the paintings sold for. I knew at once I didn't
want to operate a business, taking a percentage of the sales. I
would do it just for his benefit, and for the pleasure I would get
out of it.

"I must tell you something funny about Mr. Rodowicz,"
Miss Webster said. "He buries his money in his backyard. Nan has
seen him do it. They have a screened porch at the back of their
studio, and they can see into his yard. They have both seen him
bury the cans in the backyard."

"How do you know there's money in them?"

"What else would he be burying? Of course, years ago, a man
buried his mother in the backyard over there. He was where the

fish people are now. Someone told the police, and he had to dig her up and put her in a graveyard."

"Tell me about the sculptor."

"He's Alvin Meyer and he's considered to be one of the leading architectural sculptors in the country. He's won all kinds of awards and prizes here and abroad. The sculpture on the *Daily News* building downtown is his work. He did that in 1928. His work is also on the Chicago Board of Trade Building and on the armory at Springfield and the state office building at Columbus, Ohio, and oh, lots of other places. The colony has had a number of sculptors. Mrs. Arnold across the street used to do a lot of sculpture, but for the last few years she's been doing nothing but life masks. You must see them. The walls of her studio are covered with them. She has done many famous people. She'll tell you who they are. Before Mrs. Arnold took the studio ten years ago, it belonged to Jessie Arms. She's dead now but she was a muralist. She did the murals for the university's Ida Noyes Hall."

"What's the machinery for at the Belle Isle place?"

"He engraves glass. They've been here three years and haven't said two words to anybody except Mrs. Arnold. She just went in and got acquainted. She says his work is beautiful. He calls it crystal sculpture, and he sells to Black Star and Gorham and Tiffany's and places like that. He's also at Peacock's here in Chicago. I don't think his wife speaks English. Say, wouldn't you like a cup of tea out in the garden?"

She led me through a door that had been cut in the partition that divided the studio's front and back areas. As I followed her and Mittee, who had taken the lead, I could see a partly closed-off bedroom and dressing room. We walked through her workroom, which took up most of the space. There were heads on pedestals in a line against one wall. The kitchen was beyond, and through the screened door I saw a fenced-in garden.

The bathroom door was ajar and I could see that the large room contained a bathtub. While the water boiled, she put cups and saucers on a tray.

"You have a very comfortable studio," I said.

"We have to keep up the studios ourselves. I had the roof fixed again this spring. We've all put in bathrooms and outlets for gas and electricity. The owner doesn't do a thing for us, but none of us would live anywhere else."

I mentioned the wood-burning stove in the empty studio across the street.

"Oh, well, Charlie Biesel liked a wood stove. He just wouldn't put in a gas heater. He had a gas plate, though, for cooking. He and his brother Fred lived in the colony for several years. Fred lived where the Belle Isle is now. They had a door cut through between the two studios. They were both painters. Fred's still alive and still painting, I hear. I don't know where he's been living the last few years. Emil Armin, he's another painter, sees him. Emil and Hilda live a few blocks from here. There are at least a dozen well-known painters living in the neighborhood."

The tea was ready, and after Miss Webster had put a tin of cookies on the tray we went outside. As I was going through the door, I was startled by a six-foot-tall, nearly nude red Indian standing there. He turned out to be a statue. When Miss Webster heard my "Ohhh," she turned and laughed.

"He was a model I made for one of Mr. Taft's groups. Mr. Taft was an authority on the American Indian and he used them a lot in his work. When we closed the studio, after he died in 1936, I didn't want to leave this one behind. I keep him inside during the winter."

Miss Webster's garden was neatly divided into beds of alyssum and petunias. A path of stepping-stones led to a gate in a chain-link back fence partly covered with honeysuckle vines. While sipping tea, I glanced into the adjoining gardens, for every studio had a yard in back and all the yards were joined by the chain-link fence. On the other side of the fence there was a large empty lot, and beyond that there was a five-story apartment house. The studio yards were separated by wire fences.

In the yard on one side, I saw two pieces of crumbling statuary partly hidden in the weeds. One was a piece that had once been part of an elaborate cornice on a column, and the other was a life-size monkey. I said nothing until I noticed that in the yard on the other side of Miss Webster's fence there was a life-size nude woman lying on her face and partly covered by a bush of syringa. One of her arms was missing. Near her a shallow excavation lined with stones appeared to have once been a pool. Weeds had taken over the rest of the yard, with here and there a few spires of phlox and goldenrod breaking through. The next yard was a pretty and well-kept garden, and I walked over to the fence to see if there might be some piece of neglected sculpture in it. On a pedestal there was a bust of a man in a floppy hat. And on the other side of that fence several carnival figures were leaning against the building. These were tall, gaudily painted, and new.

"Who is the man in the floppy hat?" I asked Miss Webster.

"Christopher Columbus. The fair was held to celebrate the four-hundredth year since the discovery of America, and there must have been a lot of statues of Columbus set up around the fairgrounds. There were more of them here, but they've fallen apart. When they were tearing down the fair, everyone helped themselves to the statues and benches and anything else they could carry. They would only have been destroyed. Nobody cared if they were carted away. There are some in the backyards across the street, too. If you moved any of it, it would fall to pieces. The pieces have been mended with wire and daubs of plaster, but you can't keep plaster outdoors and expect it to hold up."

"What about the carnival pieces?"

"Oh, those are something Mr. Dietrich did for Riverview Park. He does stage scenery and billboards and stuff for outdoor parks, carnivals, and the like. He has a big studio in town, but he does some work here, too. His wife doesn't like him to work at home because of the mess. She's a very pretty woman, or was when she was young. I think she was a showgirl in New York. Anyway, that's where they met. He was a set designer for Florenz Ziegfeld and Earl Carroll. He's a great storyteller, too. Likes to put people on. I've heard him tell about the dungeon under their studio, where bodies are buried, and so on. There *are* the beginnings of tunnels, dug out years ago when someone who lived there thought of putting in pipes to heat the connecting studios from a furnace they were going to set up. When the fire department got wind of it, that was the end of that scheme. Katherine Dunham—you know, the dancer—lived in the same studio a long time ago."

An older woman came out of the house and joined us. She was Selma Gamache, who, I learned later, had been the cook at

Taft's studio and dormitory compound. Now she came every night to cook Miss Webster's dinner and to share it with her. She lived elsewhere.

I thanked Miss Webster for the tea and the wonderful afternoon, and then I left by the garden gate. She showed me how to go around the studios to a lane next to the railroad embankment. It led to the street.

The next day Bill paid the forty dollars for the first month's rent on the studio, and I wrote Henry about the colony and what an opportunity it was for him to send me his watercolors to sell. I explained that all of the money taken in would go to him.

He wrote back:

> The studio sounds good! But don't bank on me there or you'll flop. I'll support you in any way you like—except with money. Let me know later, if it develops. Books and pamphlets— sure. W.C.'s too. Tho I'm sending a batch now to Paris. Léger is arranging a show for me there.
>
> It's hard for me to get excited about Chicago. Or any other city in the U.S.A. But I am keen and grateful for all your generous endeavors. Don't kill yourself!

24

Looks like you have made a nest for me there!
Letter from Henry Miller,
(collection of the author)

While I waited for the first watercolors to arrive, Bill took his two weeks' vacation to help me get the studio ready. We worked every day, hosing down the windows, cleaning the walls, scrubbing the floor, and assembling a divider to close off the back of the room.

In the late afternoon of the second day, while we were drawing buckets of water from the faucet in the backyard, one of our neighbors arrived. She was carrying a tray with a pot of coffee, cups, and a plate covered with an embroidered doily.

"Hello," I said, opening the gate for her.

She put the tray down on a rickety table that had come with the backyard and whisked the doily off the plate. There was a coffee cake, which, from its aroma, had just left the oven.

"Good afternoon. I'm Hildred Arnold. I thought you could use a cup of coffee 'long about now."

Then, noticing the blanket that we had spread over the weeds, she said, "You'd better borrow two of my folding chairs." She was already out the gate.

As Bill followed her he was saying, "I'm Bill Mecham and my wife's name is Kathryn."

When they returned with three canvas folding chairs and we sat down, I told her how grateful I was to have something to sit on and thanked her for the afternoon treat that she had brought us. The coffee was good, and the pastry had a tantalizing flavor. I asked her what it was.

"Bourbon in the icing and cardamom in the dough."

Mrs. Arnold was a robust woman, olive skinned and dark-eyed, and when she addressed you she fastened her eyes upon you with a piercing, inquisitive stare. She whirled her graying dark hair into a knot on top of her head, a hasty gesture that was to let you know that she was a busy woman with no time for frivolity. What kept her busy, we would come to know, was looking after the needs of others, especially those of her husband, two married sons, and their wives and children.

Her sewing machine was constantly turning out pajamas, shirts, aprons, little dresses and coats, bed quilts, doll clothes. The stove in the kitchen was seldom cold, for something was either boiling, baking, or roasting. She put up fruits and vegetables, and she made jelly. She often had people in for what she called her "Sunday lunches." At least twenty people would be invited for the feast, which would begin with drinks at eleven and continue on through the afternoon with course after course.

Somehow she found time to do an occasional life mask and later to demonstrate the art on television.

That morning she impressed us with her air of taking hold of a situation, of knowing exactly what to do. We guessed that she delighted in surprise.

"Now tell me what you are planning to do here," she said.

I explained that the studio was to be a gallery for the water-colors of a friend of mine, a painter in California named Henry Miller. I added that he was a writer and that I would probably have his books for sale as well. I could see that she had never heard of a writer or a painter named Henry Miller.

"Mary Webster says you're a writer."

I explained that I was thinking of writing a book about San Francisco at the turn of the century.

"You don't paint?"

"No, not at all."

"What about you, Bill? Where do you fit into all of this?"

"I'm a chemical engineer. I work in the West Stands at the university."

"Miss Webster told me that you are a sculptress," I said.

"She's the sculptress! But then I don't suppose she told you much about herself."

"She said she had been an assistant to Lorado Taft."

"*An* assistant! She was first assistant! A lot of his work had her hand in it, I can tell you. She already had a reputation as a well-known sculptress when she came to him. Her work is in many places around the country, and in Edinburgh, Scotland, and in Honolulu, Hawaii, and I don't remember where else. The medical library at Northwestern University has her work. Do you remember the Graham-Paige automobile? She did the trademark, the heads of three men in Roman helmets. They were supposed to be the three Paige brothers."

When Mrs. Arnold left us, she took one of the chairs with her. "Keep the others as long as you need them, and when the coffeepot's empty bring it to the back door and leave it. Keep the cups. I'll be bringing you coffee again."

She brought us coffee every afternoon and usually something to eat with it. I could sometimes detect the flavoring. The orange peel in the corn bread had been soaked in Cointreau. The blueberry muffins had been touched up with rum. The green whipped cream on the kuchen had more than a dash of crème de menthe.

A few times Miss Webster sent Mrs. Gamache over with nonalcoholic sandwiches.

I wrote Henry to let him know how work was progressing on the studio. I also asked him to let me have *Into the Night Life* to sell. If I didn't sell the entire book, I could offer the illustrations or the separate pages of manuscript.

He wrote back:

> I'm really touched by your enthusiasm and all the valiant efforts you're making on our behalf. About that *Night Life* book, so far as I know only one copy was sold in the city of Chicago!— by Fink. He seems to have seen about everybody, including Marshall Field's, the Institute of Art, etc. But you may have better luck —don't fear to knock again. You do me a great service there. You know, I suppose, that we offer the text alone for $75. There are also separate loose sheets to be had of the text pages alone and the

double-page illustrations. For the former we ask $5 per page, for the latter $12. I am trying to get Schatz to raise his price. Well, I hope you have some luck. Lately, I've had a bit of luck. Let me waft you some. And deepest thanks, Kathryn, for the self-appointed crusade.

Fink was Bob Finkelstein, a chemist employed by a research testing laboratory in Chicago. He called himself Fink. He was one of the numerous persons with whom Henry kept up a correspondence after they had bought his books and sent him gifts and checks. When Fink had offered to take the *Night Life* book around to possible buyers in Chicago, Henry had sent it to him.

Our backyards, like those across the street, were separated by wire fences and had a common fence that faced an empty lot. There some sort of building had recently been torn down, leaving a rubble of bricks and plaster. Bill and I carried the best bricks to the studio to stack them between the planks we were using as shelves to display Henry's books.

As Miss Webster had said, there were pieces of broken sculpture in our backyard. (I envied the marble bench in the Belle Isle's place.) All of the yards were overgrown with weeds except Mrs. Arnold's, which was planted with vegetables. In our yard we had a rather well-preserved bust of Columbus and also an eighteen-inch-tall slab of plaster that appeared to have been broken off from a larger piece. Arranged against it, like figures in a family album, were father, mother, and infant, all of them orangutans. Every feature was still intact, even the father's frown showing displeasure at the stares of onlookers. It was a curious piece and in such excellent condition that I was sure it had not been left out of doors for long. I took it back inside but left Columbus in the yard because when I moved him driblets of plaster fell off.

When I was in the yard, I sometimes felt that I was being watched from behind the Belle Isle's screened door. When a small black and tan terrier got out and dashed to the fence to yelp at me, the trespasser, a woman came to the door and yelled, "Shut up, Billy!" But Billy did not shut up and she came out to send him back inside. She was plump and rather short. Her blouse and skirt were soiled, and her bare arms and legs didn't look clean either. She stood there looking at me.

"Hi," I said, smiling and telling her my name.

"Pleased to meet you. I'm Lily." She smiled back at me.

I told her what I was planning to do with the studio. "I'm going to sell his watercolors and books. No one else's. It's not to be a regular gallery or bookstore."

A man came to the screened door. "Did you say Henry Miller? *The* Henry Miller?" he shouted. "Is he coming here?"

"No, I'm just selling his work."

"I know who he is. I read his book. So he's a painter, too. I'd like to see what kind of painting he does. I'm a painter myself." His voice was so loud that it brought Bill to our back door.

"When the watercolors arrive, come in and see them."

"I sure will. That is, if the police don't get to them first."

"What do you mean 'police'?"

"Do you think the police are going to let you get away with selling Henry Miller's stuff?" he yelled. And then he was gone.

Lily's eyes were pleading with me. "Don't pay attention to Glen. He's not sore or anything. It's just his way. Kind of sassy, that's all."

The day we started painting the walls, Glen and Lily walked in the back door. "Need any help, Buster?" yelled Glen. "I'm taking an hour off."

"No," Bill answered, and stopped rolling on the paint to turn around and greet our visitors.

The color we had decided on was a light green. We called it lime green. "Jesus!" Glen yelled again. "What kind of pukey color is that? Put some French aquamarine and Naples yellow in it!"

"What?" asked Bill.

"Wait a minute, I'll be right back." Glen stomped out to go to his studio.

"Don't worry," Lily said. "Glen knows what he's doing."

In a short time he was back with a fistful of paint tubes. "Gimme that bucket!" He worked in silence over the lime green paint, squirting this and that color into it, the ash from his cigarette falling into the paint as well. He stirred the paint with the paddle, added something else, and went on stirring and mixing. Finally he was pleased. "God dammit! Look at that." He held up the paddle. The color was indeed beautiful, although darker than we had intended. We all admired the new green.

"Can you make enough of it?" Bill asked.

"I don't see why the hell not!"

We had only one other receptacle, the bucket we intended to use to wash the roller. We wouldn't let him have it.

"Lily! Go get the washtub!"

When Lily returned with the tub, Glen filled it with the exact color of the paint in the bucket.

In his dirty T-shirt, pants, and sandals, he was as unkempt and grimy as Lily. He had not shaved for at least two days. The crown of his head was bald and draped with a fringe of sandy-colored hair. He had blue eyes, a sensuous mouth, and a sharp jaw.

It took Bill three days to finish the walls, and while he worked Glen came in several times to admire them, his cigarette ash falling everywhere on the clean floor. I hoped that when we acquired ashtrays he would use them.

We got a phone, had electrical outlets installed and the gas connected. Then we phoned Clark Cosby to find out what was the best kind of paint to use on the floor. We told him we wanted black paint. The next morning he was there in work clothes with gallons of black paint and a variety of equipment. He and Bill had the job done by noon. The floor was a shining pool of India ink, and we were very pleased.

I thought that we, too, should have curtains in the windows and looked around until I had found what I liked in a theatrical supply house—bolts of sapphire blue cotton. I gathered ten-foot lengths of it to fall from the ceiling in back of the windows' display shelves. We bought a long trestle table and wooden kitchen chairs. I painted the chairs Chinese red. We also bought a desk and a chair for it, and put large white Japanese lanterns over the light bulbs that hung from the ceiling. On the shelves I displayed all of Henry's books that I had, and I put the three orangutans there with them. I placed the sculpture at eye level so the features of the animals could be admired.

There was one more decision to make—what to do about the

front door. We decided that I should paint the eight glass panes with the Indian symbols I had become familiar with in Santa Fe. They were easy to draw and I used poster paint. The backgrounds were filled in with copper paint.

I drew a thunderbird, the sacred bearer of happiness; rain clouds for good prospects; morning stars for guidance; a snake for wisdom; a bird for lightheartedness; a medicine man's eyes for watchfulness; raindrops for plentiful crops; and an arrow for protection.

I put *The Colossus of Maroussi* in one window and *The Wisdom of the Heart* in the other. Outside, on one window, I lettered M, THE STUDIO FOR HENRY MILLER in white paint. It was August 21, and we were ready for the watercolors. I let Henry know.

He replied:

> Many thanks for all you're doing. Looks like you have made a nest for me there! Will send you some water colors soon (as I can) to offer at any price you choose. They're all failures (for me) or almost so. But soon I'll send you a *good* one—for yourself. Little time, that's all. Are there any books I can send you for display—or other items of interest? I appreciate what you are doing. Good luck.

25

Early in September the first watercolors arrived in a mailing tube. It was an exciting, long-anticipated moment for me, and I quickly cut away the tape and unrolled the contents. I was shocked! I could not believe my eyes. There were only five paintings, when I had expected at least a dozen, and they were very poor ones. He had really sent me his "flops." On one was a splash of white paint that had seemingly been dropped by accident, spoiling it. On two he seemed to have given up after a poor start. Another had paint drizzled and running over a part of it. The last was merely bright-colored daubs. I was angry and hurt. I couldn't make sense out of what he had done.

The next day Clark came in with an artist friend of his, Jacque Jacobsen. I told them what Henry had sent me and reluctantly brought them out. At first nothing was said. Then Clark began to grin and snicker as he shuffled the sheets across the table to Jacque, and then he laughed hard.

"How much are you going to ask for them?"

"They're no good. I can't sell them."

"Sure you can. How much did Henry say he wanted for one?"

"He didn't say, but I've seen ones that were a lot better than these that he got five dollars for."

"Five dollars! Sold. I'll take this one."

"You don't want to pay five dollars for that!"

"Sure."

It was the one on which the blot of paint had splattered.

"It's the funniest damned cockeyed thing I ever saw. It looks like a pigeon crapped on it. And that's probably just what he thought of the damned thing when he finished it."

Jacque had said nothing. The amazement showed on his face. Finally, he said to Clark, "Where did you say this guy comes from?"

"Oh, some damned place in California."

Jacque turned to me. "Why are you selling him? We've got a lot of good painters here in Chicago. Why don't you get some of their work to sell?"

Clark said, "Jake here paints stuff as weird as Henry's." And to Jacque he said, "Bring some of it over sometime and show it to her." Jacque looked offended. He lit a cigarette and threw the match into a pottery saucer I offered as an ashtray.

He was large framed, tall, blue-eyed, with red hair turning gray. His corduroys were badly worn out, and over a T-shirt he wore a tweed jacket that was frayed at the cuffs. Clark was shorter than he, dark-eyed with a heavy head of dark brown curly hair. He, too, was casually dressed, but his tweed jacket was nearly new.

While they were there, Joseph Flagg walked in. It was the first time I had seen him, although we had talked on the phone a few times. He said that Henry had written him about the studio. We showed him the watercolors, and I asked him his opinion of them. He agreed with me that they were terrible.

"It's just as well that I never let him send me one."

"But you should have," I said. "They're usually much better than these. I'm sure he'll send me some of his good ones later, and then you'll see what I mean."

Flagg was a small man, very slender, perhaps forty years old, perhaps younger. His step was light and quick, as were all of his movements. He's been a dancer or an acrobat, was the thought that flashed through my head then, but when I asked him, months later, if he had been either one he laughed and said no. But he never said what he was, either. Over the years his visits to the studio would be at all hours, although he seemed to prefer the afternoons. He was always well dressed, dapper, neat, somewhat on the somber side. He did not have the manner or looks of a person who worked at a job everyday. He always had money on him, not that he flashed it, but because he became my best customer, often buying more than a single copy of one of Henry's books or of a magazine that he liked.

Invariably he brought me a gift—a piece of art, a plant, a jardiniere for a plant I already had, lengths of weaving, ten yards of bright red velvet. Once he brought me two tambourines. He often came with a loaf of freshly baked bread. He lived with his mother, and she baked the bread. He was, of course, very generous in helping Henry financially.

That day his gift to me was a piece of Mexican art, a smaller-than-life but large rooster fashioned from sharp, saw-edged ribbons of brass. Every tail feather was as hostile as a dagger. It was a handsome piece and I loved it. I put it in one of the windows.

After a few days I matted the four watercolors I had left and hung them. Glen's green background improved them as much as anything could. The one person whom I did not want to see these poor Millers was Glen, but I had mentioned their arrival to Lily and told her how disappointed I was in them. When I saw him approaching the front door, I fled to the back of the studio. I did not want to hear anything he had to say. However, I watched him come in, stare, and march out. I was surprised that he had not uttered a word of profanity; he had not even looked around for me.

Another day I saw Rodowicz come across the street. I knew it was he by the beret and smock, and I hoped he wasn't coming in, but he was. After looking at the display he looked at me. What was going on in his mind I could easily guess, but I did not intend to explain to anyone that these were not good Millers and that better ones were on the way. If they thought I was out of my mind for opening a gallery for work like this, let them think so. Rodowicz had no comment. He just introduced himself, told me which studio was his, and then he left.

People passing by sometimes stopped to look in the windows and then peer past the open blue curtains to see what might be inside the place. I had made a small OPEN sign to put in one of the windows, but only a few passersby opened the door. Those who came in usually asked, "Who is Henry Miller?" I had no books yet for sale, but I invited them to look over what was on the shelves. I explained that Henry Miller was an internationally famous writer who painted watercolors as a hobby and that I had opened the studio to sell his books and paintings. I invited them to return when I would have his books for sale. No one seemed the least impressed. When they looked at the watercolors, they said nothing and, of course, showed no interest in buying one.

"It's kinda childish stuff, don't you think?" one might say to the other if there were two of them.

"I thought this was a fortune-telling joint from the signs on the door."

"I told you this was a screwy art colony."

For the most part our first visitors were people we knew, who dropped by to see how the studio was coming along. Wallace Fowlie came alone the first time, but on subsequent visits he brought one or two others with him, among them the poets Henry Rago and Reuel Denney. Fowlie was the advisory editor of *Poetry: A Magazine of Verse* and a poet himself. Two books of his poetry had been published in French and a third one in English, but poetry was not his principal field. He was a leading American critic of French literature, and several volumes of his criticism had been published. At the university he was teaching a graduate course on Molière as well as literary criticism to third-year undergraduates.

Denney had been a Yale Younger Poet whose first book of poetry was published by the Yale University Press in 1940. I had often seen his work in little magazines. One day he came to the studio with a gift for me—the Spring 1938, volume one, number one issue of *The Phoenix*, a literary quarterly that had long since ceased publication. I looked at the table of contents to see if his name was there and saw that two of his poems were included. I also saw Henry's name and Michael Fraenkel's as the authors of essays. I saw too that the entire inside page of the back cover was an advertisement for *The Booster*.

"I thought you'd like it for your Miller collection," he said.

The novelist Jack Conroy was another early visitor. I had

corresponded with him for a dozen or so years, from the time when Walker and I had lived in Honolulu. Walker had been a contributor to Jack's magazine of proletarian literature, *The Anvil.* In those years Jack lived in Moberly, Missouri, but now he was living with his wife and sons in Chicago, where he was an editor with a book-publishing firm. Jack had written two novels, *The Disinherited,* which had brought him a Guggenheim Fellowship, and *A World to Win.*

As soon as I got in touch with him, he came to the studio. Later he brought others with him, people he thought could help me spread the word that Henry Miller's books and watercolors were available in Chicago. Until then, only the New Directions books had been carried occasionally by Kroch's Bookstore. One day Jack brought along an old friend, Studs Terkel, who had a popular midday radio program that featured interviews and folk music. Another time he brought Dale Harrison, whose magazine *Chicago* ran stories with a local slant. Later, Art Desmond came around to do a story for the magazine.

I wrote Henry begging him to send me books and some really good watercolors. He answered that all he had on hand were the Bern Porter books and *The Smile,* and that he would have Emil send me some of these. He gave me Judson Crews's new address in Taos, New Mexico, where he had recently moved his Motive Press and opened a mail-order book business. He was sure that Crews would give me a 10 percent discount on *Maurizius Forever.* He also said to ask Laughlin for the New Directions books that were returned from bookstores. He said I should get these for a dollar each. He ignored my plea for more and better watercolors.

In late October Fink came to the studio—at Henry's urging, he explained. He brought along his wife Edie. My immediate impression of Fink was that he was not unlike Glen in manner. His wife was a petite and beautiful woman, dark-eyed and dark-haired. She walked over to the watercolors and studied them with interest.

"What do you plan to do here, anyway?" Fink barked at me while striding about and looking into the rear of the studio. "What's Henry getting out of this? You're calling it his studio. Did he give you permission to use his name?"

I tried to explain, but he kept interrupting me.

"You'll never get anywhere selling a few watercolors. He doesn't need you to do that. He's mailing them out as fast as he can paint them to people who write begging for them."

I asked him how many he had bought.

"None. He's a writer, not a painter. Look what you've got here! I can do better myself. I paint, too, you know."

He walked over to the bookshelves. I told him that these were my books and were for display only. He took down one or two, flipped through the pages, and then returned them carelessly to the shelf.

"Why are you doing that?"

"I want to see what pages you've marked."

"I never write in books."

I had a pot of coffee brewing, and when it was ready Edie accepted a cup and sat at the table with me. Fink refused the coffee. He pulled a chair away from the table, tilted it on its back legs and sat there, legs spread apart, his arms folded across his chest. Edie told me that they were leaving Chicago very soon to live in the Los Angeles area, where Fink intended to open a laboratory of his own.

"Of course, we'll see Henry before we do anything. We'll drive up to Big Sur and bring him a lot of stuff we have for him —paper, paints, clothes—and see that he has a supply of food."

"Did you know that Henry's a father again?" Fink asked.

"Yes. Henry said they named him Tony."

When they left, Edie wished me the best of luck. "We'll tell Henry what you've done here."

In November, snow was banked outside the windows, and people plodding by through the slush were in a hurry to reach their destinations. They were not stopping to look in windows. I drew the blue curtains together and removed the OPEN sign.

On Christmas Eve we built as hot a fire as we could in Charlie Biesel's old iron stove and began trimming a Christmas tree. We had invited the colony in for holiday punch, which Mrs. Arnold had volunteered to make from the ingredients we gave her. Mrs. Gamache helped me make open-faced sandwiches and cut the fruitcakes. The front door was unlocked, and to our surprise a student walked in. I recognized him as a young man who had come to the studio not long after we had opened.

He went over to one of the watercolors. "I see it's still here," he said, and explained that he wanted it but couldn't pay for it. He wondered if I would take his copy of *Tropic of Cancer* in exchange, and he produced the book from under his coat. I knew that Henry was often asked for copies of the book and would be glad to have this one. I took the book, and he left with the painting.

26

*If upon my death I should have any fame as a writer
these water colors which I have been turning out for
my amusement and the amusement of my friends will
have real value.*

The Leaves Fall, August 1943

Henry received the copy of *Tropic of Cancer* and wrote back
at once to thank me and to warn me against getting caught selling
the banned books. I hardly expected another copy of *Tropic of
Cancer* or of any of the other banned books to fall into my hands,
but, in any case, I did not intend to sell them.

In the same letter he wrote:

I laid aside a few water colors to send you, then suddenly wondered if it was any use. Tell me, is the shop going apace—or
creaking? Is it really any use doing things? I feel pessimistic deep
down. From all quarters only bad news—a depression—soon a
panic! On the other hand, if it was really going, I could send in
addition to the W.C.'s—for your perennial window display—all
sorts of interesting items—photos—charts—word lists—mss.
pages corrected, agenda, etc. (Most of this material now at UCLA
being catalogued—but due back soon.) Have you ever thought,
when displaying books in window, to turn a page every day (to
exciting passages)? *Not censorable ones!* Might arouse curiosity. Well,
let me know when and/or if and how, etc.

While wondering what on earth Fink had told him, I wrote
back that, while I understood his misgivings as to the studio's
success, since all he had received from it so far was one five-dollar
bill and a copy of *Tropic of Cancer,* I knew that it would "take off"

if he would send me some watercolors and the promised books. I also repeated my intention of running the studio for his financial benefit, that he was to receive the total income from it, that there was to be no profit in it for me because I was doing it for pleasure and to help him.

I told him that I had two orders for the *Night Life* silk-screen illustrations. I told him that I planned to take out ads in the *Hyde Park Herald* and the university's *Chicago Review* and *Chicago Maroon*, and that when I had paintings to display I would invite the art critics from the Chicago papers to come and see them. I think it was my idea of calling in the critics that roused Henry to action. He wrote at once: "As I told you, these W.C.'s are all either failures or third rate. So don't play them up with the critics."

I had already written him that Fowlie had been coming to the studio and had brought a number of people with him from the university and from *Poetry* magazine. Now I let him know that I had been asked to open the studio to Sunday afternoon "round-table" discussions led by Chicago's writers, poets, painters, and sculptors. Henry Rago had volunteered to lead the first one. I sent him photographs of the studio, with his three lone paintings on one wall.

He answered:

> I am sending you definitely in day or two about 20 water colors, a few good ones (?) among them. You can sell at any figure you like, $10 or over, perhaps—*not under*. Keep one or two for yourself, if you like any. Enclosed with them the (2) silk-screen prints. Also a lithograph of Lee Mullican's "H M's Cabinet"—for display. (He's a good artist, from Oklahoma!) About Emil and his books—I'll have him explain things to you. Anyway, nothing is coming to me on these. Only on what you buy from me direct. (I have a number of the Bern Porter books, the expensive items, for example, the Paris edition of the *Alf* pamphlet ($5 now—the last of the lot!) and lots of Cossery's *Men God Forgot* ($2.50) pub. by Circle Editions, Berkeley. Money for the "prints" comes to me— I split with Schatz. Thank you for that unexpected order. (Note: Be careful *not* to expose them to sun—they fade! Ditto on water colors.)
>
> About the banned books. Get what you can for them— that's the way it's done. Certainly *no less* than ten—perhaps 15 or

20 dollars each. Be careful not to get caught. Use your discretion when talking of them or offering for sale.

I also enclose in pkge. all the double-page illustrations from *Night Life* ($15 each), plus (2) silk-screen reprod. of Schatz other than from the book, and a number of written pages from book ($5 each).

Will send you personal items as soon as I get around to it. The photos you sent look very interesting. Some place! You may yet make Chicago art conscious or at least "HM" conscious. Very grateful and pleased with all you are doing on my behalf.

The watercolors and silk screens arrived along with a carton of books and the *What Are You Going to Do About Alf?* pamphlets. I had acquired several easels, and I now displayed the *Night Life* illustrations on them, each one resting against a large sheet of colored cardboard that served as a "frame." Lily, with hands washed and hair combed, helped me mat the watercolors and hang them.

We had picked up more furniture, including an antique horsehair sofa and some chairs, but the find I treasured was an old-fashioned bisque mannequin that had been in use half a century before in the windows of a Chicago department store. We paid a dollar for her at Maxwell Street's ragtag flea market. She had lost her wig, but she had real glass eyes and her lipstick was still faintly pink. A circular iron base with an upright rod reaching up from it to the small of her back kept her erect. The marvelous thing about her was that she was constructed of removable parts, and these, when separated, had a surreal effect when used as props to display Henry's books. The books were distributed about the gallery on boxes and small tables, with an arm, a leg, or perhaps her head, beside them. When we took pictures to send Henry, she was literally everywhere.

Now all of the watercolors were good, and some, I thought, were extraordinary. In those days he painted backgrounds that filled the paper with color. There was little similarity in the work he sent. Heads or figures, his favorite subjects, emerged out of mists of color, or they loomed out of velvet dark walls, limby and outrageously bedizened. There were mountain and parapet scenes that were presumably views of the Big Sur coastline. On one of them the sea was bobbling with pink and green toy boats, and on another bathers were standing on the sand. (Henry could not depict a sitting figure.) In another, a blue underwater grotto showed a mermaid in the midst of eel-like fish. And there were still lifes of pots and pitchers with green plants and speckled fruits on tablecloths of Persian scarfs. All of the paintings were rich with color.

There was only one small one, and I chose it as the gift he had offered me. It was an eight-by-twelve-inch scene crowded with buildings of various shapes and sizes with pointed roofs and many-colored windows; there were bridges and streaks of color representing who knows what; and making its roller-coaster way up and down were the cars of a trolley on tiny black tracks.

I pinned small price cards to the wall beside each picture: FIFTEEN DOLLARS, TWENTY DOLLARS, and TWENTY-FIVE DOLLARS. I figured that, when I had sold all of the watercolors, all of the silk-screen pages from *Into the Night Life,* and all of the books and pamphlets, I could send Henry $858. Some of it he would have to share with Schatz, but there would still be a nice sum left for him.

As planned, I took out ads for the studio, a quarter page in *Chicago Review* and a smaller one in *Chicago Maroon* and the neighborhood weekly. I had ordered stationery with the studio's address and telephone number on it, and when it was delivered I wrote the literary and art editors of Chicago's four dailies:

> M, THE STUDIO FOR HENRY MILLER is a gallery and reading room which recently opened on Chicago's South Side for the purpose of showing the author's watercolors and also to offer a selection of his books for sale or browsing.
>
> There is a special exhibit from the widely acclaimed book, *Into the Night Life,* which was produced entirely by silk screen. All of the book's illustrations and the separate pages of the handwritten text are on view.
>
> From time to time on Sunday afternoons at two there will be roundtable discussions of Henry Miller's work. The first will be Sunday after next and be led by the poet Henry Rago. The public is invited.
>
> Can you come to the studio sometime? We are open every afternoon from noon to six.

The letters were ignored, and no paper mentioned the studio or Rago's planned appearance. One letter came back with long pencil slashes through it and at the bottom: "The *Chicago Daily News* is a family newspaper. Not even the name of Henry Miller will ever appear in its pages."

The wrapper of *The Smile at the Foot of the Ladder* was a bright yellow. I painted a small ladder red and put the books on its rungs and closed the blue curtains behind it. The curtains in the other window were left open so that people looking in could see the watercolors on the green walls and the silk screens on their easels. They could see into the entire studio with its books displayed on tables and shelves, and they could see me at my desk. I had finished reading through the diaries and had begun writing my book.

There was a good crowd for the first roundtable, word of which had got around to young writers and artists and to students at the University of Chicago and Northwestern University. When all of the chairs were taken, people sat on the floor. It was warmest around the stove, so we moved to the back of the studio. There was lots of hot coffee.

I had planned a surprise for the afternoon—Henry's voice on the record that George Leite had made of him reading from *Tropic of Capricorn*. Bill had set up a record player. I was bitterly disappointed when the record arrived in pieces.

It was a profitable day for Henry. The silk screens of the *Night Life* text were much admired, and I sold six of them. *Hindu Wedding* was the title of the silk screen he had sent that was not from the book. Schatz had made it from one of Henry's watercolors before Henry had sent it as a gift to Kenneth Patchen. It was not a wedding scene. On a brilliant blue background strewn with leaves and flowers, there was the figure of a dusky woman and a design of green lines beside her. Henry had priced it at ten dollars, and I sold the two he had sent me. I also sold a copy of *The Smile* and two watercolors. I had to come down from twenty-five to twenty dollars on one of the watercolors in order to make the sale. The next day I sent Henry my check for ninety-five dollars and asked him to send more copies of *Hindu Wedding*. I also let him know that the Leite record had broken in the mail.

He replied:

> Many thanks for the check and all the info! I believe that Leite has only breakable records left now. He's quitting business soon. ... ask him—by telegram—where are the 5,000 records he says he made. . . . You can get them from Gotham Book Mart, I believe, if you have to. . . . I'm making some records soon for "Sound Portraits," S.F. They made several for Anaïs Nin. You should get them! Write Louis Barron, 2533 Lake St., S.F. . . . Any bites on the *Night Life* book? Do you have *The Smile* on sale? Here's my smile [a drawing of a smile].

He had ignored the list I had enclosed with my check, which told him exactly what had been sold to make the total of ninety-five dollars. The lists did not interest him, especially when they were lengthy ones. In the future he would tell me again and again not to bother with the details. I don't know how he squared things with Schatz. As to the window I was so proud of, the red ladder, the yellow books, and the blue curtains, he had paid no attention to it.

Leite had gone into bankruptcy. The number ten issue of *Circle*, summer of 1948, had been its last. Circle Editions had not published the books it had contracted for, among them Wallace Fowlie's *The Clown's Grail*, Lawrence Durrell's *The Black Book*, and Anaïs Nin's *D. H. Lawrence: An Unprofessional Study*. Some of the books on its list were already in page proofs when the end came. With a lot of ambition but no sound financial backing, Leite had opened "the most modern bookstore and art gallery on the West Coast" and named it Daliel's. It was near Sather Gate, the main entrance to the campus of the University of California, and the handsomely designed space was a bookstore with a huge stock of prestigious books and an art gallery for planned exhibitions of the works of Marc Chagall, Frank Lloyd Wright, Man Ray, Dan Harris (Zev), Varda, and, of course, Henry Miller, as well as many others. Its "cultural center" offered lectures, chamber music conducted by the noted Darius Milhaud, and the usual autographing parties. Daliel's, according to the ads, would "supply any book you want, answer any questions you may have, and mail postage free anywhere in the galaxy." Unfortunately, the creditors closed in too soon.

Henry was writing me now every few days, sometimes a letter, at other times a postcard, written in green, red, purple, or blue ink. The postcards were signed "In haste" or "Rushed to death." The letters usually ended with "Good luck and cheerio! And thank you so much." He continued to send me books and other items to sell: *Semblance of a Devoted Past, The Happy Rock, Maurizius Forever, Money and How It Gets That Way,* the *Echolalia* portfolio, *Of, By, and About Henry Miller, The Amazing and Invariable Beauford DeLaney, Murder the Murderer,* and *Henry Miller Miscellanea.* I sent him a recently published French translation of *Tropic of Cancer,* for which I had paid $2.50 at a leading Chicago bookstore.

The studio was doing pretty well, I thought, although the income was far from sufficient for Henry's family to live on. I was sorry to hear that he was running up a big bill with the new mailman, Ed Culver, who had taken over the route from Jake Hodges. Then, late in May, I received a copy of a letter that Henry was mailing out. He asked me to display it. I did, although the studio had all of the books, except *Into the Night Life,* that he was offering in a pathetic plea for barter.

Big Sur, California
May 18, 1949

Dear Friend:

Instead of increasing, my income is rapidly diminishing. My principal publisher (Paris) was recently compelled to declare a five-year moratorium. Several have gone bankrupt, others are in serious difficulties (a few have had to pay me off in books—which are hard to eat). Moreover, publishers both here and abroad are in agreement that the situation will deteriorate still further this coming year.

What I am now earning is not even sufficient to provide the necessities of life. There are now four of us, and the children are still too young to understand the intricacies of high finance. I am thinking, therefore, that it may be better to resort to barter than to sit and wait for a miracle to happen. If I could just sit and pray, that might be the ideal solution; but I am temperamentally incapable of doing this.

At any rate, it is just possible that this idea of bartering will meet with your approval. Perhaps I have something to offer—which you would like—in exchange for the commodities I have listed. (See next page.)

If you will tell me the approximate value of what you are sending I will endeavor to uphold my end of the bargain. I shall welcome any proposal or suggestion that will make for better reciprocity. You may have something to propose which I hadn't thought of. Or perhaps you would like some special service which it is in my power to perform.

If what I set forth rings no bell in you would you be kind enough to pass this letter on to someone you think might be interested. It would be a kindness. On the Coast here "kindness" is the word.

Sincerely yours,
Henry Miller

What We Could Use

Canned baby foods	Coffee and tea
Evaporated milk	Canned vegetables

Olive oil	Dried fruits
Canned soups	Canned fruit juices
Tunafish	Bacon and salami
Nuts	Smoked ham or tongue
Cheeses	Smoked salmon (lox)

Vitamins: Squibb's special formula and
          Vitamin A—25,000 U.S.P.
Stamps, air letters, envelopes, and writing paper
          (typewriter size)
Cigarettes (Chesterfield or Camel)
Good water color paper or boards

What I Have to Offer

1. *Into the Night Life*—deluxe silk-screen book: $100.00
2. Same book, text alone, handsomely bound: $75.00
3. Separate pages from this book—of text alone, $5 each;
   of double page illustrations by Schatz, $20 each
4. *Semblance of a Devoted Past*—deluxe edition with
   several black-and-white reproductions of my water
   colors: $10.00
5. *Maurizius Forever* (The Colt Press) deluxe edition:
   $10.00
6. *Henry Miller Miscellanea*—a collector's item: $7.50
7. *The Happy Rock*—a book about H. M. by over 30
   contributors: $5.00
8. *What Are You Going to Do About Alf?*—one of the Paris
   editions of this famous little brochure: $5.00
9. *The Smile at the Foot of the Ladder*—illustrations by
   Picasso, Klee, Miró, Rouault, etc.: $5.00
10. *Men God Forgot* by Albert Cossery (Egyptian): $2.50
11. *Hindu Wedding*—a silk-screen print of an H. M.
    water color executed by Schatz: $10.00
12. Original water colors (by H. M.) ranging from $35 to
    $75

Note: Whoever cooperates with me now will be aiding me greatly as I am now on the second volume of *The Rosy Crucifixion*. This volume will run to a thousand pages or more. Needless to say, I shall be able to work with more concentration when I know that the larder is full. The whole object of bartering for the prime necessities is to be able to use whatever cash comes in to pay off debts incurred through failure to obtain my legitimate earnings.

27

> *Louis the Armstrong . . . was for peace and joy. . . .*
> *"Peace, it's wonderful!" he shouted all day long. . . .*
> *Louis put his thick loving lips to the golden torque and*
> *blew.*
>
> The Colossus of Maroussi

June 7, 1949

Dear Henry:
This week about sixty people have been in. Most were from the neighborhood or they were university students. Maybe a third bought some book or pamphlet, but no watercolors. I think it's because many of the neighborhood people are artists themselves and they don't *buy* paintings.

Judson Crews sent me, along with the *Maurizius*, a dozen tiny (4-by-5-inch) booklets of his poetry to sell for 10¢ each. The poems are reprints of work of his that appeared in twelve magazines. The cover is a very attractive black and yellow block print. In his letter he explained that besides printing his own poems he also brings out books of poetry by others and asked me if I would handle them. I don't know what to answer because the studio is just for your work. But I didn't want to return the poems so I sent $1.20 along with the $12 for the dozen copies of *Maurizius*. I am selling the *Maurizius* for $1.25. I put the Crews booklets out on the big table along with other browsing material and everybody who glanced through it bought it. They were all gone before the end of the second day. Now I don't know what to do. What do you want me to do?

The Bern Porter *Money* is my best seller. I just can't sell the Paris edition for $5 when the other is only $1.50 and is so much more attractive.

A woman who came in said she was a member of the Henry Miller Fan Club in Los Angeles. I have never heard of it. What do you know about it?

A young girl who might have been a student came in with *Black Spring* and asked me to buy it for $2. I doubt if the book was hers. From the conversation we had I'm sure she had not read it. She probably swiped it from somebody. It's the first copy I've seen and I want to keep it for myself. I hope you don't mind that I'm not sending it to you. I am enclosing my check for $59.50.

Henry answered that there was no Henry Miller Fan Club in Los Angeles and to help Crews all I could. He gave me Patchen's Old Lyme, Connecticut, address and urged me to ask him for his books to sell. And to get *Patchen: Man of Anger and Light* from Padell. He explained that Patchen continued to be confined to his bed and that he needed all the financial help I could give him. He said to drop the price of the Paris edition of *Money* to three dollars.

"*Happy Rock, Semblance, HM Miscell.* I have plenty of. I can send you a dozen more *Hindu Wedding* if you want them. Vol. 1 of *R.C.* will be out in August or Sept. (in English) from Paris. Don't know how I'll get copies. Ask your friends going abroad to bring them in. Won't cost over $2 each over there. Here worth $25."

I received a carton containing a variety of material promoting *Into the Night Life.* There were leaflets that Henry and Schatz had had printed; other leaflets advertising the exhibits of the book in Europe and America; and a stack of paperback oversized booklets of twenty-six pages that described the book's progress through to its finished triumph as a work of art. It was fully illustrated in color. I sent a copy of the booklet to the art and literature editors of three of Chicago's daily papers, leaving out those on the *Daily News.*

The studio was already attracting regular visitors, people who dropped by once a week or so to see if anything new had come in. Joseph Flagg was one of them. Henry sometimes mentioned him in his letters. "Flagg has been more than kind. Please let him pick one or two of the water colors as my gift."

I would invite Flagg to help himself but he never would. "If you don't want it yourself you can give it away," I suggested. And why not? He was always bringing me gifts, and I felt sure that he was generous with others as well. He would politely explain that while he sort of liked this one or that one he really didn't want it.

The studio was not far from the part of Chicago that was mostly black and that touched Hyde Park's small area on three sides. To me, the black men who began coming in were neighborhood people. I was pleased to see that they were acquainted with Henry's books, even if, for the most part, only those from New Directions, because I had to explain Miller to so many others who came in.

When my black visitors asked me to get *The Colossus of Maroussi* for them, I learned that some of them were band musicians and that the "Jazz Passacaglia" which Henry had included in the book had become a jazzman's classic. Henry's affectionate tribute to Louis Armstrong, Count Basie, Duke Ellington, and others was written with a riff and rhythm that can be found nowhere else in his writing. Especially, there was Louis "with that broad, million dollar smile like the Argive plain itself and smooth, polished nostrils that gleamed like the leaves of the magnolia tree."

When I wrote Henry about his following of musicians, he was as surprised as he was pleased, and said what a coincidence it was that he had read that very passage on one of the two long-playing records he had recently made for Louis Barron's Sound Portraits. There were two records: "Jazz Passacaglia" and "New York," both from *The Colossus of Maroussi*, were on one of them, and "Jabborwhorl Cronstadt" and "Third or Fourth Day of Spring," from *Black Spring*, were on the other. He urged me to order the records, which were due out in about September, and he gave me Barron's new address in New York. He reminded me that these records would be unbreakable and again said that I should order the two records that Barron had made with Anaïs.

The records could be ordered only as a set, so those who wanted the "Passacaglia" got his reading from *Black Spring* as well. When I sent in the orders, I added the Anaïs set for myself. I had not given up the idea of letting people hear Henry, and now Anaïs, read their work. When Henry told me that Frances Steloff had Leite's *Tropic of Capricorn* record I ordered it, and it also broke in the mail. But now there were Barron's unbreakable Sound Portraits to look forward to.

I had put my own copies of Anaïs's books on the special shelf with those of Henry's that were not for sale but could be taken down and looked through—or visitors could sit down and read them if they liked. The books I had were *Under a Glass Bell, Ladders to Fire,* and *Children of the Albatross.* On the records she read short stories from some of her books and all of *The House of Incest,* which I had been unable to find in any bookstore.

From time to time someone would ask me to order a book of hers. E. P. Dutton was her publisher, but some of the books were out of print. When I told Henry that her work was being asked for, he gave me her address in San Francisco. "Write her! Help her!" he wrote, and added that I should get her pamphlet *On Writing,* which was Number 2 of Baradinsky's Outcast Chapbooks. "When you write him ask for the two of mine that he has, *Obscenity* and the *Beauford DeLaney.* He'll give you a 40% discount. Tell him I said so."

In my January 1949 letter to Anaïs, telling her about the studio, I mentioned the books on the shelf and that I had had trouble getting orders filled from Dutton. "If the idea appeals to you, perhaps you would like to send me some of your work to sell. I am sure I can sell anything you send and I will pay you at once when they are sold.

"I've always wanted to know you—since I first heard about you and read your books. In 1944. Perhaps you will be coming through Chicago one of these days. Would you come to the studio if you do? I have put our phone number at the top of the page."

She answered within a few days, saying she was sending me six copies each of *Children of the Albatross* and *Under a Glass Bell.* "*Ladders to Fire* is out of print but I have a new book coming out January 27 so there is a possibility I may pass through Chicago in February when I will be lecturing to colleges. Would you like a few copies of the Prose Poem *House of Incest,* published on my own Press. . . . I hope we will meet one day—perhaps in February if Chicago University invites me to lecture."

I had subscribed to a variety of art and literary reviews, journals, and quarterlies: *The Kenyon Review, Chimera, View, Accent, Rocky Mountain Review, Furioso, Horizon, Zero, Partisan Review,* and now the new *Tiger's Eye.* I kept a selection of these magazines, marking the issues that carried Henry's work or that of Anaïs or Lawrence Durrell, out on the studio's big table with *Circle's* ten issues. When the July 1949 *Horizon* arrived from London, I saw that the eighth person in the magazine's monthly series of "Studies in Genius" was Miller. Durrell had written the essay.

He saw Henry as a "fecundating force" whose work, though formless in a static literary sense, was intricately shaped and colored by his "surrender to the flux of individual life." Henry's world was "a world seen through a prism . . . and this sense of multiple weaving is admirably conveyed by his writing, which follows ideas and memories down long labyrinths of images, long *couloirs,* of darkness, corridors full of shattered prisms." The use of obscenity was a technical device used "to usher in a sense of reality"; it was an attack upon prudery and an invitation to reconsider morality.

In selecting quotations from Miller's work, Durrell explained that it was "the only way . . . to indicate the sweep and volume of Miller's prose, the powerful swell and cadence of its music . . . [its] rare tonic quality." And in conclusion he wrote: "There is much that is below his highest standard, to be sure, much that is careless, ill-judged, rash, splenetic, shapeless, over-stated. . . . These defects are the peculiar defects of his particular type of genius. But they should not blind us to his positive qualities. Judged by his best work he is already among the greatest contemporary writers. The completion of his seven-volume autobiography, if it fulfills the promise of what he has already given us, will put his name amongst the three or four great figures of the age. It only remains for me to add that this is a considered opinion."

I knew that many who came to the studio would want to have this issue of *Horizon,* and so I ordered a dozen copies from Gotham Book Mart, which handled the magazine.

Earlier, in the spring, I had attended a reading by a young poet, Gwendolyn Brooks, and afterward, when I had walked up to speak to her, she was so pleasant and easy to meet that I had invited her to lunch. I knew her work from *Poetry* magazine, and this was the first opportunity I had had to hear her read her poems. *Harper* had published her first book, *A Street in Bronzeville,* in 1945. After

we got acquainted, she sometimes came to the studio with one or
two new poems that she invited me to read. They were for another
book, *Annie Allen*, which would earn her the Pulitzer Prize the
following year.

When Langston Hughes came to Chicago in May, she had
a party for him and invited Bill and me. Miss Brooks was married
to Henry Blakely, and the party was in their flat on East Sixty-
third Street. When we arrived we found Jack Conroy and other
people we knew there. During the evening I asked Hughes if he
would lead our next roundtable. He said he would like to, but he
was leaving Chicago in a day or so.

Reuel Denney led it instead, and again a crowd came. Many
were new faces. I sold the last of the watercolors that day and
several pages from the *Night Life* book. People also bought the
illustrated booklet that told so much about the book. Henry had
asked me to charge a dollar for it.

I had received another dozen of Crews's ten-cent poems,
which he called *A Poet's Breath*, and I sold all of them that day as
well. I thought that I should ask Crews to raise his price to twenty
cents or even to a quarter.

When I mailed Henry his check I wrote: "I think that in
another year this studio will be making money for you. It's attracting more notice all the time and bringing in people with more
money to spend than the students have."

Although the *Hyde Park Herald* gave the studio a write-up
now and then and the ad continued to run, I wanted the studio to
have citywide coverage. When I learned that the Art Institute of
Chicago published a quarterly exhibitions calendar that listed the
current art and science shows throughout the city and suburbs, I
subscribed. Thereafter, in the coming years, M, THE STUDIO FOR
HENRY MILLER appeared in the center of the triple-column spread.
This was because the forty or more museums, galleries, libraries,
art centers, and so on, were listed alphabetically and M fell into that
space. The listings were generous, six-inch-wide descriptive boxes.
For my first quarterly I included a notice of the permanent exhibition of *Into the Night Life*. When the July-August-September quarterly came out, I sent a copy to Henry.

"Delighted you are pushing *Into the Night Life*. Think if you

could send a post-card to doctors and lawyers in Chicago to come
in and look at it, you might get results."

Every few days I sent Henry whatever cash the studio took
in, when it was five, ten, or a few more dollars. I thought it was
easier for him to have cash rather than a check, knowing that he
had to pay Culver for the delivery of groceries that came with the
mail three times a week. It was only when I had a large amount
to send him that I wrote a check. One day it occurred to me that
checks with M, THE STUDIO FOR HENRY MILLER and our address on
them would be more businesslike, and I ordered them from our
bank.

When I sold one of the five-dollar editions of *Money and How
It Gets That Way,* I thought I might have a collector and I was right.
He asked for items I didn't have—issues of *The Booster,* the Paris
edition of *Aller Retour New York,* and *The World of Sex,* which had
been privately published in Chicago. When I wrote Henry about
acquiring these titles, I also asked him when I could expect more
watercolors.

So people were finding out about M after all. When I asked
the collector who had put him in touch with us, he would only say
that it was "a friend." Later I found out that Flagg was the friend.

The Henry Miller name on the windows aroused the curiosity of an elderly man who lived nearby. I learned later that he and
his wife had an elegant apartment in one of the big hotels on the
lake. The colony was usually included in his daily stroll. One day
he opened the studio door, looked inside, and when he saw me he
saluted me with an upraised right arm. This became his usual
entrance.

He appeared to be in his seventies and had a shock of white
hair and a large belly. He had been handsome, and what remained
of his good looks and stately carriage gave him a distinguished
appearance. Nevertheless, it was always afternoon when he arrived, and his open jacket usually revealed traces of a late breakfast,
drops of egg, butter, coffee on a white shirt.

In time I learned that he was an Englishman and had
come to this country as a young man and never returned to his
family. He had wanted to be a writer but had earned his living

holding a variety of editorial jobs. He had been in Chicago thirty years. When he was in his fifties he had married a wealthy widow and thereafter lived a life of ease and abundance. His name was John Stapleton Cowley-Brown. He spent the winters alone in Havana.

He seemed fascinated by the studio, which he saw as a unique tribute to a single writer. He would ask me about my interest in Henry's work, repeating the questions from to time, forgetting that I had already answered them. He was interested in Henry and would question me about his personality, reading habits, interests aside from writing, his family, and his life in Big Sur. I let him read all of Henry's letters.

When there were others in the studio, there was little talk between us. Then he would sit at the table and look through the journals and quarterlies that were new to him. He carried a bundle of rare-book catalogues with him, and, if we were alone, he would spread them out on the table and read from them, glancing up now and then to see my reaction. "Edith Sitwell, *Rustic Elegies*, 1927. Rubbish! James Stephens, *The Crock of Gold*, 1912. More rubbish! Milne, *When We Were Very Young*, 1926. Rot! Now here's something, Evelyn Waugh's *Mrs. Loveday's Little Outing*. I wonder what that's about. He'd show her no mercy. He never wrote a kind word about a woman. Here are some engravings. *Naked Girl with Cloak*. Ought to cost more without the cloak, don't you think? One of only sixteen copies. Golden Cock Press."

I knew, from looking through the lists myself, that he was referring to the Golden Cockerel Press.

"*The Bee Sting*. Female nude. Hair added to the head. Now what in hell does that mean?"

The prices of these books and engravings were given in English pounds and other currency because they came from his brother in London who was, as far as I could make out, either a collector of rare books, a bibliopole, a bibliophile, or a bibliomaniac. New catalogues arrived frequently and were shared with me. Eventually he would give me the catalogues. "Maybe someday your Henry Miller will be in one of these."

He had read the *Tropics* but nothing else of Henry's. I would put other books and brochures before him, but he would only riffle through the pages. He bought nothing from me. When I told him a new book, *Sexus,* was coming out soon and mentioned how difficult it was going to be for me to get hold of a copy, he said, "Never mind, they'll have it in Havana. They have all of his books. Do you want me to bring a copy to you?"

"What about getting it through customs? Henry said it would be banned."

"Don't worry about customs. I've been coming through customs for years and all the men know me. They don't even open my bags. If you want the book I'll get it for you."

I told him to bring it.

I was still buying an occasional copy of *Tropic of Cancer* from a student. I never asked how they had acquired the book, but I could see that they were too young to have been among the servicemen who had brought it back from Paris. I assumed that these were pirated editions. I never paid more than five dollars for them, and I sent the books at once to Henry.

In October I planned a quick trip to New York. I had several things in mind. James Laughlin had not responded to my request for Henry's New Directions books that had been returned unsold —copies that I could have for the studio at a dollar apiece, I had hoped. I wanted to call on him. I also intended to go to Sound Portraits, now established in New York, to pick up some of the records I had ordered, and to the Gotham Book Mart for another *Capricorn* record to carry home safely. In a letter a few months back, Henry had said that Michael Fraenkel would probably be happy to have me sell his books. I had written him, but he had not answered. Now I wired him, giving him the name of the hotel where I would be staying and asking him to phone me to arrange a meeting.

I also planned to call on the publisher who had given me a contract for my book. After reading the diaries through, I had found the San Francisco years less exciting than the diarist's account of how he was caught up in the "Klondike fever" of 1898 and set out for the gold creeks to make his fortune. This was the book I was going to write.

In four days I was home again. Laughlin had been easy to talk with. He was curious about the studio and asked questions.

The answers seemed to amaze him. When I told him that I bought his annuals every year, we talked about writers, especially the ones New Directions published. Before I left he gave me an auto-graphed copy of a slim volume of his own verse, *Some Natural Things*. He promised to supply me with the one-dollar books, and later he did.

Henry's Sound Portraits were not ready, but I took Anaïs's with me. At the Gotham Book Mart there were no more *Capricorn* records, and when I told Miss Steloff that mine had been broken in the mail she simply shrugged. I began to explain the studio to her, how it was helping Henry, but she was either not listening or not interested. When she turned her back and walked away, apparently to attend to other business, I left without saying good-bye.

Fraenkel invited me to come to where he was living in Greenwich Village. From what I had read in the *Hamlet* book, I had expected him to be the brainy sort, pretentious perhaps, and stiff, and he was. He ushered me inside to an all-but-empty, cur-tainless room that appeared to be part of a large flat and offered me a hard wooden kitchen chair to sit on. He drew up a similar chair, the only other piece of furniture in the room, and for a time we sat nearly knee to knee while I listened to him denounce "the philistines who have driven the great surrealist filmmaker, Luis Buñuel, to exile in Mexico."

When I was able to change the subject, I described the studio and asked if he cared to have me offer any of his books for sale. From my letter he already knew that Henry had suggested it. He was silent for a minute or two.

"What good would it do? The public does not read my books, they don't know me. Even the *Hamlet*s are known as Henry Miller's books."

"I show my copy of *Hamlet* to people all the time, and I could have sold a few copies if I'd had them."

"You have the *Hamlet* volumes? What edition?"

"The first edition, but only volume one. Henry gave it to me five years ago."

"You should also have volume two. I'll send it to you. As you see I've moved out of here. Everything was picked up yesterday and is on its way to Unionville, Indiana, where I'll be living from now on."

I wondered why he was moving to Unionville, Indiana, but thought it best that I mind my own business and not ask. As I was going out the door, he said: "I can send you *The Genesis of the Tropic of Cancer.* Bern Porter published it, and I have some extra copies."

"Oh, please do send them. And Indiana's so close, why don't you come and see us?"

28

The Millers' marriage had never been a love idyll, but now
with two small children underfoot their quarrels were less recon-
cilable, especially those that arose over the children. Tony was
only fourteen months old and Lepska could usually handle him in
spite of Henry's interference, but four-year-old Val had her father
on her side and she could do as she pleased. Henry adored her.
Lepska loved the children as much as Henry did, but she wanted
Val to respond to discipline and to have good manners. Henry was
permissive in all things at all times and took Val's side when
Lepska tried to correct her behavior. It would not be long before
Tony learned that he, too, could defy his mother.

Henry's refuge from the battles was his studio, the made-
over garage a few steps from the house. There he was finishing
the second book of *The Rosy Crucifixion*, which he called *Plexus*.

"I'm on page 1,616," he wrote me.

And when he wasn't working on the book he attended to his
voluminous correspondence: "Forgive speed of this. Devote 2 to 3
hrs. a day just *answering* mail. Frightful. Kills my energy. And it's
all sheer rot and waste."

He kept at his watercolors and occasionally attempted to do
a portrait of Val. He included one of these with the next batch that
he sent me. To me it was much the same as his other "portraits,"

and yet the pinks and yellows and tender greens suggested young innocence, and the features of the face seemed angelic.

While likenesses of others were beyond Henry's ability, the pen-and-ink sketches that he did of himself were easily recognizable self-portraits.

Before Christmas of 1949 he had asked me to send a copy of *The Smile at the Foot of the Ladder* to a certain publishing house in London. He had written them a letter, but because he had no copy of the book on hand he had asked me to mail one. Now, in January, the book was returned with this letter: "Dear Miss Winslow: Thank you very much for sending us a copy of Henry Miller's *The Smile at the Foot of the Ladder.* I enjoyed it immensely and consider it a very fine story. However, it is far too short to make a separate book. The British book trade is against short padded books and it would be very difficult to sell. However, once more thank you." The letter had come to me instead of to Henry probably because I had given the studio address when I had mailed the book. I sent the letter on to Henry.

It was the first I had known of his seeking a publisher abroad for the book. He had told many people that it was the book he had most enjoyed writing, and it was to be expected that he wanted it to reach as many readers as possible.

Into the Night Life was never far from his thoughts. In nearly every letter or card he wrote me, he asked if I had had "any bites yet?" He always thanked me for my efforts in trying to sell the book. "You are moving heaven and earth."

In one letter he wrote: "*There* is a book *Time* should have written up—or *Life.* Why don't they? . . . They can write up Braque, Picasso, Matisse, et al., why not Schatz and myself?" When I told him that Reuel Denny was a stringer for *Time,* he wrote back: "If Reuel Denny wanted to do us a favor, let him tackle that subject [*Into the Night Life*] but if it has to go through the mangler at the main office, then it's useless. They distort everything. They never say anything worthwhile about me, always cheap, vulgar, superficial. Story always rewritten by someone in New York who knows nothing. Nothing by *Time* has brought me any good."

Although I tried very hard, it would be two years before I

sold a copy of the book. A hundred dollars was a lot of money to pay for a book.

I had seven or eight tables set up with his work, and the Sound Portraits had arrived. Henry had run out of copies of *Echolalia* and *The Happy Rock* as well as the booklets *Money, Maurizius, DeLaney, Obscenity,* and *Murder.* He told me to order these now from Crews. Bern Porter and Baradinsky had supplied Crews with these titles to sell through the mail-order business he was operating along with Motive Press.

I did not tell Henry that Porter had sold *The Happy Rock* to Marshall Field's at a price low enough for them to offer it at $1.50. I had seen it in the book department and considered buying the dozen they had because the studio price was five dollars. Then I thought that, if a big store like Field's was showing the book, they might stock other Miller titles. I did not consider the studio to be the sole outlet in Chicago for Henry's books, although I always told those who bought at the studio that its income was for Henry's financial benefit. Before Laughlin had begun supplying me with books, I had urged the buyer at Kroch's to stock Henry's books from New Directions, and I had sent them customers.

When Crews filled my orders, he always sent along copies of a few thin quarterlies that he published. Their titles were *Suck-Egg Mule, The Flying Fish, Notebook,* and *The Naked Ear.* Their contents were poems, for, knowing how difficult it was for newcomers to get into print, he had opened these pages to them. He resented what he felt was the snobbishness of many poetry and literary magazines in taking only the work of recognized "names." Evidence of his zeal in getting his own poets into circulation was seen in *The Flying Fish,* which had a box with a quotation from Kenneth Patchen: "I believe the people who say they like poetry and never buy any are a pack of cheap sons-of-bitches."

To help finance these publishing ventures, Crews relied upon patrons. Caresse Crosby was one of them.

I especially liked *The Naked Ear.* It was only four by six inches in size, and the covers were reproductions of original drawings, or they might be details taken from a famous work of art. Some were photographs, the work of Mildred Tolbert, who was Mrs. Crews.

About twelve very short poems were printed in each issue, and, for the most part, they were good poems. Since the price was only fifteen cents, or eight issues for a dollar, anyone who liked poetry could afford a copy. It was an irresistible bargain, and I sold many. I ordered them twenty at a time to keep up with the demand.

One evening Clark Cosby took Bill and me to Jacque Jacobsen's upstairs flat in Old Town, a Greenwich Village kind of neighborhood on Chicago's near North Side. He wanted us to see Jacque's paintings. Jacque showed us more than a dozen of them, and none were for sale. He prized them so highly that he could not part with them. They were certainly unusual.

He worked in tempera, with brushes as fine as pen points, which produced drawings rather than brush strokes. The thread-like tangles and skeins, done in vivid colors—purple, magenta, sapphire, red, green—lay upon pools of undercolors. Some of the patterns were foamy, as if they had burst in wet spurts from a crevice.

I asked him where he got his ideas. His answer was evasive. He called them fantasies. "You could call it fantastic realism," he said. "It's just nonobjective art."

"Oh, for God's sake, tell her what they are," Clark said.

I learned then that Jacque worked in a hospital, assisting in the dark room where they developed photographs of samples of diseased tissues and various malignancies. He had acquired copies of the slides, some of which he showed us. What we were looking at in his paintings were blood, bone, cell, membrane, gland, and other pathological samples. They had inspired his designs.

"If you didn't know what they were, you'd see the beauty in them, wouldn't you?" he asked.

"They're beautiful," I said. And they were. When he suggested that I take a few back to the studio "for show, not to sell, but just to give others a chance to enjoy them," I chose four. He did not want to "spoil" the designs by signing his name over them. Instead, he wrote his name on their backs in thick black pencil.

A note from Henry came on the back of a colored picture postcard showing a brightly painted piano. The colors were in stripes and zigzags, and soaring out of the top of the piano there were four fairy-tale towers. Birds were flying, and two puppet shows were in progress. "Come Play With Me" was written across the front in large letters. A small clock told the time. A message on the back of the card described "a piano in the studio of Henry Miller." It was Zev's creation.

When Henry wanted to teach Val to play the piano, an old but playable upright was found and Zev offered to paint it. The results so delighted Henry that he had the postcards made. He was selling them for ten cents apiece. I thought they would be fun for sending out studio announcements and ordered a hundred.

In December 1949, Anaïs wrote me that she was moving back to New York and would take with her the books, manuscripts, first editions, and so on, that had been with a San Francisco bookshop for months and had not sold. She asked me if I might like to buy some of it, and she enclosed a list:

> *Tropic of Cancer,* original edition. Obelisk Press, Sept. 1934. Bound in leather. Deluxe handiwork of best book binder in Paris. $35.
>
> *Max and the White Phagocytes,* original paperbound edition. Obelisk Press, Sept. 1938. Two copies, $25 ea.
>
> *Scenario,* paperbound. Obelisk Press, with a frontispiece by Abraham Rattner. Signed and numbered copies. 1937. Four copies, $10 ea.
>
> *Money and How It Gets That Way,* paperbound original. Eight copies, $2 ea.
>
> *The Booster* magazine. Sept., Oct., Nov., Dec., 1937. Seventeen copies, $1.50 ea.
>
> *Delta* magazine, April 1938. Five copies, $1.50 ea.
>
> *What Are You Going to Do About Alf?* Original pamphlet. Fourteen copies, $1 ea.
>
> *Aller Retour New York,* original edition. $8.
>
> *House of Incest,* original ms. corrected by Henry Miller. $50.
>
> *D. H. Lawrence: An Unprofessional Study.* Original ms. $50.
>
> *Winter of Artifice.* Original ms. $50.
>
> *Under a Glass Bell.* Original ms. $50.

Two notebooks of Henry Miller's. Handwritten. Notes on D. H. Lawrence and *Miscellanea*. Bound. $100 each.

I phoned the collector, the man who came to the studio in search of *The Booster* and other Milleriana, and when I read the list to him he said he would be right over with a check. From what he and I bought, I was able to assure Anaïs that we would take everything, and when the packages arrived I mailed her the money.

In the roll of new watercolors that I received from Henry, there were ten; only one was not a "portrait." It was of three figures on half a sheet of paper, and the colors were different from those he usually worked with. These were citron, henna, brown, red, and black. The face of the central figure was in torment. Were the black slashes thorns? Were the red drops blood? Behind the figures the sky was roiling in darkness. It looked like the scene of the Crucifixion, but I could not believe that that was what Henry meant it to be. Perhaps it was a trio of gargoyles.

Marvin Halverson dropped by the studio late that afternoon. It was a snowy January day, and I had built up a fire in the old stove and stayed open, although I had hardly expected any business. He had got off the bus and was on his way home when he saw the lights on in the studio and came in. I put on a pot of coffee.

Marvin had been in the studio many times. He was not an artist, but he was interested in all of the arts and had been since his undergraduate days. He had gone into the ministry and was now dean of students at the Chicago Theological Seminary, which was on the campus of the University of Chicago. In 1948, in despair over the mediocrity and oversentimentalization of the religious art that he saw in churches, he had arranged a contemporary religious art exhibition on campus. Its purpose was to awaken clergy, and the public as well, to the vitality of various forms of religious art being done by contemporary artists.

We drank our coffee while I listened to his plans for a second similar show, this one to open on January 30 in the nearby Frank Lloyd Wright Robie House. Then, because I knew he liked Henry's watercolors, I brought out the ones that had just arrived.

I especially wanted to see his reaction to the one I saw as the Crucifixion. When he came to it, he looked at it carefully and then said, "Why would Miller want to paint the Crucifixion?"

"Maybe that's not what it's supposed to be."

"Maybe not, but there's the top of a cross, and the man's head is bleeding."

I had not been sure it was a cross. It was only a suggestion behind a crisp halo of hair.

"What title did he give it?"

"None. He never titles his paintings."

"Would you like to put it in the show?"

"All right."

The day that one of Halverson's coworkers came to pick up the watercolor, which I had matted, he also stopped at Glen's studio to get the crystal vase that Glen had engraved for the show, a scene of Saint Francis feeding the birds. I had admired Glen's design for the work before he began cutting it, and I would have liked to watch him "bring it to life," but I was not allowed to watch Glen at work. Lily had told me, "He don't ever let anyone come around when he's working. It disturbs his concentration and he's got to be careful when the wheel's spinning. If he makes a mistake —oh, boy!"

Glen's work was really extraordinary. It was no wonder that it went to the finest stores in the country and that it was exhibited at Chicago's Art Institute. I had often admired the samples of it that he kept on shelves behind glass doors. There were abstract designs and also realistically sculptured figures that seemed to be free of their sheer backgrounds. The female nudes were usually in action, walking, running, dancing, but the male nudes were posed like athletes to show off their muscles. He did animals, especially dogs and lions, but also fish and birds. The horse, though, was his favorite subject, and he had many examples of it on bowls, plates and platters, lidded boxes, ashtrays, and drinking glasses.

Glen and Lily had become our friends. In the evenings we often had coffee together either at their studio or ours, and sometimes we walked together through the park, with Billy on a leash. Glen generally did all the talking, managing to steer the conversation around to some new piece of information that he had come

y. He got his information from the magazines he subscribed to, n health, wildlife, sports, adventure, stamp and coin collecting, igeon racing, and photography, among others. (He had recently ought a Leica camera.) He said he was interested in everything nd always ready to learn something new. We had grown accusomed to his loud voice, which we knew now was from impaired earing, the result of working over whining, whirring, spinning nachinery for so many years.

"Glen's teaching me to paint," Lily told me one day. "He is first-rate portrait painter, Katy. Believe me. He painted before e got into this glass sculpture. I tell you, Glen is a very remarkable nan. You don't see that at first. He was raised an orphan, but he an away from the home when he was fourteen. Then he was just bum. He had a tough life. He hardly talks about it to me. And hen he took up painting. He never took a lesson or nothing. He ust learned by himself. That is why I say he is a remarkable man, born artist. Then, about ten years ago, he got into crystal. He was o good that Steuben hired him. He was there a long time doing ery special work for them, but you know, Katy, he can't get along vith people. Before he knows it, he's in a fight. But he's not mad. Ie just talks too much and argues. He's got a big mouth. That's vhat I tell him—to shut up once in a while."

The exhibition of religious art was well attended. People ame not only to view the show but also to see the interior of the amous Robie House. The 127 exhibits included sculpture, paintngs in a variety of media, stained glass, drawings, carvings, lithoraphs, woodcuts, silk screens, aquatints, linoleum prints, tchings, and photography. There were wall crucifixes and cross endants. A crèche was done as a silver wire mobile. Glen's handome vase was the only work in crystal.

Time magazine sent a reporter and a photographer to cover he show, and when the story appeared one of the paintings was sed with it. They had overlooked Henry's watercolor, which was lainly titled *The Crucifixion* and was listed on page two of the how's brochure. If the people from *Time* had seen it, they had robably assumed that "Henry Miller" was a local artist, along vith many exhibiting in the show. No one expected to see the vork of *the* Henry Miller in an exhibition of religious art. Had

Time made the discovery, it is interesting to surmise what they would have written.

When I wrote Henry that I was putting the watercolor in the show, he made no comment. Later, when I sent him the brochure, he never mentioned it, so I guessed that he had thrown it away without looking through it. However, in a letter I received some time later he wrote: "Don't recall what you said about the Lutheran minister and my *Rosy Crucifixion*. Anything important?"

29

*To have undertaken the thankless task of listing all the
books I can recall ever reading gives me extreme
pleasure and satisfaction. I know of no other author
who has been mad enough to attempt this.*

The Books in My Life

When a bundle of circulars arrived announcing the two-volume publication of *Sexus* "for private subscribers," it was the first I knew that the book had come out as planned. Henry had not mentioned it for six months. The small four-page folders, printed on rose-colored paper, also offered Miller's books published by Obelisk during the thirties, and a few other titles from the same press. Three of the pages carried the notice that all of these books were banned in England and the United States and should not be brought into those countries. I was puzzled, wondering why Henry had sent me more than a hundred of them when he knew the studio would not sell *Sexus*.

I was even more surprised a day or so later when I received a poster from him, one that somebody had sent him from Paris. A newspaper had printed it, and it appeared to be one of many that had been posted in public places. Among other large black letters the largest were: "Le Procureur fédéral déclare la guerre aux libres d'Henry Miller." *Sexus* had been declared obscene and further publication forbidden in France whether the book was printed in French, English, or any other language.

None of the run of three thousand copies had been confiscated, and Girodias was hurriedly sending them abroad. In spite of the ban on bringing them into the United States, the books were turning up. Henry asked me to "try and find out how Steloff gets her copies." I wondered why he did not ask her himself. *Plexus* was in Girodias's hands, but what would happen to it remained to be seen.

Henry was writing *The Books in My Life* for New Directions, and for weeks had been sending me lists of books he was asking people to send him. The first four-page, single-spaced list came with a letter:

February 24, 1950

Dear Friends:

The enclosed list, representing both books I have read in the past and wish to reread as well as books I have never read but wish to get acquainted with, comprises those books I would like to add to my small library. I say I "need" them, because I am in the midst of writing a book about books: just to thumb some of these titles would stimulate me no end. The book is being dedicated to Dr. Lawrence Clark Powell, of UCLA (director of the library there), who put the bug in my head.

Perhaps you can send me only one or two from this list. Every little bit will help, believe me. If you wish to aid me further, copy the list and send it with this letter to one of your friends whom you think could spare a few copies. I do not care about the condition of the book—any old copy will do. As regards the boy's [*sic*] books, the older they are the better, as the ancient editions will revive pleasant memories.

Perhaps I ought to add that this book will be a record of my personal experience with books, an intimate and lively work, not a scholarly one. It will supplement the autobiographical "novels" I have written—round out the picture of my life, so to speak. It should not be inferred that the enclosed list represents the books I am writing about—some yes, but not in detail. A complete list of *all* the books I can recall ever reading (including a few I still hope to read before I die) will be given in the Appendix of this book, alphabetically according to authors. I have now recalled (within the last forty days) well over a thousand. I doubt, however, that the list will reach to more than two thousand titles. I am not, as you see, a great reader.

Thanks again to all of you for any help you may extend me.

Sincerely,
Henry Miller

As the books began to reach him, he crossed them off the list, but many others still had not been sent him, and these he starred in red ink and added a footnote that they were needed *now*. To me he added, "Get your scouts out for these, if you will be so kind."

I posted the lists and continually urged people to look through their books and send him those they were willing to part with. The variety was so extensive that in a neighborhood like ours, where many people had home libraries, some of the books were likely to be on their shelves. Flagg scouted the secondhand bookstores for titles that had been long out of print. As the weeks passed, he sent Henry about a hundred books. Henry wrote me: "Tell Flagg to write me before sending any more books." His studio was overflowing with duplicate copies. Still the lists came, with more titles inked in at the bottom of their pages.

While writing the book, he had no time for watercolors. When I asked him when I could expect more of them, he answered on a postcard: "So busy writing now—new book—haven't touched paints in weeks. Snowed under."

Later he wrote that he had got in a supply of *Happy Rock* and would send some, along with foreign editions of the *Tropics*. "Will try to send you one each of foreign editions—to keep for show, not to sell. Don't have Italian *Tropics*—not out yet. Have others—and in 4, 5, or 6 languages. What do you have now?"

For some time he had been sending me foreign editions of his books. They made an impressive display, I thought. In answering his letter, I finally told him about the copies of *The Happy Rock* at Marshall Field's and asked him to sign the copies he sent. Autographed, they would justify the studio's five-dollar price.

One morning, while I was typing my book and the studio was not yet open for business, there was a knock at the door. When I opened it there stood James Laughlin. His dark hat and long dark overcoat made him look even taller than his considerable height of a few inches over six feet. I was so surprised that for a second I didn't recognize "the giant." He was in town on business and had come out to see just what it was I was doing for Henry. As we visited, he walked around looking at things. He saw what remained of the last shipment of books he had sent and noted the sign

I had made for "used copies." They were bargain priced according to their wear and tear in bookstores. However, if a book was in good condition I asked the full price for it. He made no comment.

"What are these?" he asked, looking at Jacque's rearranged arteries and cysts.

"The work of a friend of the studio. We're showing them. They're not for sale."

"Very colorful," he said.

I tried to sell him *Into the Night Life* by showing him the remaining pages I had of the illustrations and text. I handed him one of the descriptive booklets so he could follow my "sales pitch." He looked at everything very carefully and then said that Henry had been trying to sell him the book for two years.

A few mornings later two other unexpected visitors knocked on the door. Like Laughlin, they were wearing fedoras and long dark overcoats, apparel that was rarely seen in our neighborhood. One of the men introduced himself as a friend of the other, who was the famous performer known as Dunninger. I had heard of "the Amazing Dunninger," as he was billed, but had never seen his mind-reading act. Now I learned that he had come to Chicago for a three-week engagement at the Blackstone Hotel where he would do an after-dinner show. I also learned that he did not call himself a mind reader. He was a "mentalist."

"We saw the sign in your window as we were leaving the shop next door," Dunninger said.

They had been at Belle Isle ordering highball glasses. The friend, a Chicagoan, was familiar with Glen's work.

Dunninger was looking around. "Do you have any of the French books?" he asked.

When I said that I didn't handle them, he asked if Miller had any manuscripts to sell.

"I don't know. I'll have to ask him. Do you have something in mind?"

"Find out what he has, will you? I'll be back when I pick up my glasses. Let me know what his price is. Is he living here in Chicago?"

"Oh, no. He lives in Big Sur, California."

While explaining the purpose of the studio, I followed him

around as he looked at things. He picked up the Bern Porter
edition of *Alf* and handed me a dollar for it.

"I have the original edition if you'd like it."

"How much is it?"

"Three-fifty."

"No, this one will do." He pocketed the booklet.

I tried to show him the illustrations from *Into the Night Life*,
but he brushed them aside.

Meanwhile, his friend had been looking at the watercolors.
He asked me how much they were.

"They have various prices. Which one are you interested
in?" I had noticed him giving more attention to the nude I called
Portrait of Gertrude Stein. It had some black smears where the color
had run, but otherwise I thought it was pretty good. As for the
face, it had a hint of Picasso's famous portrait. I am sure that
Henry had not intended the figure to be Gertrude Stein, but whenever I had asked him to title his work he had answered, "Title them
yourself." And I often did. I wrote the titles on small cards that
I pinned to the wall below the paintings. He always signed his
work, even when it was poor.

"How much is this one?"

He looked like a man who could afford twenty-five dollars
for a painting he liked and that was what I was about to ask for
it. Until that moment the price had been fifteen dollars. Dunninger walked over and gave me a look that said, "Fifteen!" And
that is what I asked.

After they left I waited until Glen's machinery stopped
whining, which meant that he and Lily were having their coffee
break, and then hurried in to tell them about the visit and how
Dunninger had known the watercolor was only fifteen dollars.
Glen thought it was very funny. "He didn't fool around with
mind-reading me," he said. "I told him right off my price was a
hundred and eighty dollars. He says, 'A hundred fifty.' I says,
'Mister, you don't work for nothin' and I don't neither.' "

Two heavy crystal glasses in a tulip shape gleamed on the
oilcloth-covered table. Each one held a pint, more than enough for
a highball. "The crystal is beautiful," I said. "Really exquisite."

"I am to engrave twelve of them with these here pictures,"

Glen said, handing me a pile of photographs. They were of nude men and women in various erotic poses, stimuli, and positions of copulation.

"He brings me these here pictures and wants me to copy them, one to a glass. I says, 'Fifteen dollars a glass.' Shit, them glasses cost me three dollars apiece wholesale."

I was looking through the photographs. "Ain't they somethin'?" said Lily.

"Is he going to pay the hundred and eighty?" I asked Glen.

"You're damn right he is."

Lily said, "If one of them breaks as I'm washing it—oh, boy!" It was her job to wash the crystal after Glen had finished engraving it, and it was a painstaking and tedious job. What remained of the red poster paint that Glen used in drawing the design on the glass had to come off without damaging the delicate details of the work. Lily washed crystal all day long. Her fingernails broke and her hands burned from being in soapy water for hours at a time. After the crystal was washed and dried, she wrapped each piece in tissue paper and packed it in the cartons that were picked up for shipment almost every day.

When I sent the fifteen dollars to Henry for the *Gertrude Stein*, I described Dunninger's visit and his request for handwritten excerpts. I also told him about the highball glasses. He wrote back: "I could always dig up or do something special for Dunninger, but he would have to prove to me that he is not a piker. He should pay *handsomely* for anything of mine he wants. Tell him I said so."

After mentioning other matters, he added this postscript: "Ask Dunninger if he will buy handsome single (only) copy, bound, etc. of all trial drawings and writings—huge—of *Into the Night Life*—fat volume—price $1,500.00."

I knew that Dunninger was not interested in *Into the Night Life*. When he came for his glasses and stopped in to see me, I suggested that he write Henry himself if he wanted to purchase a manuscript. Nothing ever came of this, according to Henry.

Henry had interrupted his work on *The Books in My Life* to come to the aid of Kenneth Patchen, whose continued illness and disability alarmed him. He painted a few watercolors to be raffled for Patchen's benefit and wrote me: "Students at *Occident* (Berkeley) will raffle off some of my paintings soon for the benefit of Kenneth Patchen—bedridden and penniless. Can you do something similar there? Or get University students and profs to stir themselves? Patchen lives at Old Lyme, Connecticut. Am writing to big lit. reviews to draw attention to his plight."

Occident was a new magazine published by the Associated Students at the University of California. In its first issue, in the spring of 1950, it printed a brief article of Henry's "Is Fiction," in which he urged aspiring young writers, who might be hesitating to begin, to start by putting words together, "stammering and stuttering as most writers do—whether in good taste or bad, whether intelligible or nonintelligible." Patchen also contributed an article on fiction for this first issue of the magazine. I sent for ten copies.

I wrote Patchen to tell him that the studio would soon have a fundraiser for his benefit and asked him to send me some of his work, collect, by express.

In the meantime, one late afternoon I answered the phone to hear Michael Fraenkel on the line. He was calling from the tony Hotel Windermere just a few blocks away on the lakefront. I invited him to come right over, and in ten minutes he was at the door with—as a surprise—Daphne Moschos, the woman who had been his companion since the Villa Seurat days. She was small, a little on the plump side, and had a lovely face. Her brown eyes were smiling at me.

Fraenkel's warm greeting, so different from our first meeting, was another surprise. He was impeccably dressed, although somewhat in an out-of-fashion style, which only added to his air of an established man of means who was not tempted by tailoring fads. Daphne wore a bright, flowery dress that could be seen under her partly open long black cape. A black beret-style hat was pinned to her curly brown hair, and she wore black gloves and carried a huge black leather bag.

I was so pleased to have them at the studio that I locked the door behind them and drew the draperies in case some passerby should wander in. We often had more curious browsers than buyers anyway.

The studio was a surprise to them. They didn't expect the green walls, red furniture, purple, magenta, and yellow cushions on some of the chairs, the blue curtains, the painted door. Lily had given me two tall openwork screens that the former occupant of their studio had left behind, and I had painted them orange.

They smiled at the mannequin, which at that time was holding a page of Henry's script from *Into the Night Life*. They glanced at Henry's watercolors but said nothing. They were more interested in Jacque's paintings. Henry's books, booklets, and foreign editions were examined one by one by Fraenkel while Daphne looked over the magazines on the long table. I had sold all of *The Naked Ear*, so I could not show her this gem, but *The Tiger's Eye* had just come. She had never heard of the magazine, which I thought the best of the new literary publications.

"In Unionville we don't have anything very interesting," she said.

They enjoyed looking at the photos of Henry and his children, the house, and the claw-footed bathtub in the yard. I explained that it was connected to a spring. Henry's book lists hung in assorted streamers from the bulletin board. Reading them, Fraenkel often smiled but made no comment. I was proud of the Art Institute of Chicago's exhibitions calendar, the current issue of which was tacked to the wall. I pointed out the studio's space in it, for I wanted them to know that it had an active part in the city's cultural scene.

Bill and I took them to dinner that evening and would again several times during their two-week stay. I saw them almost every day. Because we had talked about *Hamlet* at the roundtables, I knew there were people who would like to meet Fraenkel, and I arranged an afternoon coffee klatch to bring them together. We also asked people to a party that first Saturday night, with Fraenkel as guest of honor. Part of the evening would be given over to listening to Henry reading on Sound Portraits. While many more came to the coffee klatch than I had expected, the evening party was an even greater success, with people, as usual, sitting on the floor for lack of seats. I knew that Fraenkel was pleased. He had brought a number of his books with him, a set of each to give me, and the others to sell "if I cared to." We sold all of these copies, and he accepted requests for others to be mailed from Unionville.

The sculptor Eoina Nudelman, who was a frequent visitor to the studio, came to the party with the toy manufacturer Marvin Glass, who was his employer. (It was then I learned that Eoina made his living designing toys.) Glass was an unfulfilled man whose yearning for creative expression, as a writer-artist-or-whatever, made his enormous success as a manufacturer of children's playthings almost an embarrassment to him. He owned most of Fraenkel's books and believed with him that it was "death" to live only for material success. When Eoina told him that Fraenkel was in town, he was eager to meet him.

The two men liked each other and met several times in town to have lunch and talk. When Glass learned that Fraenkel would like to have a studio in Chicago, he offered to lease a small suite for him in a certain office building. Glass, of course, would pay the rent. Fraenkel saw the suite and longed to have it, but there was some matter that had to be ironed out with the former tenant whose lease had not yet expired. Nothing had been resolved by the time Fraenkel and Daphne left Chicago.

I asked Henry if he had a message for Fraenkel and told him that he had asked to be remembered to him. He answered: "Sure, do give my best to Fraenkel."

Listening to Henry's voice on the records was a nostalgic experience for Fraenkel. He asked to hear them again when there were no visitors in the studio. One record included a "greeting" from Alfred Perlès speaking from London. Fraenkel said, "Kathryn, now you know the three voices that once began *Hamlet*."

Glass gave a small farewell dinner for Fraenkel and Daphne and invited, among others, Bill, me, and Wallace Fowlie. Fraenkel had especially enjoyed meeting Fowlie at the studio and asked Glass to be sure to invite him to the dinner.

In a thank-you letter from Fraenkel after they had returned to Unionville, he wrote that Glass had called him up to say that he had been unable to get the suite for him because the owner of the building wanted a photographer in it. "Why a photographer and not a writer, I didn't ask. Anyway, I am sorry the thing fell through, because it would have been good to have a little place of my own in Chicago to which I could repair now and then for a change of air and a spate of work in the seclusion of a city— something by the way which I am particularly fond of."

I reminded Henry to send the watercolors for the Patchen fundraiser and told him I had already sent in the copy for the April-May-June issue of the exhibitions calendar, to announce that all of the paintings sold during those three months would be for the benefit of Kenneth Patchen. He wrote back: "Will do what I can to send W.C.'s Can't promise. Am now sending all my good ones to France—disgusted with America. Try to think up some other way to aid Patchen. Maybe other, better artists, will offer their work to aid him."

Bill and I decided to have an all-day "Fair for Patchen" on Sunday, May 21.

30

Today he is practically an invalid . . . a sick giant consumed by the poisonous indifference of a world which has more use for mouse traps than for poets.
Patchen: Man of Anger and Light

Jack Conroy was the first person I called on to help us. He was on friendly terms with the newspaper columnists who would give us publicity, and he knew celebrities to invite. Nelson Algren was the only one who turned him down. I had met Algren at a party at Jack's and saw him leave as soon as the house began to fill up. He didn't like crowds.

The studio's following of writers, poets, painters, students, and other friends could be counted on to attend. And because Patchen was a much-admired poet, the people at *Poetry* wanted to help, and also the staff of the *Chicago Maroon*. There was work for everyone. We needed auctioneers, people to take turns selling Patchen's books, and others to sell the twenty-five-cent tickets for the door prizes, grab bag, and raffle. The women students said they would wear costumes and carry trays of paper cups full of Mrs. Arnold's peach brandy punch to sell for a dime. Two young men who played the guitar would take turns providing music throughout the day.

We sent out letters, made and distributed posters, collected articles for the grab bag, and asked for door prizes. Early on the day of the fair we would festoon the tree out in front of the studio with balloons and serpentine, and set up tables and chairs on the sidewalk in front of our place and the Belle Isle. We would decorate with greens and flowers purloined at dawn from Jackson Park.

Patchen had sent us a good supply of his books. We had *The Journal of Albion Moonlight, Sleepers Awake, Selected Poems, First Will and Testament, Cloth of the Tempest, Panels for the Walls of Heaven, Red Wine and Yellow Roses,* and a thin violet-covered book of love poems written to his wife that was titled *To Say if You Love Someone.* He replenished our stock of Henry's *Patchen: Man of Anger and Light.* He sent us single-page handwritten poems that he had illustrated with drawings and collage, and also two of his "painted books." These were books of his poems that had been finished with special spine cloths and handmade Japanese papers. On each side of the book's hard covers was a painting he had done, a different subject for each side. These were so exceptional that we decided to auction them rather than limit them to their ten-dollar price.

We had Henry's four remaining watercolors and also the paintings donated by neighborhood artists to put in the auction. With a little coaxing Jacque parted with one of his temperas. Glen gave us a large-footed bowl, a splendid piece engraved with a Pegasus. He also gave us smaller pieces that he had bought and then decided not to work on, such as salt and pepper shakers, sugar-and-creamer sets, ashtrays, and paperweights. They were all fine crystal.

The showstopper of the day was a Rolls-Royce that Severn Darden asked to sell for him "for no less than four hundred dollars." If we sold it, he said he would donate a hundred dollars to the Patchen fund.

Darden had been in the studio a number of times. He was a young actor working with the improvisational theater group at the university that was under the direction of Paul Sills. Ed Asner and Mike Nichols were fellow actors in the group, but if he had ever brought them to the studio I would not have known their names. I did not always know by name the people who came in, but I did know Darden's. On his first visit he had left his calling card. It was a one-by-three-inch sliver with *severn teackle darden 2* engraved on it in very small print in lowercase. Since he was taller than six feet, the miniature card made an unforgettable impression.

No one could miss Darden when he was striding about the campus or on the streets of Hyde Park, for he always wore an opera cape, a melodramatic getup that was spoiled by his going hatless. He had sandy-colored curly hair, blue eyes, and a boyish face. When he was not on foot, he was driving his Rolls.

The car was a 1930 or 1931 Phantom II limousine landaulet with an Italian-made body and left-hand steering. It had wire wheels that had recently been painted cornflower blue. A large trunk was on a platform extending from the rear of the car, and two spare tires were in aluminum sheaths on either side of the hood. The white cloth top was rather new and had replaced the original one that had covered only the passenger compartment. The new top covered both the passengers and the footman and chauffeur up ahead. Overall, the car was seventeen feet in length.

In the midst of getting the studio ready for the fair, I was surprised to see my friend John Stapleton Cowley-Brown, who had spent the winter in Havana, walk in with a shopping bag. He went to the back of the studio and I followed him, sure that he had the two-volume set of *Sexus*. To my surprise, the volumes were not paperbacks but nicely bound in blue buckram and printed on good paper.

"The damn things are heavy," he said. They were.

"Did you have any trouble getting them in?"

"I had them strapped up with a half-dozen Agatha Christie books. They paid no attention at all. So here you are."

The bill from La Casa Belga was for the equivalent of eight dollars, which I paid him. I put the books away to look at later.

The fair turned out very well. Darden had the Rolls parked in front of the studio by nine o'clock. He propped a FOR SALE sign against the windshield. The crowds were already beginning to surge in and out of the studio, and they kept coming until after six in the evening. The police came. They were the motorcycle cops who patrolled Jackson Park, and when they saw the Rolls, the crowds, and Glen shooting the scene with his Leica, they came over to find out what was going on. Glen took pictures all day so that we could send some to the Patchens.

At day's end we counted $274.62 taken in, not including

the five- and ten-dollar promised checks that would be mailed to the Patchens by the donors within the next few days. We did not sell all of Patchen's books and kept them to sell later for him.

No one bought the Rolls. People with cameras who happened to be passing on their way to the park or the beach stopped to take pictures of the car or to have someone snap them standing in front of it beside the Silver Lady radiator cap. Some people opened the doors and climbed into the back seat. They pulled out the folding table and jump seats; they examined the gray astrakhan fur rug, snapped the tea-colored silk window shades up and down, and otherwise amused themselves by opening and closing the sliding glass partition between them and the chauffeur's seat. The doors had no locks because the car was supposed to be attended at all times by the footman.

Communication between the chauffeur and the passengers was by electric signals flashed to a series of commands that lit up on the dashboard: STOP, GO, TURN AROUND, RIGHT, LEFT, QUICK, or GO HOME appeared before the chauffeur when a finger was touched to the selected button on an arm of the back seat. Those who got into the car soon discovered the system. Finally, Bill had to stand guard and keep people out of the car.

When Darden drove it away that evening, I did not expect to see him again, for he had said he was going to New York to continue his acting career, but a week later he was still around. Meanwhile, Bill regretted not buying the Rolls, and he looked up Darden to buy it. It took him a few days to get used to handling the car, and then we invited Fowlie, Rago, and some of those who had helped at the fair to join us in a picnic on the Indiana Dunes, about a two-hour drive to the Indiana shore of Lake Michigan.

About a week later Glen bought a Rolls older than ours, a gray coupe with a body made in Springfield, Massachusetts. It needed a coat of paint, and it was not in the best running condition, but he had bought a Rolls-Royce manual that he intended to follow in working on the engine.

I had written Henry about our success with the fair. He replied: "Answering at once to thank you for all you did for Patchen. Fine! Congratulations! It occurred to me that you might be able to help George Dibbern." He sent along fifty reprints of the article he had written for *Circle* four years earlier and said he had several hundred more that I could have. He wanted me to sell them for a quarter apiece. "An occasional individual might be moved to send Dibbern a contribution," he explained.

31

Who knows what will come out of the soul of man?
The soul of man is a dark forest, with wild life in it.
From a Henry Miller Notebook

In a June 4, 1950, letter from Henry, he mentioned that the federal government's case against the importation of the *Tropics* was to be tried soon in San Francisco. The defending lawyer representing the American Civil Liberties Union had asked him for the names of literary critics and English professors in universities and colleges who would be willing to make a deposition stating that the books have literary value. "I have given him a few names," Henry wrote, "but I need more. Should you or any of your friends think of good names—which would weigh with the court—please let me know."

I asked Fowlie and others to help, but no one could come up with the name of anyone. In the meantime I had received a copy of the *Author's League News* for May 1950, which had something in it that I believed would interest Henry. There was an article about Judge Curtis Bok, "who last year tossed out a series of indictments of obscenity charges that grew out of a vice raid on Philadelphia bookshops." Now his ruling had been upheld by the Pennsylvania Superior Court. Judge Bok had found that these books were protected by state and federal guarantees of free speech and free press. (The *Tropics* were not among the books at issue in this case.) In his decision he had written: "The power of a State to abridge freedom of speech . . . is the exception rather than the rule and the penalizing even of utterance of a defined character must find its justifica-

tion in a reasonable apprehension of danger to organized government."

I asked Henry if he had given the name of H. L. Mencken
to the attorney, for Mencken had praised the writing in *Tropic of
Cancer*, and when Henry wrote to thank me for the Bok material,
he said that he had given the attorney Mencken's name. Henry,
however, wanted as little as possible to do with the case. "Had I
been advised by the Civil Liberties Union before they took action,
I would have advised against it. I don't think the time is right," he
wrote.

In 1946, the *Tropics* had been attacked in France, and twenty-
two of the country's leading authors had come to Henry's defense.
Led by the editor Maurice Nadeau, they included Jean-Paul Sartre, André Gide, André Breton, Albert Camus, Paul Eluard, Raymond Queneau, Pierre Seghers, Jean Paulhan, Frederick LeFevre,
and others. The case was dismissed.

Referring to the present suit in the United States, Henry
wrote: "Here, at least it seems to me, the situation is quite otherwise. The men whose names might mean something to the public
will be the last ones to join up. There are not more than a half-
dozen writers in the country for whom the problem means anything. The rest have capitulated long ago. I don't feel that there is
any solidarity among writers in this country—not on such issues."

The case in San Francisco was ultimately lost.

While Henry continued to write *The Books in My Life*, he sent
excerpts from it, as well as from *Plexus* and other works, to magazines in London, Brussels, Paris, Stockholm, and New York. He
always let me know which of these magazines were coming out
with his work so that I could order copies.

A young man, John Kidis, had printed a letter that Henry
had written to Emil Schnellock on February 22, 1939. It came out
as a booklet with the title *The Waters Reglitterized*. Henry urged me
to order it and, since it sold for only a dollar and I would get a
dealer's discount, I ordered my first twenty-five copies. That year
The Colossus of Maroussi became a Penguin Book selling for thirty-
five cents. With my dealer's discount of forty percent, I was able
to keep the book in stock for years. As with all of Henry's books

that I had to buy, I gave him the difference between the cost and the selling price. Many times he asked me to keep something for myself, and, because I did not, he made me gifts of his watercolors.

By now I had finished reading *Sexus,* and I was disappointed with it. It reopens and enlarges upon the story he had begun to tell first in *Tropic of Capricorn.* The book carries no name in its dedication, written only "To Her"—who is "Mara" and sometimes "Mona"—and she is the central subject. Scenes and episodes pile up as he describes his yearnings, hurt, desperation, and distrust. His rivals, friends, fellow workers at the telegraph company, his estranged wife—all have parts to play in the story.

He writes of wanting to get rid of his wife so he can marry Mona. He wants "to take his wife for a walk some evening and push her off the end of the pier."

What begins to read like a soap opera is now and then interrupted by lyrical passages on art and writing. But then these too are suddenly dropped for a return to lusty, anatomical descriptions of his having sex with numerous women.

So much attention to sex puzzled me. He had said that he wanted *The Rosy Crucifixion,* of which *Sexus* was part one, to be the most important book he would ever write. I could not understand what he was trying to do.

Sexus shocked and disturbed many who had formerly admired his work. Durrell wired him to "withdraw and revise" the book, and, in a lengthy letter that followed, he called *Sexus* "lavatory filth."

Henry replied angrily, "I am trying to reproduce in words a book of my life which to me has the utmost significance—every bit of it. . . . I've been as sincere as I possibly could, maybe too sincere, because it certainly is not a lovely picture I made of myself. . . . if it was in bad taste, it was on the side of life."

My attention was called to an article in *Soviet Literature,* a monthly magazine published in Moscow and distributed in twenty-four countries around the world. Each edition was printed in the language of that country. The article in English was titled "Literature of Decay." Among the American authors accused of "psychologically conditioning the masses . . . as a strategy of the cold war which the rabid American reactionaries are waging against the freedom-loving peoples," the writer of the article names Yale Professor F. S. C. Northrup, the author of *The Meeting of East and West;* Eugene O'Neill; John Steinbeck; and Henry Miller. He also denounces "the traitors" Jean-Paul Sartre and Albert Camus of France and England's George Orwell and Aldous Huxley.

But it is Miller he calls "the most typical representative of the corrupt literature of imperialism." He cites Miller's statement in *Tropic of Capricorn* that "capitalism is rotten to the core" and assumes that he is pointing to himself as the only genius capable of establishing a new order. He points out that Miller is "the spit image of one Corporal Schicklgruber, alias Adolf Hitler." He calls attention to Miller's "real name," that of Gottfried Leberecht Müller—which Miller called himself in a piece of satire.

"Another aspect of Miller's writing," the author goes on to say, "is his pornography. Here he goes to truly monstrous lengths, so much so that it cannot be called simple pornography. It is a moral plague, a leprosy of the mind, whose evil stench hits you in the face the moment you open a book of his. . . . with importunity he presses his mad ideas on the reader and enumerates his sexual sensations with nauseating pertinacity. . . . he leads his reader into a world of perversion and sexual licentiousness and moral degradation with the object of inculcating upon him slavish obedience to the ruling classes."

I asked Henry if he had seen the magazine, and when he answered that he had not I sent him my copy.

In September I saw an announcement on one of the university's bulletin boards that Art and Science Press was bringing out unabridged editions of the *Tropics* for $4.50 apiece, *Sexus* for $22.50, and the four volumes of *My Life and Loves* by Frank Harris for $9. Sold by subscription only, it read, for professional use by literary scholars and critics, psychologists, psychiatrists, and other qualified mature persons, and accredited libraries and institutions. Orders had to be on official letterheads of a university or institution, with the position of the subscriber indicated.

I passed this information on to Henry who wrote back that it was news to him. He wrote them and received an answer that the project had been called off because they were unable to get the books from France. "Dreamers!" he called them in writing me about it.

I asked him if he had any fliers or advertisements about certain of his books, giveaways that my customers could pick up. "The only things I have to give away," he wrote back, "are about two dozen of Anaïs Nin's Prefaces to T. of C. [*Tropic of Cancer*]. Do you want these? You can get more from Maxwell, you know. They sell for 25¢."

In another letter he wrote: "Sending you (6) water colors today—prices marked on back—only one at $50. If you want more I'll send some—but they will be over $50—$75 to $100—large ones. Drew pencil lines to indicate border of mats on 2 or 3. Others mat to edge of color."

When I wrote that things were slow he answered: "Don't worry about making a few dollars for me! We always get by. I hate to sell things cheap. Rather give them away. Besides, I want you to look after your own interests. The 'propaganda' value of your efforts is worth much more to me than the few dollars you can gather in."

One day I received, of all things, a Chain of Good Luck letter from Henry. One of those "going around the world . . . the person who breaks this chain will have bad luck. . . . F. D. Roosevelt was elected president of the U.S. forty-two hours after he mailed this letter. . . . Captain Havarre, who broke the chain, died seventy-two hours after he received this letter. Cancel the first name and add your own to the list, make twelve copies and mail them within seventy-two hours."

I saw that Pat Wall's name was ahead of Henry's, so it was he who had mailed him the letter. Wall had an art gallery in Monterey and showed Henry's watercolors from time to time. I don't remember having any bad luck after I broke the chain.

When Nan and Hugh Rice moved to California, we took their studio on the corner across the street. It was by far the best and largest one in the colony with a bedroom, bathroom, kitchen and a sleeping porch. The gallery in front was about twenty by forty feet and a great improvement over our other studio for showing Henry's artwork and displaying his books. An access road ran between the studio and the railway embankment. It was lined with cottonwood trees that were coming into bloom.

We took a month to move, to repaint the walls and floors, buy more furniture, and hang new curtains. Carl Van Vechten sent us for the studio two enlarged photographs of Henry that he had made in 1941, and these we framed and hung. We removed the wallboard sides of a small rectangular enclosure in a back corner of the gallery where Nan Rice had stored her canvases, and, after painting the supporting two-by-fours black, we had what appeared to be a cage. We made this into a dressing room for our mannequin. The disengaged parts of her body lay about, and a wig was on its stand. Evening gowns from the twenties hung on the wall, and there was an ostrich-feather fan with tasseled dance programs and a pair of long kid gloves on a tiny table. Summer hats with flowers around their crowns were on a gilded rack.

One day we were looking out the front windows when we saw Glen come out of his studio with cans of paint and a brush. When we called over to him, he said he was going to give his Rolls its much-needed coat of paint. It took him all day to sand it down and put on a fresh gray coat, and he did a beautiful job of it. He expected the car to be thoroughly dry by morning because there was a warm breeze blowing. During the night, the breeze picked up to a wind and blew away the tufts of seeds on the cottonwood trees. They drifted across the street and onto the Rolls, turning it a feathery white before dawn.

32

> *An artist who is non-commercial has about as much*
> *chance for survival as a sewer rat. If he remains*
> *faithful to his art he compromises in life by begging*
> *and borrowing, by marrying rich, or by doing some*
> *stultifying work which will bring him a pittance.*
>
> The Plight of the Creative Artist in the
> United States of America

On January 15, 1951, James Laughlin wrote Henry that the $17.85 in royalties due him for "My Friend Stanley" and "The Robot Picodiribibi," both excerpts from *Plexus,* which had appeared in 1950 in the New Directions twelfth annual, had been credited to his account. Laughlin also mentioned that the manuscript for the book about books, which Henry had finished on December 15, had not yet arrived. Henry enclosed the letter with one he wrote me:

> Am so terribly broke and so many bills to pay and don't know where next cent is coming from. (All I can count on is Laughlin's $50 a month.) Would suggest that you sell *all* my water colors on hand—to one or to several persons—with the idea of raising $75 at least. Nothing less will do me any good.
> My main problem is to maintain credit with our mailman, who not only supplies me with stamps but milk, bread, butter, cheese and eggs, which we need for the kids. I owe him $40 now and I'm getting worried. Maybe you can do something. If not, OK. But let me hear from you in 2 or 3 days after receipt of this, will you? I was depending on my French publisher to come across—but he seems sunk.

I sent him $50 by return mail and wrote:

It is all I can raise tonight. I have been trying, trying, trying—even before your letter reached me. I wrote Red Skelton during the week he was playing a Chicago theater, but got no answer. [Skelton was friendly with Henry and had been to Partington Ridge to see him.] I have been trying to get Tennessee Williams to come in, in view of the records. We talked on the phone and he promised to come. He especially wanted to hear your records. He is going to make a Sound Portrait, too, you know. I was the first one to tell him about the publicity for it, which was on the blurbs that Barron sent. But he didn't show up. Then Dr. Karl Menninger was here last week to speak at the Theological Seminary's annual "Ministers' Week." I wrote him and even took the letter to his hotel to be sure he received it before he left town. He didn't come either. I have contacted a number of regular customers, and got promises but nothing sold so far. The weather may be to blame. We're having blizzards and it's two or three below zero.

It was a long letter, for I had several things I wanted to bring up, including how I felt upon discovering that Kidis had sold a lot of *The Waters Reglitterized* to a bookstore only three blocks away and closer to the university. I had found it difficult to compete with the shop, for it also had the Penguin *Colossus of Maroussi* and some of the New Directions books. "This makes it very difficult for me. They grab off all the cream. And they were really stinking about helping me with Patchen. Gave me the cold shoulder and said they didn't have to engage in cheap publicity stunts to sell books. And I have learned that if people ask for the books of yours which they don't carry, they won't send them here."

Henry wrote back: "I can't tell you how much it meant to me to get that fifty dollars yesterday—at just the right moment, too. . . . As for Kidis selling that bookstore his brochure . . . he's just a boy, printed it himself after working to save money to do it, and could hardly offer exclusive rights to one shop in any city. When you read what I say of him in the preface you'll forgive him."

His letter continued for several pages:

You must write to Editions Denoel, 12 rue Amelie, Paris, to send you the "plaquette" on Blaise Cendrars which they will bring out soon. It is in French (same as chapter in *World Review*) but will contain a word or two by Blaise Cendrars on myself, and perhaps photos. Tell them I requested you to write and it is to be gratis, on my account. Mention you have studio for me, and send dope on it.

A Swiss publisher just brought out a handsome book of photos of Paris *(Paris des Rêves)*, with texts by famous authors opposite each photo. There are three texts by myself, in English and in French. Price $4. (Special price to me. Tell him you are vis-à-vis me and he will give you same price. You could sell the book for five or seven-fifty easily, I imagine.) I am the only American contributing text for it, incidentally. I have only one copy or I'd give you one gratis. Many things I get only one copy of, and no payment for writing either.

I am sending you on loan *The Angel Is My Watermark*, which belongs to Anaïs Nin. She lent it to me until she wants it again. I have no copy myself. I am also sending you four copies of the European *Alf* pamphlet, a little battered but contents OK. As for *Booster*s, I don't know myself how many we got out. Do you have the Xmas number of *Delta*? May have an extra copy for you, if not . . . probably my last.

Glad to hear of interest in the recordings. Don't like sound of my own voice reading—too monotonous. Glad they like the *Black Spring* bit though. One day, when I get the chance, I'll make a big recording (impromptu) of what I've long wanted to say about Blaise Cendrars. If we get electricity here, maybe soon, I may be able to borrow a machine. Then I will make a number of spontaneous, humorous ones.

You mention your husband Bill. I never speak of him only because I never met him. Do please let him know I appreciate all his efforts.

When I read that your street and studios were occupied by Hecht, Anderson, Dreiser, Bodenheim I feel a bit flattered. But it is still a deserted area, I mean "shunned." No? The studio, size of it, sounds enormous. I must send you more things to hang up— not just water colors. In fact, with the *Angel* book I'll send two big sheets of my original plan for the Lawrence book. Get some one to do me this favor, will you—go over my writing with black India ink, so that it is clear and legible, then return it to me, and I'll have photostat made for you to keep. If I think of it I'll enclose a few photos for you—fairly recent ones.

If you know anyone who can read Swedish easily, I'll lend you a copy of a book of critical, interpretative essays, which I'd like someone to read (for chapter on myself—short) and let me know roughly what it says—particularly if it says anything about the *Tropics of value*—as my case comes up for a final hearing in April.

Well, I think this is about all. I'm enclosing various announcements. I'm killing myself with work. No rest, no vacations, no play and no money. But I enjoy it.

One more thing I just thought of. For that appendix to my new book I also made up a reference list, indicating books or authors mentioned in *all* my previous works—runs to about 30 typewritten pages. I have an extra copy, which I may need, but if you thought it of interest I could send it to you and let some one copy it off for you. It's an astounding list. There will be another list—even bigger, much bigger, though it may not be included in this first Volume, and that is of *all* the books I can recall ever reading. I am still working on this. Will have to go to L.A. library soon to complete the list. Perhaps two thousand titles—and more, of course, in succeeding volumes. Kidis is printing, or said he was, a list of books I have recommended from time to time. That might be useful too.

Well, good luck, and if I forget anything, omit anything, overlook anything—especially acknowledgments and thanks—be indulgent. I have a thousand things on my mind. My best always to Flagg and Cosby—and that fellow from Kankakee, a real friend.

The "fellow from Kankakee" was Bob Campbell, an artist who had sent Henry books from his wanted lists and was a good friend of the studio, buying Henry's books and records. He also made all of our display cards for the windows, large boards with handsome script that repeated a variety of descriptive sentences taken from the dustcovers of Henry's New Directions books. These messages all began with: WHO IS HENRY MILLER? The answers were like this one:

Iconoclast, Prophet, Poet, Painter, Philosopher, Acute Observer and Recorder of the Vagaries of His Fellow Humans, Severe Critic of Modern Civilization, Partisan of the Underdog, Champion of Frank Expression, Explorer of New Realms of Feeling—Henry Miller is a writer like no other writer living today. He cannot be explained or criticized in the usual terms. He must be read to be understood.

We had half a dozen of these cards, each one describing Henry in a different way.

As for being in a deserted area, I had sent Henry photographs of the studio, inside and out, in 1949, and I had told him that we were located on a block with a major bus line through the city at one end and the Illinois Central local trains at the other. But he seemed unable to rid himself of the impression he had got of the South Side during his first trip to Chicago, which he described in *The Air-Conditioned Nightmare*. Because we were on the South Side did not mean that we were in a blighted area. In fact, the residents of Hyde Park had a snobbish opinion of themselves as well-heeled intellectuals.

When Henry sent me a bundle of new brochures about the *Night Life* book, I noticed that Chicago was not included in the list of cities where the book was on exhibit, and I brought this to his attention. "We've steadily advertised it in the Chicago exhibitions calendar for more than two years." I also asked him why he never mentioned the studio when listing the shows of his watercolors. He had written once that he wondered if the Gotham Book Mart would ever show his paintings. I reminded him: "This is not Gotham, but it is a whole studio devoted to you."

He answered:

> You know, Kathryn, if I sometimes forget to mention your place when I ought to, it's for two reasons: one, because it's not yet quite a reality to me; second, because it's a bit embarrassing for me to recommend a place dedicated just to me. It's like advertising oneself. But I do think of you and I am truly grateful for all you are doing. . . . Just the other day, in writing the preface to the book I just finished (on books) I made mention of two "new" friends who had done a great deal for me—i.e., in getting me the books I needed and in many other ways, viz.: Dante Zaccagnini and John Kidis. Then I thought of you and I wondered how to speak of you. I couldn't in *this* connection because truly there wasn't much to say. And again I didn't want to drag in that studio—because it would seem like puffing myself up—the "H. M. Studio" and all that. So I said nothing. But one day, somewhere, there will be a chance for me to speak of your roles, and I will do it with a full heart.

In the same letter he let me know that he was sending me more watercolors and gave me instructions on how he wanted them matted. "They may as well hang in your studio as to be hidden away in a closet here. I'm not eager to sell them either. Only if they fetch a good price. Otherwise I'd rather keep them for myself, or for my children when they grow up."

I read the letter through more than once. Henry had never before said anything about being embarrassed because of the studio. He had always seemed appreciative, had sent so much for me to sell, had asked me to buy for the studio all the magazines that carried his work, had even sent us out-of-towners who were passing through Chicago. As for mentioning me in his book, the thought had never occurred to me. But his phrase, "because truly there wasn't much to say," hurt me. I had not forgotten, even if he had, the piles of books I had mailed to him, my own donations and those from the people I had asked to help, or the boxes of food staples that the studio had collected for him and that I had sent parcel post. I had lost track of the income that M had earned for him.

I looked around the studio. I was proud of its color and warmth, of the watercolors on the wall, the glass-doored cabinets displaying rare copies of Henry's books, the tables of books and magazines to sell, the way I had fixed up the windows with exhibits. I thought that if Henry could see it he would like it too. I knew he had never seen all of his work in a cumulative display such as this.

One of the fliers on the studio's bulletin board was an announcement from the Kenneth Patchen Fund, which was being organized in New York under the auspices of W. H. Auden, T. S. Eliot, Archibald MacLeish, and Thornton Wilder. "We should like to call your attention," it began, "to the tragic plight of the young American poet, Kenneth Patchen, and urge that you join with us in bringing him the medical treatment which he desperately needs. . . . A substantial sum is needed for prolonged treatment, about $10,000. . . . We hope to find among artists and lovers of the arts 100 patrons who will each subscribe $100 or more."

The appeal was answered by 750 people, but only a few gave as much as a hundred dollars. Edith Sitwell suggested a benefit poetry reading to augment the fund, and one was organized for March 10 in the Community Church in New York. Seats were $10, $4.80, and $2.40. She and her brother Osbert would read, and also Auden, MacLeish, William Carlos Williams, and e. e. cummings.

I had been following the progress of the appeal while letters passed between Miriam Patchen and me. Ever since the studio's Fair for Patchen a year before, Miriam and I had corresponded frequently. She wrote: "The fund so far has brought in about $4,000 with expenses over $2,000! So many people spent so much of our money. . . . I saw a doctor yesterday. He advised us to wait until we have a good deal more money."

After the reading she wrote: "The reading? I don't know—not quite good enough, I'm afraid. But we had too little help and so very inexperienced and immature. Anyway it looked good and everyone probably thought it all right, so what the heck!"

Another letter, a day or so later: "Kenneth was rushed off to the hospital Sunday in a state of total collapse. He should have gone earlier." She blamed this on the strain the reading had been for him. "He had to mastermind the whole thing and it took full toll of his nerves and was the thing which pushed him in such a state to the hospital."

I offered to have a reading by Chicago poets, set the date for April 14, and asked Karl Shapiro, who had just become the new editor of *Poetry* magazine, to read his poetry and also help me in choosing other poets to read. I had announcements made and sent to two hundred people. We got good publicity in the papers.

That evening Jonathan Williams and Robert Glauber read Patchen's poetry and prose; in addition to Shapiro, the poets who read from their own work were Reuel Denney, Elder Olson, Selwyn Schwartz, and J. V. Cunningham. A neighborhood combo provided music, refreshments were free, and admission was $1.25. Patchen's books, which I had quickly bought from Padell and New Directions, were on sale.

Somehow we squeezed 170 people into the studio that night, and the following day I sent the Patchens a check for $268.75. There were no deductions for "expenses."

The young poet Jonathan Williams had only recently arrived in Chicago. He was an admirer of Patchen and had visited
him in Old Lyme just before coming to the Midwest. The Patchens had asked him to look us up, and he had arrived just in time
to help me with the poetry reading. Later, when I showed the
two large sheets of Henry's penciled notes on D. H. Lawrence, I
told him that Henry had asked me to find someone to go over
them in India ink. The fifteen-by-twenty-inch manila paper
sheets were crowded with diagrams, numbered notes, large capi-
talized words scattered here and there, typed inserts, marginal
notations, and more. He had done the sheets in 1932, and now
most of it was hardly legible.

Jonathan said that India ink would not do, that it would
smear on the soft paper. "Tell Henry it should be gone over with
a heavy black pencil." And then he added, "I'll do it if he wants
me to."

Henry agreed to forgo the India ink, and in a few days
Jonathan began the painstaking task of copying every pencil
stroke. He did some of it at the studio and the rest of it in his
furnished room on the north side of town.

When I let Henry know that Marvin Halverson had found
someone who could translate the chapter in the Swedish book,
Henry sent me the book. The translation was mailed directly to
him, so I did not have an opportunity to see if the references to the
Tropics would be of use to him in court.

Jens Nyholm, head of the library at Northwestern University in Evanston, was among those who came to the reading. He
had not known about M until he had seen the Patchen publicity in
the paper. A few days later he and the Special Collections curator,
Felix Pollak, came in to buy Henry's books that the library did not
have. I learned that they were collecting the works of Miller, Nin,
and Fraenkel. I tried to interest them in buying the fifteen-hun-
dred dollar material from *Into the Night Life*, but Nyholm said that
the university did not have funds available for such a large purchase.

The next day I wrote Henry to ask him if he had any manuscripts to sell the university. I thought they might be interested.
He answered: "I have carbon of *Sexus* with 3rd or 4th revisions

which I'd sell—but want *at least* $500 for it. If Nyholm wants more of my things let him write Powell (UCLA) for complete list."

Another letter from Henry: "If Cosby or Flagg could conveniently get me a small cheap 4-drawer file cabinet in which to file library cards I would appreciate it greatly. I have about 3,000 authors to file on cards. If they could also send me 500 or 1,000 ruled cards (library size) it would help. I am utterly broke and little sign of getting money as yet. Though a half-dozen big publishers abroad owe me for royalties. Frightful."

I answered: "On April 20 'Dances of the Southwest' will be performed by an Indian from the state of Washington who dances professionally. He's an ex-GI student at the University of Chicago and dances to the music of records he made at the reservations. This is to be a benefit for you—to pay for the file cabinet and cards. Cosby is in a hell of a fix right now. May be losing his business. And Flagg owes me $10."

From Henry: "Never mind. I'll use shoe boxes."

I sent him the list of sixty-three sales, which included books and records sold from January through April, although he had told me time and again not to bother with files and reports. I did it anyway because I could not believe that he had no interest whatsoever in which of his books were selling, which records bought, and so on. In this way I accounted for the money I sent him. I had not sold any watercolors because, at three or four times what they had been selling for, nobody would buy them.

With the checks I sent him I usually added a few dollars for stamps because he had told me how high his postage bill was—"twenty or thirty dollars a month." I knew that the mailman was no longer giving him credit for stamps.

Letters from friends in Carmel and Big Sur kept me in touch with what was happening. Henry seldom gave me any "news," although he was the first to tell me that Walker was back in Big Sur and writing a book about the Menninger psychiatric clinic in Topeka, Kansas.

Emil had continued to paint, and the year before had begun showing his watercolors in an outdoor "gallery" at his place. Tourists driving by usually slowed down as they approached the rambling structure separated by miles from other habitations on the highway. The paintings were in full view, and many cars stopped. His style continued to be tiny, multicolored strokes in tightly controlled patterns that were part fantasy. People said his work resembled embroidery.

When the *Monterey Peninsula Herald* sent a reporter for a story about Emil's gallery, my Carmel friend Bobby Ferro read it and drove down to take a look. She liked the paintings so much that she offered to buy them all, but Emil would let her have only two. The next day her sister Marjorie Grabhorn came and bought two more.

Emil had no trouble selling his work, and he was invited to exhibit in group and one-man shows. The San Francisco Museum of Art showed his "neoprimitives" in its annual watercolor group show, an invitation that was repeated in the years that followed. When his work was shown in Pasadena, Vincent Price and Adolphe Menjou were among the buyers.

Emil's marriage to "one of the most ravishingly beautiful women ever to pass through Big Sur" (according to Henry) lasted about two years. She was a singer, and she had brought her piano with her, as well as two small children by a previous marriage. When she and the children moved out, she left Emil the piano. This enabled the German pianist Gerhardt Muench, who was then living in Big Sur, to give a few free concerts in the guardhouse.

I learned that Lepska and Lolly Fassett were taking lessons in dance from a retired danseuse who had come to Big Sur; that Shanagolden was writing her third book; that Walker Winslow had a woman living with him; and that Lynda Sargent was living in Carmel Valley working as the caretaker of the weekend house of the playwright Martin Flavin and his wife.

In July Jonathan Williams went to San Francisco where he stayed with the Patchens' friends, David and Holly Ruff. He met Kenneth Rexroth and wrote me: "an interesting man, a welter of confusions. Lawrence could have been quite like Rexroth."

The Ruffs and Jonathan drove to Big Sur to visit Henry, and Jonathan wrote me: "Spent two days on and off there; told him about Studio M; and in everything he was warm, gentle, kind. Superb!"

Soon after that I heard that Lepska had fallen in love with "a Roumanian doctor" (also said to be a biophysicist with a Ph.D.) who was staying with neighbors of the Millers and that they had run off together.

Emil wrote that Henry wasn't surprised that she left him, but that he was shocked when she walked off without the children. "He couldn't believe it."

Emil left at once for a three-month vacation in Palm Springs in order to escape what he called "the ordeal that lay ahead." He knew that Henry would call on him for help with the children, a future he could not face. "I turned those two spoiled brats over to Walker."

From Palm Springs he went to Mexico for three more months. Years later, in telling me about it, he said, "Henry never held it against me."

33

I have tried more perhaps than any other living writer to tell the truth about myself. . . . I don't say I have succeeded—but I have tried.
The Plight of the Creative Artist in the
United States of America

A young man, Larry Krebs, had opened a student travel service in the colony, and through him I was able to get Henry a free round-trip flight between Chicago and Paris on a "nonsched" airline. Henry had written me that he wanted to visit Paris again. When the arrangements came through, he asked me to give Larry two of his watercolors in token of his appreciation. Then he wrote that he was taking the child Val with him, and that was all right too. I was looking forward to seeing them, and I let Henry know that his friends in Chicago, Flagg, Cosby, and Campbell, would be on hand to greet him. If there was a layover, he and Val could stay at the studio. I would have had a party for him, but he begged me not to.

After a couple of weeks passed, I wrote him to find out what was delaying him. He answered: "Must raise big sum to pay off debts before I can leave."

After my book *Big Pan Out,* the story of the Klondike gold rush, was published in January 1951 by W. W. Norton, I was called upon to make promotion trips between New York and Seattle, and in August I was invited to Alaska and the Yukon. When I returned and learned that Henry had not yet left Big Sur, I wrote him. He replied: "No—I didn't go to Europe—nor do I know when, if, or ever. Everything is perfectly lousy with me." He did not explain.

Miriam Patchen wrote about the same time:

Things have been so very difficult and confused that I've been unable to think clearly enough for the simplest letter. Nothing has been working out the way it might, and we are worn out by frustrations. Our friends have given and loaned money to the limit of their capacity; people who might be expected to help won't; others who promise, don't keep their promises; others who might help are off and away and we are stymied in trying to get in touch with them. And so it's been for months. . . .

There was a possibility that Kenneth would receive free treatment in Massachusetts General Hospital, and we were all excited about an immediate trip there a few months ago—when it had to be dropped instantaneously. The hospital demanded an advance fee of $2,400! Exclusive of doctors and drugs! At the time we had $2 and hundreds in debts. So that was another rather typical will-o'-the-wisp for us.

Kenneth is getting a little more uncomfortable with the approach of winter, as he always does. The Fall is really his worst time.

Then in November I was surprised to hear: "We're on the eve of departure for San Francisco. Decided just four weeks ago tomorrow. Since then we've sold everything we own—almost."

She did not say what had prompted the move across the country, but she gave the Ruffs' address, which appeared to be their destination. The Patchens were unaware that their train was not a through one to the coast, that there would be a wait between trains of several hours in Chicago. When this was discovered, they spent that time with us. We had met before. Bill had accompanied me on one of my New York trips, and we had gone up to Old Lyme to spend an afternoon with the Patchens.

The latest news from Big Sur was that Lepska had the children again and that they were living in Long Beach, California. She sued for divorce in October. The separation from the children was difficult for Henry, for they were everything to him. His only consolation was Eve McClure, a young actress who was writing to him from Beverly Hills. Her sister Louise was married to Bezalel Schatz, whom she had met in Berkeley, where the McClures lived. Eve wrote Henry that she and the Schatzes had driven to Big Sur to see him but had not found him at home. She told him how much she wanted to meet him, having read his books. Henry, of course, answered.

She wrote often and her letters were warm. Emil said that Henry pinned them up on the walls all over the house. He was falling in love with Eve through her letters. She had sent him a photo portrait, so he knew that she was a beautiful young brunette. She was twenty-eight years old. The age difference between her and Henry did not matter to her. At seventeen she had married the former movie star Lyle Talbot when he was nearly sixty. They were now divorced.

Late in March 1952 Henry drove down to Long Beach to see the children, and after being with them a few days he looked up Eve in Beverly Hills. It was love at first sight, and she returned to Partington Ridge with him. It was such a happy, fulfilling relationship that Henry found he could write again. There was *Nexus*, the third and last volume of *The Rosy Crucifixion* to begin, and he went to work.

Now Eve was writing to me: "May I take the opportunity to say how do you do for myself since we are meeting through correspondence. I'm writing for Henry, since he must get on with the new book *Nexus*, and in order to add a few hours writing time to his day, I will attempt to take over as much of his correspondence as possible." As time went on we did become friends through our letters. Sometimes Henry scribbled a sentence or two at the bottom of the page. He sent me a few watercolors.

The Books in My Life had been published, and I was selling it along with the February and March issues of *World Review*, which had his pieces on Blaise Cendrars. I also had the *Paris des Rêves* that he had asked me to order. Excerpts from the new book and others were appearing in French, German, Swedish, and Dutch magazines, and he sent me a copy of each to exhibit.

I saw Henry and Eve in August 1952. On a return trip from a brief visit to Alaska, I stopped over in San Francisco to see the Patchens and other friends, and with one friend drove to Carmel, where Lynda met us. She was still working for Martin Flavin and his wife, whose main residence was in Pebble Beach. They came to the valley only occasionally, which gave Lynda plenty of time to herself. She was writing again, the same book that she was never satisfied with. I had not seen her for six years, but we had written to each other. In her letters she had mentioned the ailments of her "scrawny old age" but seeing her was a shock. She was indeed scrawny, weighing hardly a hundred pounds, and gray haired, her skin like parchment and her eyes going blind from cataracts. Her clothes had belonged to others and had been given to her. They were too large, already worn out, and ugly.

The three of us drove down the coast together. I found Eve as beautiful as she had been described, but more than that she was a gracious, friendly person. Henry had not changed. He was as thin and spry as ever, and there was still some white hair behind his ears. We didn't stay long because the place was overrun with children, including Henry's two, and Eve was trying to hold them together while teaching them to paint. Henry explained that Eve was a natural artist who had never had a lesson in her life but was "loaded with talent."

On December 29 that year they flew together to Europe for an extended holiday. Before they left, Henry asked me to send whatever was coming to him from the studio to his former wife June. "She is ill and without funds," he explained, and gave me her Brooklyn address. "Send by American Express or cashier's check if you can and let me know later when, if, and how much."

Somehow it irked me. I did not feel like giving my time and efforts in order to keep June in funds, small as they may be. But I did it, for, after all, it was money that I had promised Henry.

He and Eve remained in Europe eight months, traveling from France to Spain. Louise and Bezalel Schatz joined them for part of the trip, coming from Israel where they were then living. In Barcelona Alfred Perlès and his wife met them. They stayed away from Paris as much as possible, where Henry's arrival had made headlines. He had been besieged for interviews, and he and Eve were entertained continually with banquets and receptions. He was invited to speak over the radio. People wanted his autograph. While it was flattering and exciting at first, he soon had had enough of it, and he and Eve escaped, first to the Riviera and later to the countryside. Finally, they went to Spain.

While Henry and Eve were in Europe, Girodias published *Plexus*, the book he had been holding since the ban on *Sexus*. He had gone bankrupt with his Obelisk Press and had recently resumed publishing with the new Olympia Press. The paperback two-volume set was printed only in English.

Correa brought out *Plexus* in a French edition in 1952 and in 1953 published a bilingual edition of *The Smile at the Foot of the Ladder*. Another edition of *The Smile* was published in English in the Hague, Holland, by L. J. C. Boucher. Its twelve black-and-white illustrations by Dick Elffers were a robust improvement over the clown figures taken from the works of world-famous artists and reproduced without distinction or life in the original New York edition of 1948. Because the book was for sale only in Holland, Henry sent me an autographed copy.

When my friend John Stapleton Cowley-Brown brought me the two-volume *Plexus* from Havana, I hesitated to open the book, remembering my disappointment in *Sexus*. I was pleasantly surprised to find volume one a rather merry recollection of his first year of marriage to June, during the months when they had lived extravagantly in quarters beyond their means while he was writing and trying in vain to be published. This was Henry at his best as a caricaturist of people and events. In his style of writing, which moves along with whatever comes to mind, the brilliant passage on the life, art, and the letters of Vincent van Gogh suddenly appears without prelude or postlude. The pages have since been published separately a number of times.

In the second volume there are a few carnal diversions but hardly in the excessive detail of *Sexus*. Their life together continues with scenes in the speakeasy that they ran for a while, his hitchhiking misadventure to Miami, a later trip to the South that he and "Mona" took together, her infatuation with a lesbian friend, and other episodes. He steps away from such scenes as these to write about Nostradamus, Buffalo Bill, the famous black leader W. E. Burghardt Du Bois, Oswald Spengler, Nietzsche, Karl Marx, and a dozen others. And then there is the stranger with "second sight" who reaches into Miller's psyche and reveals Miller to himself. There is also the twelfth-century robot Picodiribibi. It is both a continuing autobiography and a pungent mix that somehow holds together.

When they got home in August 1953, Henry wrote me: "We had a wonderful eight months abroad. Now, back home, things are just as tough as ever."

34

A book is a part of life, a manifestation of life, just as much as a tree or a horse or a star. It obeys its own rhythms, its own laws, whether it be a novel, a play, or a diary. The deep hidden rhythm of life is always there—that of the pulse, the heart beat.

Un Etre Etoilique

Back in January 1950, when Anaïs had written me that she was giving up her apartment in San Francisco and going to New York, I had hoped that she would stop over in Chicago, as she had said she might. But I did not see her or hear from her until she wrote to me from Acapulco, Mexico, some weeks later. Apparently, she had made other plans. In the meantime, a badly damaged package had arrived from her. The post office had taped it together to keep more of the glass from falling out. She had sent me four framed watercolors that Henry had given her in 1938.

From Acapulco she wrote: "I should have let you know about the Miller paintings. When I had to give up my home in San Francisco I sent them to you on an impulse—I wanted you to sell them for me if you can—will you?" In the letter she also wrote that she planned to ask Lawrence Powell to send me her Miller notebooks, which he was keeping for her in the Special Collections division of the library. These were Henry's bound manuscripts, ones he had given her in Paris.

"Would you like me to ask him to send you all my Miller items to take care of since you have gathered so many already and people know you have them?"

When I told her I would take whatever she sent and sell them for her, she gave me the New York address where she and Hugo lived so that I could send any checks there.

Her new book, *The Four-Chambered Heart*, had been published by Duell, Sloan, and Pearce, and she was working on a play based upon the book. "No success so far with my play—I thought it would go because the theatre is more mature for symbolism than the novel—and so much subtlety has been accepted (should I say with resignation?) by the public, such as *The Innocents, Member of the Wedding*, and Fry, etc. whereas in the novel they still have tantrums when you don't write journalism."

She asked me to take her booklets *On Writing*. "I can get them for you at $.15 from Alicat and you can sell them at $1." She said she was also writing Powell to send me all of her own manuscripts, hoping that I could sell them. She said how much she needed the money in order to be free financially. "I have had everything one can have," she wrote, "except economic independence. I'm a dependent with all the guilt it develops towards the master when you do something not approved—and guilt is always atoned for, and I dream intensely of the one freedom I can't reach, which you must understand (such as your sending me the $35 your husband wouldn't have sanctioned!)."

In June 1950, she sent me her record, *House of Incest*, as a gift. I was glad to receive it since I had sold all of her Sound Portraits and had not yet reordered from Louis Barron. I had told her this and that her records were well liked. Now that we had become friends, listening to her voice was a new experience for me. She was signing all of her letters "Your friend" or "Affectionately your friend."

She sent me a review of *The Four-Chambered Heart* that she said was "the most useful review" she had had. "I've mimeographed it and I can send you a few if you can use them—I am so eager not to be a failure—(the worst selling author in U.S.A.) because I have got so many books to write and want merely that the publishers shouldn't give me up!"

The review by Lloyd Morris appeared in the *New York Herald Tribune* on March 12, 1950. It began:

> Though her books have not yet won a large audience, few contemporary writers have caused so much commotion in literary circles as the author of this novel. A fine short story by Anaïs Nin

appeared in *Transition*, but her first books were privately printed, and did not reach the general reading public. At this stage of her career, the admiration of two critics brought Miss Nin sudden celebrity in the literary world. Miss Rebecca West hailed her as a writer possessing "real and unmistakable genius," and Mr. Edmund Wilson described her as "a very great artist." Since then, many other professional colleagues have praised Miss Nin's work in scarcely less impressive terms, and her most recent novels have been published commercially.

Of the novel itself, Morris wrote:

Miss Nin is not in the usual sense, trying to tell a story. Her object is to reveal experience directly. . . . she exalts love as the exclusive goal of living; and she can be fulfilled only by that absolute and total union with a lover which, intellectually, she knows to be beyond the reach of human nature. It is, of course, one of the oldest subjects in literature, for it springs from an awareness of the ultimate isolation of every individual, against which the human spirit permanently rebels.

Anaïs felt that no one had better understood the book and her work. When she sent me copies of the review, she asked that I sent it to "unbelievers."

In the summer of 1951 she wrote that she was on her way to Southern California and would later go again to Mexico. From Sierra Madre, California, she wrote that she had given up the play. "It could have been done—but I am not in favor just now —and am tired of making such efforts—My writing has been the most intense obstacle race ever staged—Every step has required a struggle. Nothing has ever come to me fully or spontaneously. . . . I wrote a play skeleton and no one was interested—I wanted to make films of the stories and I can't get backing, I can't get fellowships, can't get child diary published, can't get into magazines—Just recently *California Quarterly* turned down a story."

From Acapulco she wrote: "I had delays and difficulties getting Powell to mail you original manuscripts. Whenever I ask him he holds on to them saying he is going to buy them, and it was all a ruse to hold them hoping I die and they would be left to the library. *Please* help me sell them. I only ask $50 for each one and they are interesting documents. As you will see, *Winter of Artifice* was edited by Henry Miller. Do the best you can—I need the money. I am struggling to be independent from Hugo and seem unable to achieve it. Write me as soon as you receive the box." She enclosed the letter she had received from Powell, which had been sent to her in Mexico in August 1951.

Powell finally wrote to her: "The price you have placed on your manuscripts is certainly very reasonable. I am sorry nevertheless that I have no present prospects of raising this total amount. Thus I will have to ask you to give me the address in Chicago to which you want them sent."

She wrote me: "You might try Chicago University. You might write to Harvard which collects contemporary M.S. To Dartmouth—I can give you more names of people to try. Huntington Cairns, 2219 California St., Washington, a collector. If it is possible to sell them all to one person of course it would be wonderful. Above all Kathryn, I want to sell them *now*, I need it *now.*"

Her letter came while I was in Alaska. When I returned, there was a letter from her from New York:

> I haven't heard from you and I would like to know whether you received the box with all the manuscripts. Please let me know at above address where I will be for a month. I do so hope you can dispose of these M.S. now when it means something to me—I know it will be easier after I am dead.
>
> I'm here to see about a new publisher for the last M.S. Duell Sloan and P folded up and remaindered all my books. I wonder if you were notified. You can get them for $.49—Do you want me to send you a few? Do you want an inventory of the M.S. which Powell sent me? Write me please.

After receiving my answer, she wrote back:

> Your attitude about my M.S. was very kind and helpful. I have not been able to sell to UCLA so whatever you can get above $50 is for you. I know you need money too—so let us agree on that. I will be content with 50 because I cannot take care of selling. I'm enclosing the inventory—I'm also mailing you 20 copies *Four-Chambered Heart*—5 copies of *U A G Bell* for which I paid .49 at Womrath's.

These too you can sell as you wish—I don't know what the proce-
dure is when people can go to Womrath and buy it at .49 but to
a bookshop one block away and pay 2.75! The truth is there are
only 200 or 300 copies left that I know of.

Now—I have a suggestion—Would you like me to come the
4th and have a film showing of Hugo's *Ai-Yé* the 5th of November
together with showing of my books, my reading anything you
please—to help sale of manuscripts-records-etc.? (Have you any
records left?) Hugo's film takes 28 minutes and is in the mood of
my work, harmonizes with it—Do you like this idea? I have a radio
program the 3rd I could be in Chicago the 4th—be at your gallery
on the 5th and go on to Hollywood the 6th where I am due—Let
me know—

Soon after, in September, I received the box of manuscripts
from the UCLA library, I had an announcement printed to publi-
cize the coming exhibit.

HERE'S NEWS—
      By arrangement with Anaïs Nin the manuscripts of Miss
Nin's total published writing have been loaned to the studio for
exhibit and public purchase. Many contain handwritten comment
and editing by Henry Miller. All versions of various texts have
been sent with the exhibit. This is one of the most remarkable
shows that M has had for a long time. Try to see it.
      October 28 through November

Now, when I received her letter about coming on November 5 I began calling people to let them know that the party I had
planned on October 28 for the opening of the exhibit would be
postponed to November 5 when Anaïs would be there with the
film *Ai-Yé*. I sent her some of the announcements and a copy of the
publicity release I had sent to the papers and magazines in the
Chicago area. My letter crossed hers in the mail, in which she let
me know that she was sorry but she could not come after all and
that there was also some mix-up with the Chicago office of the
agent who handled the film for Hugo. The letter was written not
from New York but from Sierra Madre. She mentioned that she
was showing the film and giving a talk in Los Angeles on October
28. She added:

I'm grateful you are making this effort for me now when the money means so much liberation so much in terms of human life —Specially at this moment when I'm thwarted with my newly finished manuscript on Sabina—*A Spy in the House of Love.* So far only rejections from Houghton Mifflin from Random House from Scribner's, etc. At some time pretty soon there will be no more copies of any of my books—and I will be where I was 6 years ago —May have to get my own printing press again! I do hope you'll be able to sell the manuscripts. I know you'll do the best you can. Write me soon.

A day or so later she wrote again, this time from New York.

Dear Kathryn, I'm sad to disappoint you and myself again. The truth is, dear Kathryn, I am caught in a dual life and my "duties" at each of my two lives two loves are so tremendous that I can barely finish what I must do here for Hugo before I must rush back to take care of my life in California. Please forgive me. Now Hugo has started a new film and needs me until the last minute—When I leave I have to go direct to L.A. You don't know how many times I have tried to stop off at Chicago. Please don't be disappointed— I will come sometime—I want to—I feel I have a friend in you— and I hope all goes well for you. Write me.

I was more than disappointed by this sudden reversal of her plans; I was provoked with her unreliability. I was also sorry that a showing of *Ai-Yé* had been indefinitely postponed. After I had read the folders she sent me about the film, I was eager to see this documentary that Hugo had made from several years of travel along the Pacific Coast of South America. It was the result of thousands of feet of colored film edited to about one thousand.

Ai-Yé was not about a particular place, but, through its variety of scenes, it was "the universal story of mankind . . . from birth to death." In the Nigerian language *ai-yé* means "mankind." Osborne Smith, a drummer and chanter and a member of the Katherine Dunham troupe, provided the original musical score. There was no voice narration.

The film had received awards in the 1950 film festivals in Cleveland, Ohio, and in Venice, Italy. It had been described as "a visual poem." I had noted the mention that Hugo was "an artist, etcher, engraver, and the illustrator for the books of his wife, Anaïs Nin." His engravings had been bought by the Museum of Modern Art in New York, the Library of Congress, and by several private collectors.

I had been looking forward to meeting Anaïs. The year before, when Daphne Moschos and Michael Fraenkel had visited us, I had asked them about Henry before and during the Villa Seurat period, and some of our evenings were spent listening to their reminiscences of that time. Anaïs was very close to Henry during those years. Daphne said she was beautiful, "but not in a sweet, natural way. She had theatrical beauty, an affected manner like an actress. Even when she spoke it was in a stage voice. She always seemed to be hiding her real identity."

"She has marvelous eyes," Fraenkel said.

"What color?" I asked.

"I don't remember. Whatever color, they were always shining, as if a fire were burning behind them."

Daphne said that Anaïs was the woman in all of her novels. "She only wrote about herself. The way Henry did, except that she used a stream-of-consciousness style. Did you know that she was once an assistant to the psychoanalyst Otto Rank? He studied with Freud, you know."

The studio's display of manuscripts included her handwritten notes, handwritten manuscripts, typescripts, and carbons of all of her books, published and unpublished, some in different versions. There were thirty-nine separate folders of this work, and they covered a borrowed Ping-Pong table. I put them away during the Christmas holidays when I could not look after them carefully enough with people wandering about the studio and lingering and handling things. They were in the drawers of a chest in case anyone asked about them. I still hoped that someone from the University of Chicago would visit us in answer to my letters to the librarian and the head of the English Department.

Many people had looked over the manuscripts, a collector or two among them, but no one showed more than a passing interest. In January I wrote Anaïs: "I don't know what's the matter with people. With all the work I've put in on this, I haven't sold any-

thing yet. I haven't the right customers. Universities and colleges
around here were between semesters and then the holidays, and I
don't know what else. Please let us wait until Huntington Cairns
comes next month. I think he might help me with contacts. He
wrote me that he would be here early in February, when he was
coming to Chicago on other business."

While I was waiting for Cairns, I wrote Jens Nyholm again,
practically begging him to take a look at the manuscripts. It was
my second such letter.

"Don't worry about *time*," Anaïs wrote back, "and don't
worry if nothing happens. All of it is due to the fact that I have
no established commercial value, and people with money want
names, as they want famous painters only. Those who read me are
poor and unable to buy even books. Only friends showed up loy-
ally at my reading for new manuscript in New York and we sold
only 3 books and 2 records. Later—too late—the M.S. will increase
in value, I know."

Cairns' visit in February 1952 did not result in a sale, and he
had no useful contacts to give me aside from mentioning the interest that some universities might have in collecting Anaïs Nin. It
was March before Nyholm came by to see the manuscripts. He
brought along Professor Richard Ellmann of the English Department, who had only recently come to Northwestern. He had
taught at Harvard and lectured at other colleges and universities
and was eminent in his field, which was that of twentieth-century
literature.

They showed interest in the leather-bound, handwritten
notes she had made while writing *D. H. Lawrence* and agreed that
the seventy-five-dollar price was not too high. They were also
interested in the original version of *Winter of Artifice* at fifty dollars, and three typescripts of other versions of the book, for which
they were willing to pay ten dollars apiece. They explained that
they had no authority to purchase these items but that they would
present their offer of $150 for the five items to the library board
if Anaïs agreed to sell at that price. They had lowered their offer
by five dollars.

I wrote her immediately and told her that I had tried to
impress upon them the value of acquiring the entire collection

rather than picking out a few pieces, and I urged her to agree with me:

> They are interested in your work, they have all your books except *Winter of Artifice*. (Can you supply a copy of the book?) They were able to get your Lawrence book in Paris last year so you see they have gone to some trouble to "collect" your work. . . . The possible figure that I think I may get for everything is $500. I know that blow must stun you! But it is the top price that I have been able to get—the only price. I haven't been able to get the response anywhere that your work deserves. At least Northwestern holds you in your rightful esteem. They understand and admire everything of yours. But that is all I believe I can get—and that offer may come from them. I have no commitment, remember, it's only a hunch from something that was "dropped" while they were examining the manuscripts.

She wired back: "Feel as you do prefer sale of all manuscripts to university for 500."

A letter followed: "I like the idea of selling M.S. to a University and all the M.S. in one place—I liked the way you handled it and our reaction is the same. I hope it goes through—As you know one half of my life is always the one I have to support, and only the half here with Hugo is the one I do not have to work for—so I'll be glad of the 500."

When I let Nyholm know that Anaïs preferred not to break up the collection, they made me the expected offer of five hundred dollars. I said I would write Anaïs. When she learned that the offer had been made, she again agreed upon the price. Several weeks passed while the purchase was discussed with the library board, the heads of certain departments, and "a committee."

Meanwhile, Anaïs wrote me from one coast or the other as she flew back and forth between Sierra Madre and New York, begging to know what was holding up the sale. I suggested that she write Nyholm herself, explaining the value and rarity of her manuscripts, that there were no duplicates, no other carbons, no other versions elsewhere. She did this and explained that she held all of the rights for reproduction, including by microfilm, and that these rights would be included with the sale. They had asked this.

Next, they lowered their offer to four hundred dollars, which both she and I considered unthinkable. She wrote back that she would not accept a price lower than five hundred. The university said they would have to pay her in two installments. She wrote me that this was acceptable, but I refused to let Nyholm know, insisting that the five hundred dollars be paid in full. I also asked them to send the check to me for forwarding to Anaïs. I wanted to be sure they paid the full amount. It was June 24 before the check arrived, and a few days later they picked up the thirty-nine folders.

Some days after Anaïs had received her check from me, which I sent on as soon as I had received it from Northwestern, she wrote:

> I wanted to write you a long letter when I received the check for $500 because I was grateful and pleased, but I was leaving in a hurry to appear at my preliminary examination—I'm on my way to becoming an American citizen! So once more I had to bypass Chicago! From the plane I went straight to get my documents translated and to be taught ages and numbers of Senators, contents of Bill of Rights, etc. . . . I wrote to Henry letting him know how well you had handled this—All his manuscripts are in the hands of Larry Powell at UCLA who boasts of offering storage space and nothing else to the writer. I told him once he should be ashamed (he wrote me celebrating a truck load he got from Henry) especially in Henry's case, who has nothing. I received very charming letters from Pollak and the Librarian—which I answered—I will have to come for a real visit with you and these courteous and appreciative people. Thanks again.

35

> *To Emil White of Anderson Creek—one of the few*
> *friends who has never failed me*
> The dedication to Big Sur and the
> Oranges of Hieronymus Bosch

In 1954 Henry's financial fortunes suddenly changed for the better. The Japanese had discovered his books and were asking to publish them. The lean years were over. And now, with money worries behind him, and married to Eve since December 1953, and with his children staying with them on a part-time arrangement, he was in the mood to start a folksy ramble about himself as a family man and a friend to his neighbors. He called the new book *Big Sur and the Oranges of Hieronymus Bosch.*

Friends, strangers, neighbors continued to visit him in his little house on Partington Ridge, but the two who surprised him most were George Katsimbalis, the "colossus" of Maroussi, who visited him during the fall of 1953, and his long-lost daughter Barbara. Katsimbalis had come to the United States on a cultural-exchange program, and before returning to Greece he came west to see his old friend.

Henry had not seen Barbara since she was a small child, and the reunion was accidental. In Pasadena, where she was living with her mother, she came across an article about Big Sur in the December 1951 issue of *Family Circle,* a five-cent magazine sold at supermarket checkout counters. She thought a man with the name of Henry Miller in one of the pictures might be her father. When Beatrice saw it, she knew it was the man whom she had divorced in 1924.

Barbara wrote Henry in February 1954, and he answered at once, inviting her to visit him. She arrived in June, stayed for a few weeks, and begged to remain. But Henry could not see her living permanently with him and Eve and reluctantly sent her home. Now he was afraid that Beatrice would sue him for back alimony since she knew where to find him, but she didn't.

Later that year Alfred Perlès, his old friend from the Paris years, arrived from England to stay six months. He was working on a book about the years that he and Henry had been friends. Henry was to help him with their mutual reminiscences. When the book was published in England in 1955 it was titled *My Friend Henry Miller*.

During the next few years, while Henry's books were becoming best sellers in Japan, other editions were coming off the presses in Germany, France, Italy, and England as well as in the United States. The favorite titles were *Sexus, Plexus, The Smile at the Foot of the Ladder, The Books in My Life*, and the essays he had written on Rimbaud and turned into a book, *The Time of the Assassins*. The antiwar booklet *Murder the Murderer*, which Bern Porter had published in 1944, was reprinted in Copenhagen. A collection of short pieces written and published years before became *Nights of Love and Laughter* for Signet Books. Girodias published an old manuscript, *Quiet Days in Clichy*, and a revised edition of *The World of Sex*. Henry's work was included in new anthologies. He was not giving anything away anymore to little magazines.

He asked Jack Stauffacher to print an edition of *The Smile*, limited to five hundred copies, and sold the book himself from Big Sur. He wrote prefaces for Perlès's *My Friend Henry Miller*, which was published in England and France, and for Walker Winslow's French edition of *If a Man Be Mad*, which Correa published.

He had written a detailed account of Conrad Moricand's visit to Partington Ridge in 1948, which he wrote in self-defense against possible legal action by Moricand, and he now turned the material into *A Devil in Paradise* and sold the book to Signet for another pocketbook. He also included it in *Big Sur and the Oranges of Hieronymus Bosch*, which New Directions would publish in 1957.

The colony in Chicago had taken on new life since 1951. The tropical-fish store was still there, but other tenants had moved away and new people coming in had opened art classes, an art gallery, an antique shop, a Japanese art shop, and a "repeat sale" bookstore that overflowed onto sidewalk tables set up under the trees in summer. Folding chairs were provided for readers and browsers. From May to September people passed by from morning to night, many on their way to the park or to swim in the lake. The crowds were window-shopping, browsing, buying, or just standing around taking in the "arty" atmosphere. The residents brought out chairs to sit under the trees and watch those who were looking at them.

Glen had bought another Rolls, a maroon-colored sedan with an English body and right-hand steering. It was not quite as old as his coupe. For a while then, there were three Rolls-Royces parked on the block, and since no one else in the colony owned a car, and only an occasional one pulled up to the curbs, they had the street to themselves. They drew their share of rubberneckers. One night someone came back and stole our Silver Lady radiator cap. Bill moved the car to the lot in back of the studio and covered it with a parachute. A few days later the parachute was gone.

Those who stopped to look in the windows at M saw only the books of a writer they had never heard of. To answer their question, "Who is Henry Miller?", one of Bob Campbell's tall show cards was always propped on an easel behind the display. I could see people reading the cards: "Henry Miller Is the Most Original, Most Unusual, and, in the View of Some Critics, the Most Significant of Living American Writers. Come In and Discover Henry Miller."

Now and then someone did come in. They looked around but seldom bought anything. They stared at Henry's paintings on two walls that were painted indigo blue and a third one painted kelly green. Henry was no longer sending me his work; he was sending it to Japan and Europe, where it brought good prices. The days would never come again when a watercolor of his could be picked up for ten or fifteen dollars. Those on the walls were my own collection and were not for sale.

The length of the long room was broken by screens of various heights, which became the somewhat surrealistic settings that focused on the works of Miller, Patchen, Nin, and Fraenkel. The dissembled parts of our mannequin were always used along with other ornaments.

A six-foot-long bulletin board displayed a variety of Milleriana, including new book covers, letters, photographs of the family, and newspaper clippings. Whenever Henry was interviewed and photographed at home, the old-fashioned claw-footed bathtub in the yard was usually part of the story. Eve kept me supplied with clippings from all sources. When the people in the studio saw the bathtub, they asked me what it was doing there. I had to explain that it was connected to a nearby spring and that the Millers used it and, yes, the water was cold.

M did not depend upon passersby for customers. It had never ceased to be a rendezvous for our regular customers, more of whom were painters now instead of poets and novelists. I continued to sell Henry's books and the records from Sound Portraits. I had copies of the literary quarterlies that had Henry's work in them. Some of the books and booklets were out of print, and when my stock was gone there wouldn't be anymore. I had all of Anaïs's books that were in print, and also her albums from Sound Portraits. I did not have any of Michael Fraenkel's books left, but I had enough of my own for a display.

Anaïs and I had finally got together in New York, and after that she came to the studio a few times. Whenever she had a financial crisis, she found tempting manuscripts of her own or of Henry's to sell me. He had given her the notebooks he had kept in Paris when he was working on a book about Lawrence, and these she sold to me.

I asked Emil to send me lithographs that had been made of his paintings. His work had been given shows in a number of cities, and people had begun to call him "the Pointillist of Big Sur." In 1954 he married again, this time taking a twenty-two-year-old as his bride.

Part of my Patchen exhibit were his books of poetry for which he had painted special covers. I asked Miriam if he had more of these books, and if he would like me to sell them for him. I knew that the Patchens relied mainly on Miriam's job with the City of

Paris, a San Francisco department store where she worked at one of the cosmetic counters. She wrote me that they were spending a hundred dollars a month on painkillers and muscle relaxants for Kenneth.

In December 1954 Miriam injured her head in a bad fall, and in April she had begun to lose the sight in her left eye, which was gone by September. She wrote that "a friend who is a doctor" had taken her to a clinic where "the astonishing verdict is multiple sclerosis and diabetes! So now I am home, pretty useless, completely ridiculous, and damned inconvenient! What exactly happens from now on, I don't know. Wednesday some more consultations are scheduled, and the start of insulin—a real nuisance, darn it!"

I thought that an old friend of mine, Gordon Claycomb, might be able to help the Patchens, and I wrote to him. He was one of California's leading public-relations consultants, working generally in the field of medical research while organizing and directing surveys of numerous health and medical projects. At that time he was on the executive staff of the Palo Alto Medical Clinic and the administrative assistant to its founder and chief executive, Dr. Russell V. A. Lee.

After letting Gordon know that the Patchens were cherished friends of mine and that I was deeply concerned about their circumstances, I gave him some background on Kenneth's disability, the bedridden years, the everlasting pain, and his courage nonetheless in the face of what was a very bleak future if help was not forthcoming. In case Gordon didn't know who Patchen was, I explained that he was one of the most important young poets in America, with nearly a dozen books of poetry and prose already published. I mentioned his Guggenheim Fellowship and named the poets in this country and England who had praised his work, among them T. S. Eliot, W. H. Auden, e. e. cummings, William Carlos Williams, Edith Sitwell, and Kenneth Rexroth. I told him that in 1950 the prestigious New Directions annual had been dedicated to him, and I explained that this was a signal honor of recognition. I quoted James Laughlin's words: "Kenneth Patchen is the most compelling force in American poetry since Whitman." I begged Gordon to help this kind and greatly talented man if he could. I also told him about Miriam's recent medical problems. "Gordon, please help them if you can."

He showed the letter to Dr. Lee, who took up the matter with the clinic's executive committee. Gordon had attached his recommendation, asking that the clinic provide Kenneth and Miriam Patchen at no charge with complete medical care by physicians, staff, and all ancillary departments of the clinic, including X-ray, laboratory, physical therapy, and dietary services. The committee gave its approval, and the Patchens began their visits to the clinic, undertaking the fory-mile commute by train from San Francisco.

Miriam wrote: "If it hadn't been for Palo Alto who knows what would have occurred. For I have secretly seen several doctors in the last six months, and they actually, as is always the case, harmed things by wrong treatment, diagnosis, and time-waste. Finally, as the condition worsened, Kenneth heard about it. So Gordon took over. What I would have done in my ignorance if it hadn't been for your Palo Alto, I don't know."

In November 1955 Henry Rago happened to be in the studio. He was now editor of *Poetry* magazine. I showed him the two painted books that Kenneth had done especially for me, and his new work, *Portfolio,* a collection of illustrated pages of poems. We talked about ways to help the Patchens. I suggested that a write-up in *Poetry* would bring his work to the attention of many people, but Henry thought that a full-page ad in the magazine would have better results and offered to give Kenneth the space without cost. He asked me to write them at once, asking them to send him whatever copy they wanted but to rush it for the December issue, which was due soon at the printer's. I wired the Patchens and then wrote a letter to explain things further:

> Henry Rago wants to give you a full-page ad absolutely free (usually costs $145) for the Christmas issue to announce your Portfolio and painted books. You probably have my wire but I thought I should write to explain that this is Henry's idea. I wouldn't have dared suggest a page ad when the idea of an ad was discussed. I assumed he meant an inch or two (o ye of little faith). I have given him the marvelous blurb that came with the Portfolio. Kenneth Rexroth had already written to him about it but gave no details as

to price or where to order it. If you make the layout the same size as a page in the magazine—you know the size—it will save time and possible errors. Please send it to Henry as soon as you can. Isn't it a wonderful break? Blessed is Henry Rago.

Kenneth answered my letter at once. It was one of the few I ever received from him, for he left letter writing to Miriam. His letter was typewritten, which surprised me. Hers were all hand-written, and I had sometimes wondered if they owned a type-writer. The other letters that Kenneth wrote me were painted on rice paper with a very slender brush with which he stroked tall dancing letters into words. Now he wrote:

> What a thing! such a fine gracious thing all around! for Rago and the other editors, for you. Your huge telegram came at three Sunday afternoon, some forty-five minutes before the last mail collection. I did the copy in that time. After hasty consultation we decided to make it an ad for *Glory Never Guesses* alone, and figuring on following up any orders with the Painted Books mailing piece. I got a second letter off to Rago telling him to tack on a notice of Painted Books if he thought it a good idea. Hope the ad does what you good people have so beautifully indicated you hope it will do. Frankly, I am disappointed in our sales from about 600 mailing pieces on the Portfolio to a list given us by Laughlin of the subscri-bers to *Perspectives;* although I may be beating the gun on it a bit, since the bulk of them went out only ten days ago. But I don't think it will do much on the basis of the three orders we have had so far. We may have shot our bolt into quicksand. If so we'll move on to another try. The *NY Times* will probably have a squib on Portfolio in its issue of Sunday, Nov. 20. The enclosed *Examiner* puff did nothing: for some reason no title is given. I have been working ten–twelve hours a day readying the pages of the two Portfolios, when not taking Miriam to the clinic in Palo Alto and to the office of their SF doctor—etc. etc. You know about the shocks and fears of such a situation as this. You are wonderfully kind and good. Our love to you.

Gordon realized that the train trip between San Francisco and Palo Alto was too much for the Patchens and asked that a small redwood shingle cottage owned by the clinic and located directly across the street from it be made available to them at a minimal rental. The request was granted, and in February they left San Francisco. Miriam described Palo Alto as "so quiet, so peaceful, so nicely rundown unlike dreary San Francisco's rundown quality." She added that the house was very small. "It's tiny and in poor condition but with some work by us will be cozy. The rooms are fantastically tiny, smaller than the house in Old Lyme—but it's going to be darling when I'm through."

Gordon and his wife Antoinette invited the Patchens to spend a weekend with them at their ranch in the nearby Los Altos hills. It was not a working ranch. There were horses for the two young daughters and a variety of children's pets, including goats and rabbits. The Patchens finally went, and found it too exhausting for Kenneth for them to return on subsequent invitations. Being guests meant hours of conversation and the sociability expected of them, but Kenneth was unable to keep this up. He needed to lie down frequently, to rest and relax, which he could only do, undisturbed, at home.

Besides, there was little for them to talk about. Kenneth had given Gordon a book of his poems and had expected some comment from Gordon after he had read it. But, as Gordon wrote me, he could not understand the poems and couldn't talk to Kenneth about them. Of course, Kenneth was disappointed. On the other hand, Gordon and Antoinette were passionately fond of music— she had been a concert pianist—but classical music and noted musicians were subjects the Patchens knew too little about to hold up their end of the conversation.

However, the Claycombs continued to look after the Patchens in one way or another. Gordon often dropped by "for a cigarette break." Miriam wrote me: "I think Gordon has been hurt because we don't socialize. He has been so friendly and outgoing, but Kenneth is not even up to the little visits we've had with him. The evenings he's popped in for a few hours have left Kenneth totally exhausted."

Once the Claycombs were invited to dinner. Miriam wrote: "And they stayed until after one o'clock in the morning!"

Early in June 1956, Kenneth underwent surgery at Stanford Hospital. The clinic did not operate a hospital, but its team of specialists did the surgery. She wrote: "Kenneth had his operation

Monday week, and yesterday he was placed in a torso-length cast in which he will live for many months. The operation was extensive, much stuff turned up—multiple lesions, scar tissue, another disc which had collapsed—which has all been taken care of. The doctors are wonderful and the care terrific."

In August 1955, Bill had been invited to attend a scientific meeting in Los Angeles and I went along. Afterwards we rented a car and drove up to Big Sur. We spent half a day with Henry, eating the lunch we had brought along and talking. Eve was not there. She had gone to Berkeley to be with her mother, who was ill, and I was sorry to miss her. Henry gave me an armload of his latest books. He was especially pleased with the Japanese editions, even though he could not read them.

He showed us two guidebooks that Emil had decided to publish after answering questions about Big Sur for years. When motorists stopped at his roadside gallery, they asked, "How far is it to the next town, where can we find a place to eat, where can we get down to the ocean, where can we get off this winding road?" His guides had all the answers. They featured short articles written by Henry, Gilbert Neiman, Shanagolden, Lynda, and others. There were numerous full-page scenic photographs. Everything of interest between the Carmel Bridge on the north and San Simeon on the south was described, and for a centerfold Emil had painted a serpentine design that showed the highway's mileage and other details.

The first guide was so successful that a second one came out later, with additional material that included the Monterey Peninsula. At a dollar apiece, Emil could not keep up with the demand and had to print several editions of each. Later he brought out three more guides with information about other nearby areas.

After we left Henry, we drove on down the highway to visit Emil and to pick up some guides to take back to M. They would help me answer the questions that were often asked at the studio: "Where is Big Sur? What is it?"

Henry was in New York in the spring of 1956 when he sent me a brochure describing a two-record album that had just come out called *Henry Miller Recalls and Reflects*. It was a series of conversations between Henry and the radio and television commentator, Ben Grauer. Henry had chosen the subjects, which ranged from his early years when he was striving to become a writer to the successful decade in Paris. He had something to say about many subjects, from philosophy to food, from women to his opinion of present-day writers. I sent for five albums to have on hand for those whom I knew would want to buy them.

Eve was with him in New York. They had arrived in February, called there to be with his mother who was terminally ill. During the next three months before she died, Eve nursed her and remained near to be of comfort, but Henry stayed away as much as possible. It was during this time that he made the records. Eve's attempts to bring about a reconciliation between Henry and his mother failed for reasons that were as much his mother's as his.

When Henry's mother died, they brought Lauretta back to California with them and settled her in Pacific Grove at the Del Monte Rest Home. Eve wrote me that Lauretta was happy there, that Henry spent a day a week with her.

For a year we kept hearing reports that the little buildings on both sides of our block were going to be torn down, for the property had been sold to a developer. In the summer of 1958 we received our notice to vacate. I did not look for a new place to take M, and we moved out of the city.

Part Four

Big Sur

Minneapolis

Europe

Pacific Palisades

36

*For Edward P. Schwartz, a friend if there ever was
one. Your reward will come in the next century—or in
'De va chan' when you are selecting a new earth body!*
Inscription on a book given to
Edward P. Schwartz by Henry Miller

Hokan Ljunge of the Swedish consulate in Minneapolis, his wife Harriet, and Edward P. Schwartz, a businessman in the city, were at a social gathering one evening in 1954 when the talk turned to books written by American authors. Henry Miller's name came up. The Ljunges had read his books in Europe, including those forbidden entry into the United States, and their enthusiasm for his writing awakened in Schwartz his own excitement upon discovering Miller ten years earlier. He had read a smuggled copy of *Tropic of Cancer* and would then have hunted up other books of the author, but wartime disruptions and the pressures of starting a printing business had interfered.

Thereafter, on occasions when the three friends met with others who were interested in Miller, they exchanged scraps of information picked up in newspapers and magazines about him or his books, and they played the records he had made with Ben Grauer. They resented the fact that he was a literary outcast in his own country while recognized as a major writer where he was read in translation—in France, Italy, Germany, the Netherlands, Belgium, Denmark, Czechoslovakia, Sweden, and Japan.

Schwartz shared the letters he received from Henry, for, after he had written him, "You wouldn't know me from a bale of hay but I like your books," the two men corresponded.

When it was discovered that a young couple in town had

visited Big Sur and had looked up Henry in his Partington Ridge home, they were invited to meet with the group to relate the experience.

Through Harlow Ross, co-owner of the Ross-Haines Bookshop in Minneapolis, Schwartz met another Miller enthusiast, Thomas Moore. At a newsstand Moore had picked up a copy of Henry's Signet Book, *Nights of Love and Laughter,* and after reading it went to the bookshop in search of other Miller titles. Ross suggested that he look up Schwartz.

Harlow Ross, it turned out, was H. Orvis Ross, one of Henry's old friends. They had known each other years before when Henry and his first wife Beatrice were living in an apartment in Brooklyn and Ross had rented a room from them. He was a friend of hers and, like her, was an accomplished pianist. Later, when he returned to Minnesota and Henry had gone on to Paris, the two men had kept up a correspondence. When *Tropic of Cancer* was published, Ross was among those who had received an autographed copy.

Moore, a machinist at the Minneapolis Honeywell plant, spent a lot of his leisure time reading. When Miller became his favorite author, he wrote him a letter to tell him so. Henry was soon corresponding with Moore as well.

It was not long before Schwartz and Moore hit upon the idea of suggesting to the now eleven Miller fans in Minneapolis that they call themselves the Henry Miller Literary Society. The group organized as the Upper Midwest Chapter of the society, and its members looked forward to the time when other regional chapters would follow. This, however, did not come about. It was not necessary. The original chapter took in members from across the country and Europe as well.

It was not a society in the usual sense, since there were no organization rituals, no regular meetings, and no dues. Anyone interested in Henry Miller and his books could join. They did want officers and, because "nobody wanted the jobs," Schwartz became president and Moore secretary.

They decided to bring out a quarterly newsletter, or bulletin, and in 1959 the first one appeared as a two-page mimeographed letter. The fifth newsletter was the first one to be printed.

Schwartz's Ad Art Advertising Company published it in November 1960 under the society's letterhead, one that Schwartz had designed.

The purpose of the society was to help sell Henry's books by listing shops where they could be purchased coast to coast. The newsletter gave this free advertising space. It reprinted from magazines and newspapers the reviews of his books and everything else that was written about him. Members clipped these items and sent them to Schwartz for the newsletter. Whenever they received a photograph of Henry or a letter, they printed it, too. A newsy item about anyone associated with him in any way was always used. There was plenty to read in the newsletter, including bits about Lawrence Durrell, Alfred Perlès, Karl Shapiro, Gilbert Neiman, William Carlos Williams, Edith Sitwell, Osbert Sitwell, Abe Rattner, Judson Crews, Louis and Bebe Barron, Blaise Cendrars, Walter Lowenfels, and many, many others. Maurice Chevalier's name got in when he joined the society.

The editors promised to answer "any reasonable" questions about Henry except those asking for the names of places where the banned books could be obtained. "This we cannot do," they explained, "as Customs plus the Postmaster General have a phobia towards four-letter words and erotic realism."

Henry and Eve took the children to Europe in 1959 for a vacation, and while they were in Paris Girodias arranged a meeting between Henry and Barney Rosset, the publisher of Grove Press of New York City. Rosset wanted Henry's permission to acquire the sole American rights to both of the *Tropics*. They had never been copyrighted in the United States and were open to piracy. But Henry turned him down. Not even the ten thousand dollars that Rosset offered in advance royalties could sway him from his fear of personal attack if the books were to be published in America. The certainty of a sensational trial with its publicity and personal harassment dismayed him. Moreover, he had no hope of ever seeing the ban lifted. In 1953 the American Civil Liberties Union had lost its case in San Francisco. There was then a trial going on in Norway, where two booksellers had been prosecuted in a lower court for selling *Sexus* and were now appealing the case to the Norwegian Supreme Court. *Sexus* had also been taken to court in Paris. Henry did not want to get involved in further trials. As for the ten thousand dollars, he knew that tax collectors and agents would leave him only a small part of it—not enough to tempt him.

In Oslo, Trygve Hirsch was the defense attorney fighting the case for the two booksellers. He had written Henry for a statement that he could read to the court, for it was a point of law whether to condemn a book for certain passages or to judge them from the standpoint of the author's overall intention. In a lengthy letter to Hirsch, Henry stated that, in writing *The Rosy Crucifixion*, he had had but one thought in mind, "to tell the story of the crucial years which marked a turning point in my life, and to relate my experiences (good and bad) as honestly and as faithfully as possible."

Two years later Hirsch wrote him again, for the trial was not yet over, asking for more about his views in writing *Sexus*. Henry answered, "It is not something evil, something poisonous, which this book *Sexus* offers the Norwegian reader. It is a dose of life which I administered to myself first, and which I not only survived but thrived on. Certainly I would not recommend it to infants, but then neither would I offer a child a bottle of *aqua vite.* I can say one thing for it unblushingly—compared to the atom bomb, it is full of life-giving qualities."

It was a lengthy letter and, after sending it to Hirsch, he gave a copy to the editor of *Two Cities*, a bilingual journal being published in Paris, where it appeared in the July 1959 issue under the title "Defence [*sic*] of the Freedom to Read." That same month the *Evergreen Review*, a bimonthly magazine published by Rosset, also ran the letter. Henry made sure that Durrell included it in *The Henry Miller Reader*, which he was compiling for New Directions. Later Emil White would also publish the letter in his book, *Henry Miller—Between Heaven and Hell.*

The Henry Miller Reader came out late in 1959 and became Henry's best-selling book ever from New Directions. It was Durrell's idea to collect pieces from fifteen of Miller's books, including some that American bookstores were forbidden to carry, and to offer them as a cross section of his writing skills. Twenty-one selections were divided into "Places," "Stories," "Literary Essays," and "Portraits." In addition there was a collection of Henry's ideas presented as aphorisms. In writing the introduction, Durrell described his old friend as "the rogue elephant" and "the great vagabond" of American literature.

All the reviews of the book were good. Henry's mastery of such a wide variety of writing took many reviewers by surprise and revealed how little had previously been known about his work. The *New York Times* reviewer, Harry T. Moore, wrote: "Perhaps this first American publication of samples from Miller's banned books points to the appearance of their full texts in this country."

I heard from Eddie Schwartz that the popularity of the *Reader* caused the circulation of the Henry Miller Literary Society's newsletter to increase to seven hundred.

When the Millers returned from France at the end of the summer of 1959 and the children were with their mother again, Henry and Eve did not settle easily into their usual routine. Somehow things were not the same. Everything was wrong between them, and as tension increased Eve took out her frustrations in drink. One day Henry found her with a young lover, a neighbor. He did not blame her; he had no reason to. He was also finding sexual partners elsewhere and had not kept it a secret from her.

In the spring of 1960 Henry wrote Schwartz:

> Dear Eddie:
> Have been invited to Cannes, France, for the International Film Festival May 3 to 20 to act as one of the judges. I've accepted! Will leave Big Sur April 4—ahead of time as I have to go to Germany, Holland, Denmark to see my publishers. (You have details pretty well covered in current H. M. Society Newsletter.) After festival will go to Italy and maybe Greece—getting back here the end of July. Then to Japan about Sept. 1. *Nexus* should be out any day now. Ed. du Chene, Paris, are doing it in English. French version is now out—by Correa, Paris. More anon.

Henry left in April and arranged for a young waitress at Nepenthe to follow and meet him in Cannes. Their relationship had led her to believe that they would spend the summer together. Eve was left behind.

First he flew to Hamburg to see his German publisher, Ledig Rowohlt, and was met at the airport by the firm's translator of English books. She was Frau Renate Gerhardt, a dark-haired, dark-eyed, young widow with two little boys. She was too young, too tall, and too European for Henry, but at the sight of her he felt himself falling in love again.

When he arrived in Cannes he found himself a celebrity and as sought after as any of the movie stars. He was interviewed, lionized, and photographed. He told the reporters, "I have retired in the Chinese sense. I work but I am serene. At peace with myself. I am anchored at Big Sur. I've never become reconciled to America. Living where I do I have slowed down. I no longer have any compulsions or obsessions. I can go on writing interminably. I can go on every day. I am not drying up."

He also said that he was working on the second volume of *Nexus*. "After that I don't want to write another book about myself. In 1928 I projected a program of writing about seven years of my life, and it has taken me thirty years to get through it."

He wrote Schwartz, "Two films a day, receptions, cocktail parties, reporters, radio and television in between. A tough grind."

The girl from Nepenthe joined him in Cannes, and when the festival was over they traveled around southern France for a while before he sent her home. He stayed on to visit friends— Brassai, who was married and living on the Riviera, and Durrell who was living at Nîmes. Then he flew to Milan to see his Italian publisher who was bringing out the *Tropics*. With new Italian friends he visited Pisa to see the Leaning Tower and then on to Florence to see the house where Dostoyevski had written *The Idiot*. When Henry discovered that Boccaccio had lived on the outskirts of Florence, he visited that house as well. Then he was back in Paris to catch a plane home and while in the city saw an announcement of an exhibition of the paintings of his old friend Beauford DeLaney. He looked him up and learned that DeLaney had been living in France for the past seven years.

On his return to Partington Ridge, he found Eve living with Harrydick, comforting him over Shanagolden's death earlier in the year. They were both drinking heavily. Instead of going on to Japan as he had intended to do, he picked up Vincent Birge, a friend in Big Sur, to accompany him on a flight back to Paris. Between planes in New York, Henry phoned Ben Grauer to ask him to come to Paris to tape some three-way conversations with Durrell. Nothing came of this because Grauer was unable to get away long enough and Henry discouraged his coming for only a few days. He felt that he and Durrell needed a week or more to make the proposed sessions worthwhile.

In Paris Henry bought a 1953 Fiat, and with Birge at the wheel they set out for Reinbek, the village near Hamburg where Renate lived with her children. It was not long before she accepted Henry's proposal of marriage, but with the understanding that after his divorce, he would return to Europe to live because she refused to bring up her sons anywhere else but Europe. It was not decided where they would make their home, but both agreed that it would not be Germany.

In his hotel room in Hamburg, Henry painted watercolors and did some writing. When Rowohlt asked him if he had written anything about Christmas, he had Renate translate a selection from *Remember to Remember* and called it *Ein Weihnachtsabend in der Villa Seurat* (A Christmas Eve in the Villa Seurat). Rowohlt published it as a booklet, and it was also used in the first issue of a new German revue called *Rhinozeros.* He wrote a preface for a Cologne publishing house that was bringing out *Frauen und Gottenin* (Women and Goddesses). Then he tried writing something in German, his first and only attempt to do so. The result was a humorous sketch with the nonsense title, *Ein Ungebumbelte Fuchselbiss.* It went to *Rhinozeros* for its third issue.

He was in such a happy mood that, when Barney Rosset and Henry's agent flew to Hamburg to reopen their discussion of giving Rosset the American rights to the *Tropics*, he relented. The fifty thousand dollars that Rosset gave him included a forty-thousand-dollar advance on royalties. Henry was glad to get the money. He saw that he was going to need it in this new marriage.

The romance was interrupted by a lonely Christmas week for Henry when Renate took her children to spend the holiday with her father. She did not want Henry to join them, and so his sixty-ninth birthday on December 26, 1960, was as unhappy as many that had gone before. To chase away the blues, he wrote a comedy in three acts that he called *Just Wild About Harry.*

In March he had an unexpected visitor—Emil White, who was vacationing in Europe. When they decided to tour a few countries together in the Fiat, with Birge again doing the driving, he explained his departure to Renate by telling her he would be looking for a place for them to live when they were married. She had been urging him to do this because they could not marry until there was a suitable home for them to live in with the children. Without consulting Lepska, Henry was planning to bring Val and Tony to Europe to live with his new family.

Renate thought that Henry and his friends were going to look around in France, and possibly Switzerland. They did drive all over France and Switzerland, and also Austria, Italy, Spain, and Portugal. He kept writing her that he was searching for the ideal place.

To Schwartz he wrote longer letters describing the weather and scenery, the hotels they stopped at, the meals they ate, the art galleries and bookshops they visited, the films they saw, and such sights as cathedrals and cemeteries. He mentioned how often the Fiat broke down. Schwartz shared these letters with me and later published them in the society's newsletters.

When Henry returned at last to Renate, he described her welcome as glacial. Seeing that it was over between them, he went to Copenhagen to see his Danish publisher Hans Reitzel, who had been the first to publish *Nexus.* In Copenhagen he met the Italian composer Antonio Gino Bibalo, who was writing an opera based on *The Smile at the Foot of the Ladder.* Bibalo's Danish friend, the painter Borge Sornum, was designing the sets. Then it was back to Milan to sit for the sculptor Marino Marini, who had been commissioned by Galerie Springer in Berlin to do a head of Miller. Still not ready to come home, he flew to England to visit Perlès and take a trip to Ireland with him.

He was in California by Christmas, but not in Big Sur. Wanting to be near his children, he had found a furnished apartment in Pacific Palisades not far from where they were living with

Mirror facing front door of м. Portrait of Miller at left rear is by Carl Van Vechten.

KEN UYEHARA

Portion of Jackson Park Art Colony, Chicago, 1951. M studio is in foreground.

GLEN BELLE ISLE

Kathryn Winslow with Obelisk Press edition of *Tropic of Cancer,* 1949.

"Echolalia," watercolor by Miller (1943). *Author's collection.*

Interior of M studio. Note Glen Belle Isle's Rolls Royce roadster through window.

Interior of M studio showing an array of Miller's watercolors.

Dear Kathryn —   1/24/5?

am so terribly broke and so many
bills to pay and don't know where
next cent is coming from. (all I can
count on is Laughlin's $50 = a month.)
Would suggest that you sell _all_ my
water colors on hand — to one or to
several persons — with idea of
raising $75 = at least. Nothing
less will do me any good.

My main problem is to maintain
credit with our mailman, who not
only supplies me with stamps
but milk, bread, butter, cheese
and eggs, which we need for
the kids. I owe him $40 =
now and I'm getting worried.
Maybe you can do something.
If not, OK. But let me hear
from you in 2 or 3 days after
receipt of this, will you?
          I was depending on my French
publisher to come across —
but he seems sunk.
                    In haste,
                         Henry

Letter from Miller at Big Sur to Kathryn Winslow in Chicago, January 24, 1951.

Display of Miller's books at M.

The Rolls Royces in front of the Jackson Park Art
Colony studios.

Kathryn Winslow in the office area of the M studio.

Anaïs Nin exhibit at M.

KEN UYEHARA

MIRIAM PATCHEN

Kenneth Patchen (l.), Kathryn Winslow, Bill Mecham at Old Lyme, Connecticut, June 1951.

Henry Rago (l.) and Wallace Fowlie at a picnic on the Indiana Dunes,
1950.

At the Minnesota Press Club, June 1962. Attorney Elmer Gertz is at Miller's right. Edward P. Schwartz is partly hidden by the camera. Tom Moore is off camera at Miller's left. *Courtesy of Edward P. Schwartz.*

Orvis Ross with Miller in Minneapolis, 1962. *Courtesy of Edward P. Schwartz.*

Tom Moore (l.) and Edward P. Schwartz with Miller bibliography in 1961. *Courtesy of Edward P. Schwartz.*

KEN UYEHARA

Display of "little magazines" on wall at M.

WILLIAM J. MECHAM

Kenneth and Miriam Patchen with Kathryn Winslow during their stopover visit to M in Chicago en route to California, November 1951.

ROBERT FINK

Henry Miller in 1961.

their mother. In a letter to Schwartz Henry wrote: "I am living without a car and without a telephone. I am still stout of limb and not in a hurry to get anywhere. When I walk the streets at night, I think it must be Christmas Eve on the planet Venus." He was alone and, as usual at this time of year, he was blue.

37

God . . . doesn't go in for the latest fashions. . . .
usually he makes only miraculous clothes that carry
you through with a whole skin . . . and when he makes
you a suit it's better not to make too many inquiries.
Just take it and charge it up. Of course, you are apt to
look a little ridiculous in the eyes of the fashion-plate
men and women. You may not be invited for the grand
ball or for the Fete at the Opera. On the other hand,
because of the miraculous quality of God's garments,
you are apt to find yourself in strange places, strange
situations.

Hamlet, Vol. 2

After Rosset had acquired the American rights to the *Tropics*, he chose to begin publication with *Tropic of Cancer*. An earlier attempt to prohibit the sale of Grove's publication of D. H. Lawrence's *Lady Chatterley's Lover* had been successfully defended in New York, and Rosset felt that the time was right to bring out Miller's book. He asked Karl Shapiro to allow him to use his essay, "The Greatest Living Author," for its introduction.

Shapiro's admiration for Henry's writing went back a long way. In 1951 he had left Chicago to teach at the University of Nebraska, and while there he had written the book *In Defense of Ignorance*. One of its chapters was this essay on Miller, whose writing he described as "not a mixture of truth and fiction . . . but an expansion and deepening of truth. . . . It is not the flimsy truth of facts but the truth of emotion, reflection and understanding, truth digested and assimilated." Before the book was published by Random House in 1960, the essay appeared in the December 1959 issue of *Two Cities,* where Henry had read it and ever after spoke of it as one of the few pieces that revealed a genuine understanding of his work.

In June 1961, *Tropic of Cancer* came out in a $7.50 hard-cover edition that sold 68,000 copies the first week and put the book on best-seller lists across the country. In the *New York Times* Harry T. Moore wrote: "It might be said of him, as Yeats said of Miller's forerunners and true masters, Whitman and Emerson, that he lacks the vision of evil in his assertion of self-reliance, in his song of himself." Of the humor he wrote: "Now it must be granted that parts of *Tropic of Cancer* will hammer away at some of the strongest stomachs, even in this epoch in which so many books are really scabrous. However, in the present volume, among other things, Miller projects with gusto some of the great comic scenes in modern literature." Moore briefly describes a few before he concludes: "If literary quality is a criterion, these passages run far ahead of any considerations of obscenity, in themselves they guarantee that Henry Miller is an authentic, a significant author whose ripest work has been too long forbidden in his homeland."

In the *New York Post* Gerald Walker wrote: "*Tropic of Cancer* has been published at last. . . . let's be grateful. How many great books are there that we can afford to ignore one of them?"

Day Thorpe of the *Washington Star* wrote: "a wonderful geyser of life. Miller is a superb story-teller."

Webster Schott in the *Kansas City Star* saw that the book "possesses vigor, humor, and honesty . . . passages of beautiful poetry in prose . . ." and added that "it seems all for the good that it has at last been published in the United States."

In the *Saturday Review* Ben Ray Redman described Miller as "one of the most remarkable, most truly original authors of this or any age. He is a word-master whose range, so far as I know, is unique in breadth and depth. . . . any public censor who touches this book will touch living tissue."

The reviewer for *Time* magazine did not hesitate to wield an ax and draw blood. He called *Tropic of Cancer* "a very dirty book indeed" and one that Shapiro had introduced "in the characteristic style of the muddled and ecstatic cultist." It required a full page to get in all of his rips and slashes.

In October Grove brought out a ninety-five cent paperback that quickly sold a million copies. While no word had been heard of suppressing the book while it was in hard cover, the deluge of cheap paperbacks raised an unexpected clamor of outrage from Massachusetts to Hawaii. When semiliterate men and women discovered the steamy descriptions of sex, which Miller usually described in Elizabethan language, they demanded that the book be taken off the market, and to see that this was done they called upon their leagues of decency, morals squads, and police departments. As Jay Edgerton wrote in the *Minneapolis Star*, "indignation flamed like a bonfire on a windy night."

Police raided bookstores, stationery shops, and drugstore counters; they rifled newsstands; and some even charged up to the desks of public libraries. Wherever *Tropic of Cancer* was found, it was seized and removed from the premises. In some cases, customers were forced to reveal their purchases in case they had already bought the book and were concealing it. If the book was found on them, it was confiscated along with the others in the store, although search and seizure of this kind was clearly illegal. Booksellers were hauled off to jail to be prosecuted on criminal charges. At one time there were more than sixty cases in the courts of twenty-one states, and there were more waiting to be heard. Rosset had assured the book dealers that if there was trouble, he would pay the costs of their legal defense, and within six months he had spent more than a hundred thousand dollars in lawyers' fees and court costs.

The attorney general of Massachusetts called upon the state's Obscene Literature Control Commission for a decision on *Tropic of Cancer,* which he personally found "filthy, rotten, positively repulsive and an affront to human decency." He also said, "I have never in my life read anything that was so disgusting and demoralizing and so brazenly animalistic."

In Massachusetts the book was outlawed on the grounds that "among other things it has no connected plot and is in many respects filthy, disgusting, nauseating, and offensive to good taste."

In Sioux City, Iowa, the county attorney said while being interviewed by a reporter: "I am not qualified to judge the literary value of the book, but I can say that it is full of lousy language and is obscene."

In Duval County, Florida, the chief of the vice squad was burning the books.

People who did not have a copy of the book were trying to get hold of one to see for themselves what "the Tropical storm" was all about. The only way to get a copy was through the mail —the Post Office Department had revoked its ban on mailing

Tropic of Cancer after the Justice Department had decided to look the other way.

Newspapers and magazines throughout the country carried stories, editorials, letters to the editor, and interviews with a variety of people in order to keep up with the battle. There was no hesitation in expressing an opinion: "If the sexual passages offend some people they have the privilege of not reading them. They have the right to speak out against such books, but they do not have the right to impose their restrictions on the free choice of others." The general feeling was: "Does Henry Miller's book offend us? The public libraries are full of books which offend somebody."

The writer of an editorial in the *Honolulu Advertiser* chastised the local police for acting on their own initiative in seizing the book. "This approach," he wrote, "might be all right for handling minor traffic offenses. But to invade the complex and delicate realm of free expression in such an arbitrary fashion is censorship pure and simple. We doubt that thoughtful citizens, regardless of individual opinion of the book in question, care to have the police department deciding what they shall or shall not read." He pointed out that "despite the foul words, others—including leading critics of literature—would and do consider the book a work of art. Those who have hailed the book include such well-known and highly regarded figures of literature as Aldous Huxley, John Dos Passos and Norman Cousins. The latter called it 'one of the noteworthy books of this century' and its author 'one of the adornments of modern American literature.' "

In a story in the *Milwaukee Journal* readers were reminded that objections to obscenity in literature go back as far as Aristophanes in ancient Greece. Trials of modern times were cited, including the famous one against H. L. Mencken in Boston in 1926, which was over a story he had published in the *American Mercury*.

Columnist Herb Caen of the *San Francisco Chronicle* described "the insane farce" that was being conducted by men "who didn't know Henry James from Harry James" but had set themselves up as literary arbiters. "Miller," he wrote, "is a long way from being my favorite writer although his *Colossus of Maroussi* is one of the best travel books I ever read—but I will defend him, or any other writer, from now until doomsday against the prurient prigs who pretend to 'protect' us from him. Miller is a joyous, outgoing man, filled with the zest for living. The same most emphatically cannot be said of his tormentors."

Witnesses for the prosecution were rarely capable of giving a literary opinion of the book. When asked by the defense attorneys if they had ever heard of—let alone read—*God's Little Acre, Sanctuary, Sister Carrie, The Sun Also Rises, From the Terrace,* and other books by America's leading novelists, the answer was no. *Don Quixote?* Surely they had heard of *The Odyssey?* No, they had not. Because of the memorable passage in *Tropic of Cancer* about the paintings of Matisse, at one trial a man was asked if he knew who Matisse was, if he had ever heard of him. "I may have heard of him at lectures and so forth," was the answer. When asked if he could give a positive answer, yes or no, he replied: "No, I can't."

When a group of American Legionnaires in New York City tried to have the book removed from the shelves of the Queensborough Public Library, the librarian wrote to the local post's chairman of the Americanism Committee. "When the book was purchased its controversial nature was fully recognized as well as opinions running the full range from condemnation to praise as a literary masterpiece. Precisely because of this wide range of opinion, the book should be available in the public library. Our free society is based on the right of each individual to form his opinion and I have faith in the ability of our people to think for themselves."

About this time a translation of *Tropic of Cancer* appeared in Finland and was suppressed. However, before the police went into action, almost all of the four thousand copies had been sold. An earlier Hebrew translation that had come out in Israel was not suppressed, nor did the book have trouble in Argentina. England had lifted the ban on bringing in the book, and it was not long before both of the *Tropics* were published in that country.

Grove Press's chief counsel, Charles Rembar, advised Rosset to retain the noted Chicago attorney, Elmer Gertz, to handle the situation in Illinois. Gertz specialized in First Amendment and civil rights cases but also took criminal cases and ones that other lawyers were reluctant to defend. In 1958 he had won a parole for

Nathan Leopold, who, with another young man, Richard Loeb, had committed "the crime of the century" in Chicago in 1924. They had murdered a young boy, which they had said was "for the thrill of it" and then demanded a ransom from the victim's family. Clarence Darrow was hired to defend them and was able to have their death sentences commuted to life imprisonment. Loeb was killed by a fellow inmate. After thirty-four years, Leopold had little hope of leaving the penitentiary, having been denied parole many times. Finally, his brother asked Gertz to help. If anyone could win the battle for *Tropic of Cancer*, Rembar believed, it was Elmer Gertz, and he was hired.

There was plenty of trouble in and around Chicago. Downtown in the Loop, detectives with search warrants had already arrested two men at their newsstands, charging them with selling an obscene book. One of these stands was in the Greyhound Bus depot, and the other was in a cigar store. Each man had to post a two-hundred-dollar bond in order to be released pending his appearance in court. From time to time other newsstands were searched and other arrests made. In ten suburbs of Chicago the police were apprehending clerks in shops and confiscating any books they found. Grove was concerned over its considerable loss of property as well as business and had Gertz file a suit for $3,900,000 in damages. The Illinois division of the American Civil Liberties Union had already filed a suit against the police chiefs in these suburbs over the right to read. For Gertz, the important issue was to have *Tropic of Cancer* declared "not obscene" and to have further interference with the sale of the book restrained in Illinois.

In preparing for the trial, Gertz read the transcripts of cases of note that had taken place in the past in Boston, New York, San Francisco, and London, and he familiarized himself with the opinions handed down by their judges.

He asked me for material that Henry had sent м regarding the publicity that had been given to the literary merit of his books in French newspapers and magazines. He read everything he could find that had been written by or about Miller, for although he was a well-read person he had never heard of Henry Miller before he was asked to defend *Tropic of Cancer*. His reading tastes favored Shaw, Molière, Ibsen, Wilde, and O'Neill, and he read the eighteenth- and nineteenth-century poets. When he was a young man, he had coauthored a book about Frank Harris. He had been the editor of a small weekly newspaper, and he had written numerous magazine articles and book reviews. His work was in various anthologies. Such a rare combination of literature and law made him an ideal protagonist for Henry. From the first of Henry's books that he read, he admired his work, and it was not long before he regarded him as "one of the great personalities of our age."

The trial opened in Chicago on January 10, 1962, before Chief Justice Samuel B. Epstein of the Cook County Superior Court. The insurance lawyers immediately sought to dismiss the monetary damages asked by Grove. Their arguments were so time-consuming that Gertz feared the trial would be prolonged for weeks. Anxious to get on with the obscenity issue, he dismissed the damages.

As in trials over the book in other states, it was expected that the defense would bring in "literary experts" to attest to the novel's worthlessness as obscene trash. Gertz was ready for them. He had brought together a group of qualified persons and was working with them on the questions that would be asked and what should be the response when he learned that Northwestern University's Professor Richard Ellmann favored Miller's books. He invited him to appear at the trial on Henry's behalf, and Ellmann agreed to do so. In the more than ten years that Ellmann had been at Northwestern, he had earned wide prestige in the field of modern literature. He was an authority on the works of James Joyce, William Butler Yeats, and Oscar Wilde, and his book on Joyce had won the National Book Award.

None of this impressed the lawyers for the defense, who bedeviled him with questions that were often as pointless as they were picayune and peevish. In referring to remarks in *Cancer* about body lice, the lawyers asked Ellmann how he would get rid of them. Another lawyer asked him what he thought of fornication among elephants. He answered that *fornication* is a word that means sexual relations between a man and woman who are not married to each other. Judge Epstein had to rap his gavel for order in the courtroom.

Ellmann was also asked if his associates at the university used the kind of language that was in *Cancer*, and he said that they did. He was asked if he would recommend the book to his students, and he said that he would. He refused to accept the insinuations that he ought to be shocked and repelled by the language and contents of *Cancer*, and he refused to agree that a particularly obscene passage on page five was pornographic.

In reference to that passage, Judge Epstein asked Ellmann: "Would you recommend that this portion and perhaps other abridgments be made in the book without seriously affecting the literary merit of the book?"

"No, your Honor, I feel that the whole literary merit of the book depends upon its bluntness and honesty in this kind of representation of somewhat exaggerated feelings."

Epstein continued: "You don't consider that this paragraph is just an outpouring of a lot of filth that has no relation to the book?"

"No, your Honor, it seems, to me, basic."

Barney Rosset was the next person to be called to the stand and after him, Hoke Norris. Norris was the literary editor of the *Chicago Sun-Times* and he had written in defense of *Cancer*. Five lawyers questioned these men but got nowhere in their attempt to discredit the book.

When the trial ended on February 21, 1962, Judge Epstein handed down an eighteen-page decision in which he stated, in part, that: "Literature which has some social merit, even if controversial, should be left to individual taste rather than to government edict. Let not the government or the courts dictate the reading matter of a free people." He had decided that *Tropic of Cancer* was not obscene under the law because it must be taken in its entirety and not piecemeal. He judged the book to have literary merit, although he was personally shocked by it and considered some of the passages to be vulgar and disgusting. His decision protected the book within Cook County.

Gertz asked the police chiefs of the cities and towns within the county if they were willing to be bound by the judge's decision, and all but three said they would. The three took the case to the appellate court, a delaying tactic that meant the book could not be sold during the time of their appeal. Gertz managed to take the case from the appellate court to the Illinois Supreme Court, which he expected to act promptly. He was mistaken. It took two years for the court to act and then it was to reverse Judge Epstein's decision and to find the book obscene.

This blow did not stop Gertz. With Charles Rembar, he was ready to take the case to the United States Supreme Court. This was not necessary, however, for in July 1964, the Supreme Court reversed a *Tropic of Cancer* case that had been appealed from Florida after that state's Supreme Court had ruled that the book was obscene. In reversing the Florida court, the book was given constitutional protection everywhere in the United States.

Almost immediately the Illinois Supreme Court reversed itself by acting upon "the controlling authority of the decision of the United States Supreme Court in its finding in the Florida case." It ordered its earlier opinion to be withdrawn, and it affirmed the February 21 decree of Judge Epstein in full.

The New York Supreme Court similarly reversed itself. Influenced by Judge Epstein's decision two years earlier, the Supreme Court of Massachusetts and Maryland had already reversed the findings of their lower courts.

All of us who were the members of the Henry Miller Literary Society had kept up with what was happening to *Tropic of Cancer* by reading the newsletter. Members were asked to send in whatever was in the newspapers in their parts of the country, and leading periodicals were watched for their reactions to the trials. It amounted to a formidable collection of material, but most of it got into the four large pages of the newsletter's frequent issues. What was left over was printed on various sizes and colors of paper, whatever was handy in the print shop, and it was all stuffed into an envelope and mailed to about nine hundred people here and abroad.

Henry was mistaken in believing that American writers were not concerned about censorship. He had felt this way in 1953 when the American Civil Liberties Union lost its case over the *Tropics* in San Francisco. It was an overwhelming experience for him now, in 1962, to be handed a copy of a statement condemning police censorship of books and declaring support of Judge Epstein in his decision on *Tropic of Cancer.* The statement was signed by 198 of the country's best-known novelists, playwrights, poets, critics, and publishers. Among these writers were Saul Bellow, James Baldwin, Jacques Barzun, John Dos Passos, Clifton Fadiman, Herbert Gold, Harry Golden, Lillian Hellman, John Hersey, Aldous Huxley, Alfred Kazin, Max Lerner, Carson McCullers, Norman Mailer, Bernard Malamud, Arthur Miller, Elmer Rice, Philip Roth, Mark Schorer, William Styron, Robert Penn Warren, Edmund Wilson, and Philip Wylie.

38

I honestly think a large part of the writing preoccupation is an egotistic thing, a desire to assert oneself. I don't seem to need that anymore.

Semblance of a Devoted Past

During the *Tropic of Cancer* trials, Henry was never called into court, for, as Rosset had promised him, he was protected from harassment. Anyway, he could not be found. In Pacific Palisades he gave his address to only a few trusted friends. He was not worrying about the outcome of the trials, for he had consulted a favorite astrologer who had told him that it was in the stars that the book would win.

He kept in touch with Gertz, writing him frequent letters on a number of subjects while Gertz kept him informed about the litigation in Illinois.

"Of course," Gertz explained to Henry, "I am working day and night on the case now on trial before Judge Epstein, but it is always a delight to interrupt it to read letters from you and to respond."

As the correspondence progressed and they exchanged books and articles that each had written, a warm regard for each other developed.

In March 1962 Henry was invited to the Spanish island of Mallorca to be one of the American judges of the Prix Formentor, an international award for unpublished fiction. While in Europe he visited friends in London, Paris, and Berlin. At the Galerie Springer in Berlin he saw the bronze head that Marini had done of him the year before. Copies of it were selling for ten thousand dollars. "Magnificent, if I say so myself," was how Henry described the sculpture in a letter to Schwartz.

He let Edward Schwartz know that on his way home he would fly from New York to Minneapolis for a few days' visit to give the two men a chance finally to meet each other. He wrote that he was also looking forward to meeting Tom Moore and the local members of the Henry Miller Literary Society.

Schwartz alerted Gertz in Chicago and Ross, who was now living in Rochester, Minnesota, with his ninety-seven-year-old mother. When he let other out-of-town members know of the coming visit, one of the eleven original members flew down from Winnipeg to meet him. Gertz joined Schwartz at the airport to meet Henry's plane on the evening of June 3. For the following three days Henry was a guest in the Schwartz home.

Schwartz hosted a luncheon at the Minnesota Press Club for Henry, members of the society, and other invited guests. Jay Edgerton, book editor of the *Minneapolis Star*, who had defended *Tropic of Cancer* during the trials, was among the guests whom Henry especially wanted to meet. After lunch Henry was interviewed by the press.

The next day he was asked by KUOM, the University of Minnesota's radio station, to tape an interview for them. Schwartz and Moore accompanied him to the station, where an hour-long interview took place. He talked about the authors who had inspired him when he was a young man attempting to write. When he was asked what criterion he had for selecting a book when he was officiating as a judge, he answered: "That's very difficult to answer. . . . Well, now, I judge a book . . . because it pleases me, don't you know? I don't pretend to know the value of them, but I certainly know the effect they have upon me. And it's from that that I judge, do you see?"

He was asked which of the books he had written were his favorites, and he replied that they were *The Colossus of Maroussi* and *The Smile at the Foot of the Ladder*. He said that these were the books he would like to be remembered by.

He was asked which contemporary American authors he admired most, and he answered that they were Saul Bellow and Jack Kerouac.

When the subject turned to politics, he said that people in politics were trying to play God. "Yes. Yes. We think that we know how other people should live. . . . we pity them, we feel sorry that they do not see things as we see them."

The interviewer said, "In a sense, one could call you an anarchist."

"That's exactly what I am. Have been all my life. Without belonging, you know, subscribing."

"Without labeling with a capital *A*. . . ."

"Yes, yes."

In discussing what makes a person's life rewarding, Henry said, "I don't think what we do is so important, it's what we are, what we learn to be, do you know? Discover your own being, and live with it. . . . One can have a rich life without the expression of some medium, I think—I find people who are just in themselves a piece of art. Do you see? . . . listen, I must add this—you know I never have had inspiration from meeting the really big person. The big people don't really communicate or give you anything. They've given it in their works, do you see what I mean? But with ordinary [people] or eccentrics or strange individuals whom you don't know, who are anonymous, you know, you suddenly stumble upon something interesting. You . . . get curious."

Henry said that it was the best interview he had ever had, and he complimented the interviewer, Audrey June Booth.

Henry learned that Tom Moore was working on a book to be titled *Henry Miller on Writing*, and he set aside time to help him with it, particularly in selecting work of his to be used. The book was divided into four parts: examples of Henry's early and frustrating attempts to become a writer; his later success; his methods of working; and his statements on the use of obscenity in his books. For this fourth section, his letters to Trygve Hirsch were to be used.

After a busy three days of being on the go continually, seeing people, giving interviews, autographing books for the university's Henry Miller Collection, and sightseeing around the Twin Cities of Minneapolis and St. Paul, it was time to say good-bye. Moore drove him to Rochester to spend a day with Ross before leaving for the West.

Years before, when Henry had known Ross in Brooklyn, his

name was Harold, which Henry always misspelled Harolde. Later
Ross dropped the Harold, as well as his middle name of Orvis, and
called himself Harlow Ross. Later, in the mid 1970s, Henry was
to write a book that included his friendship with Ross. In it he
would still call him Harolde.

Before writing a book about Henry's writing, Moore had
compiled a thirty-two-page *Henry Miller Bibliography* that was
sponsored by the society and published in the fall of 1961. Bern
Porter had given Moore permission to include the earlier bibliography that he and Henry had put together in 1945. The new one
went to press with 421 entries, including translations and reprints.
While it was being printed, sixteen more titles turned up that
Moore had not known about. These were inserted in the booklet
as a leaflet, and, in the future, as numerous other omissions came
to light and new publications appeared, these were printed in the
newsletter.

Even Henry did not have a complete record of his work.
Virtually everything he had ever written was in print on some
continent in hard cover or paperback. New translations were coming out all the time. In addition to books, deluxe editions of his
watercolors were being published. Bibalo's opera of *The Smile at the
Foot of the Ladder* was scheduled for a production in the fall at the
State Opera House in Hamburg, to be repeated later in other
cities. *The Smile* was also to be a play performed in Paris, and *Just
Wild About Harry* was to be a play in Berlin. In June 1962 New
Directions brought out *Stand Still Like the Hummingbird*, a collection of short pieces that had been published before. In September,
Grove Press was publishing a hard-cover edition of *Tropic of Capri-
corn.* No bibliography could keep up with him.

Nexus, the final book in *The Rosy Crucifixion* trilogy, had been
in print since 1959 when the Danish edition had appeared. The
following year French and English editions came out in Paris, and
in 1961 the book was published in Germany and Italy.

Those who knew Henry's work saw that he had put his best
work in *Nexus*. He could not have known that this was to be his
last major book, but perhaps he sensed it and wanted the book to
represent the best of his skills.

As in *Sexus* and *Plexus*, June is ever present, although he no longer feels the pain of her rejection. He can write about that long-ago time but the need for June is over. There is no sadness in *Nexus*, no despair. From a brief surrealist beginning, reality takes over in the basement rooms occupied by Henry, June, and the woman June loves. Once the situation in this frantic ménage is understood by the reader, Henry skips ahead, writing episodes, sketches, stories, caricatures, monologues, rushing from one to the other as was his style. Except for the monologues, most of it is funny, lively stuff happening in scenes of the wildest shenanigans. In writing comedy Henry was at his best.

He interrupts these scenes to express his thoughts on such subjects as Oriental art, the Book of Job, the novels of Dostoyevski, the Brooklyn Bridge, a childhood sweetheart, learning to drive a car, working for the New York City parks department.

When his thoughts return to June, he remembers that when he first began writing about her he poured out his soul hoping that he could reach her sympathy and perhaps her love. He asks himself, "Was it love that kept me chained? . . . Was it blind admiration for one beyond reach?"

But then, he reasons, pure love is totally unselfish. He was not unselfish about June, he was in a "perpetual panic" over his desire to possess her and not to lose her to the woman who meant more to her than he did. He writes, "And so, moving about in the dark or standing for hours like a hatrack in the corner of the room, I fell deeper and deeper into the pit. Hysteria became the norm. The snow never melted."

He was powerless to hold her, and in his anguish and hysteria he attempted suicide. He recalls how it came about and why it failed. In going over the past he remembers how much easier it would have been then to accept her death rather than to lose her to another. That she preferred a woman to him was almost more than he could bear.

In writing *Nexus* so many years after all this had mattered to him, he seeks to understand love. He sees it as a miracle, "the miracle which demands no intervention, no supreme exertion of will, the miracle which is open to the fool and the coward as well as the hero and the saint."

A force that he calls energy also fills his thoughts. "Man has never created an ounce of energy nor did he create love. Love and energy have always been, always will be." He believes that perhaps this all-invasive force is but the manifestation of love. He writes that love and energy are indestructible and are the same thing and that they are "God in action."

From time to time Henry thought of continuing *Nexus* with volume two. He occasionally wrote a few pages for it. He said he could finish the book if it were not for the interruptions. But he welcomed interruptions.

First it was the Cannes Festival and then it was the week in Mallorca. There was all the traipsing through Europe to visit his publishers and friends. After he left Minneapolis and was back in Pacific Palisades, it was only a few weeks before he was off again to Europe to attend a Writers' Conference in Edinburgh. Lawrence Durrell was there with him, and afterwards the two of them returned to Paris for a sentimental visit. Then Henry went on to Copenhagen to see his Danish publisher. In Copenhagen he was introduced to an artist who showed him how to make copperplate engravings. Then he was off to Munich for a week, and then to Berlin to see Renate and look over the publishing business which she had set up for herself. It was nearly the end of October before he was ready to come home. Even when he was back in the United States he put off returning to California. He stayed around New York for a while and then flew to Chicago where he spent a week with the Gertz family.

In Chicago he was astonished to learn that he was wanted on a criminal charge, that of writing an obscene book and conspiring with Barney Rosset and Grove Press to print and circulate it in Brooklyn. The book was *Tropic of Cancer*, which the criminal court in Kings County, New York, claimed had been written in Brooklyn between January 1, 1961, and June 30, 1962. Brooklyn's district attorney had been unable to locate Henry, but he had ordered his arrest and extradiction from California.

The charge was so absurd over a book well known to have been written in Paris twenty-seven years earlier that no one expected the case to continue. Yet it did, for two years. Not until the ruling by the United States Supreme Court had cleared the book was the Brooklyn case dismissed.

Henry returned to Pacific Palisades, where he spent Christmas and reached his seventy-first birthday on December 26. He was happy to be home and near his children. When Lepska urged him to buy a house in Pacific Palisades where they could all live together, one large enough for him to have a part of it to himself, he agreed. She soon found a suitable place, a two-story, white stucco, Georgian-style house on tree-lined Ocampo Drive. There was a lawn in front and a large swimming pool in back. In February they moved in.

Pacific Palisades, which overlooks the Pacific Ocean, is a fashionable suburb of Los Angeles. The streets are quiet, the houses are attractive and expensive, and the people who live in them are cautious and remote. When Henry gave me his new address, he said, "I am living in a cemetery full of rich people whom I never see."

39

Life itself is just one prolonged miracle.
Insomnia or the Devil at Large

The techniques that Henry had been shown about copper-plate engraving the summer before in Copenhagen now encouraged him to try his hand at what was for him a new art form. After he had done a number of engravings that had turned out well, he thought of another art that he would like to try, that of making silk screens. Because the College of the Immaculate Heart in Holly-wood was famous for its Art Department, and especially for the serigraphs that it produced, Henry inquired about taking instruction there in March 1963. He was accepted at once and, as he wrote Gertz, was "royally received." He worked at the college for many weeks and, whenever making the long trip to Hollywood was too much for him to undertake, because of his arthritis and a stretched sacrosciatic muscle, the Sisters drove to Pacific Palisades to work with him at home.

Henry kept the swimming pool heated to bathtub tempera-ture and used it to ease his aches and pains. When these subsided, he sat at his Ping-Pong table and worked. When he was able to, he played Ping-Pong.

Almost all of his income derived from foreign publications, from books he had written, fifteen, twenty, or nearly thirty years before. It tickled him that he was not doing a stroke of work and was collecting a fortune.

"I rely on foreign publishers for my income. In France and

Germany and especially in the Scandinavian countries, my books are very popular. There you find a much more literate population."

He figured that he had gone through two hundred thousand dollars in the last three years.

"All this happens so late, so late. Why couldn't it have happened sooner, when I could have enjoyed it more? Why does recognition come thirty years afterward!"

Friends and strangers alike asked him for loans, or outright handouts, and he seldom refused anyone. There were those he wanted to help although they did not ask. Renate was one of these. Within a few years he had given her as much as sixty thousand dollars.

While he was giving away money, he forgot about the day when the federal government and the State of California would claim their share of his income. In September 1963 he wrote Gertz that a tax accountant had told him that if he was not to be utterly ruined by taxes he would have to make donations of up to twenty thousand dollars a year and also make a further cash payment of ten thousand dollars before the end of the year. He said that he had given away so much money that he was at his wits' end to make ends meet. "What I have to shell out this year, despite deductions, makes me sick at heart. Now I really have money problems." He also asked him about giving away his paintings for a tax deduction.

Gertz answered that there was no reason why he should not take the deduction, that it was being done all the time. However, it was necessary that schools, museums, colleges, and other institutions be on the Treasury Department's approved list. Henry would be required to provide an acceptable valuation on each watercolor, and this had to be done by a qualified art appraiser or critic.

Henry went to work painting as many as four or five watercolors a day. At a recent small showing of his work, one painting had been sold for two hundred fifty dollars, and this was the valuation he placed on each of those he gave away. He also gave away copies of *Into the Night Life,* which had risen in price from a hundred dollars to two hundred fifty dollars.

The books were stored in Big Sur at Henry's house on

Partington Ridge, and as the requests came in he alerted Eve. She had offered to mail them, for his relationship with her was now warm and friendly. She looked after Lauretta for him, visiting her frequently in Pacific Grove.

Gertz provided the names of libraries, colleges, universities, art galleries, hospitals, and other institutions that were likely to accept gifts, and he also drafted the proper letter that accompanied them so that the donations would conform to the necessary requirements for tax purposes. He also mailed the watercolors that Henry sent him, while his wife Mamie purchased the materials needed to wrap them. If they were to go to recipients in the Chicago area, she personally delivered them.

When Henry had given away a hundred paintings and as many books, he wrote Gertz that he was holding off for a while although the tax deduction had been substantial.

A twenty-five-year correspondence between Henry and Lawrence Durrell had been published by Dutton in March 1963. George Wickes had edited the letters under Henry's watchful eye, for he had insisted that the letters meet his approval. Other letters of this had come out without his knowledge, those he had written years before to Walter Lowenfels, which were appearing in issues of *Outsiders*, a new avant-garde periodical published in New Orleans.

In 1962, Anaïs had asked Lawrence Clark Powell of the Special Collections library at UCLA, where Henry had sent her letters to him, to exchange them for his letters to her. With Henry's permission this was done. Now he had given his permission to select from these letters a book of them to be published by Dutton in 1965.

Grove Press published *Black Spring* in February 1963 and would publish the three titles of *The Rosy Crucifixion* in a boxed edition in 1965.

In 1962 Joseph E. Levine had paid Henry $125,000 for the film rights to *Tropic of Cancer*, but the filming had been beset with trouble from the start. Henry doubted if the picture would ever be made, even after Shirley MacLaine had replaced the original star chosen to play June.

On the other hand, he expected a film to be made in France of *The Smile at the Foot of the Ladder* to be a success. It would star Marcel Marceau.

A deluxe edition of *The Angel Is My Watermark,* produced with color plates of his paintings, was published in Cologne, Germany, in 1962 and brought out later in New York. Another book of his paintings with the essay "To Paint Is to Love Again" was coming out in New York. This essay was something he had written in 1960 for his friend Bill Webb's Cambria Press to publish. Since then it had been translated into French, Italian, German, Dutch, and Danish.

An enormous amount of Henry's work was appearing in America and elsewhere—reprints, records, play adaptations, and more. Numerous articles and books about his work were being published. There were television films and radio programs. A dozen universities were conferring master's degrees on students whose theses concerned Henry Miller.

He was often interviewed at home. Usually the subject turned to *Tropic of Cancer.*

"I think of this work as a sincere, honest effort which, in liberating me as a person and a writer, has somehow done the same for many others. I make no attempt to evaluate it as literature, since that is the task of posterity. But I feel certain that it is a work which will live, no matter what is said or done about it. I have found life worth living, even when unbearably difficult, and I think this view of life permeates not only the book in question but all my work."

When his reputation as a writer of explicit sex came up, he always bristled at the remarks of his interviewer. In discussing this part of an interview, he was bitter. "The majority of the readers of *Tropic of Cancer* have never read another book of mine, and they only looked for those pages where there was sex. That disgusts me!"

He did not mind being labeled as an obscene writer. "Obscenity, like sex, has its rightful place in literature." He was strongly opposed to pornography, which he said presented sex for purely prurient purposes. He maintained that his books were not pornographic.

Besides the interviewers there were photographers. He had dozens of pictures taken, most of them to accompany an article in a magazine or newspaper. Some of them carried his picture on their covers. The only man with a camera that he was glad to see was Ansel Adams. He framed the photograph Adams took of him.

When Lauretta died in the summer of 1963, he was too busy to make the trip to Pacific Grove, and Eve took care of everything for him.

Val got married on Valentine's Day in 1964. The wedding took place at home and was attended by 150 guests. Henry gave the bride away.

Lepska remarried and moved out of the house in April, and when Tony went away to a military academy in the fall Henry had the place to himself and called it "a morgue." He was cheered up from time to time by houseguests Emil White, Bern Porter, Lawrence Durrell, and Jean Varda. Elmer Gertz, Eddie Schwartz, and their wives visited him. Anaïs, too. She had finally divorced Hugo and was living in Southern California, married to the man she had fallen in love with so many years before. She brought him along when she came to the house.

Eve died in her sleep in August 1965. When Harrydick let him know, the shock and sadness of it stayed with Henry for a long time. It was Joe Gray, a new friend half his age, who brought him out of his depression.

Gray was an ex-boxer, a bit actor, a stunt man for the movies, and, because he was a look-alike for Dean Martin, he often played his stand-in. He stood in for George Raft as well, and other actors. He was a raunchy womanizer, and he did not forgo the details in relating his escapades to Henry. His carefree life, self-confidence, and good nature delighted Henry. Henry could not get enough of him.

Gray got him in with a Hollywood crowd where the women especially made a fuss over him. When Henry didn't go to Hollywood, Gray brought the stars, starlets, would-be actresses, and never-would-be actresses to Pacific Palisades for jolly times. Henry felt ten years younger.

Steve Allen invited him to his television show, and Henry appeared several times. The more popular he became, the more interviews he had to give, but he didn't mind. He enjoyed giving his quotable opinions on his work, his life, his marriages. He was also "falling in love," he said, dividing his attentions among several young women at the same time. They were exotic creatures, actresses most of them.

At a party one evening he met a young Japanese woman who turned out to be a jazz singer and pianist at a bar in a Japanese restaurant. Once they got acquainted, he was at the place early every night to get a table where he could gaze on her until closing time. Was she disconcerted by this? She did not reveal her personal feelings because it was her job to entertain the customers.

Her name was Hiroko Tokuda, and she was twenty-seven years old. In Japan she was a singer who had appeared in a few films. In this country she entertained at bars and called herself Hoki. She had memorized the words to every popular song about love. Otherwise, her English was limited to what she had picked up during the two years or so that she had been here.

Henry was not slow to make his infatuation known to her, but she put him off politely, although not enough to discourage him altogether, for to have admirers was good for business. He liked to think that she was singing the words of love especially to him. "All the things you are," "I can't give you anything but love," "I can't stop lovin' you."

A slight friendship developed during the more than a year that he pursued her, and then fate played into his hands. When he saw her dismay upon hearing from the United States Immigration Service that her visa had expired and that she would have to leave the country, he explained that married to him she would not have to leave.

The ceremony took place on September 10, 1967, in the home of one of Henry's friends, and he took her to Paris for their honeymoon. He was going there anyway because the Galeries Gervis was giving him a one-man show, and he wanted to be present at the opening on September 22.

"I'm mortally afraid of it," he said. "Wait 'til the French critics tear me apart! They'll compare me to real painters and I'm not a real painter. They would only forgive me because they love me as a writer. They might be amused by or interested in my work, but that's all."

There were sixty watercolors and ten etchings in the show, and the average price was five hundred dollars. Henry had donated the entire show to the Westwood Art Association in West Los Angeles, which was planning to build an art center from the proceeds. After the show had been on view in Paris for a month, the unsold works would go to Uppsala, Sweden, then to the Museum of Modern Art in Stockholm, and finally to London.

When the newlyweds returned to Pacific Palisades, Hoki did not spend much time at home after the sun went down. In the white Jaguar that Henry had given her for a wedding present, she drove off early in the evening not to return until dawn. She was playing mah-jongg she told him. At his insistence she was no longer working.

If she stayed at home, she did so to entertain her Japanese friends. Henry was jealous of the men she invited, and when she arranged for two of the women to move in with them he was not too pleased either.

She took his watercolors to Japan to oversee a show there, and not until she came home did she tell him that she had given the entire proceeds to her parents. When he gave her the money to go into the dress-shop business, she opened a boutique on Sunset Strip in Los Angeles and rented an apartment nearby. From time to time she came home for a day or two, until in 1974 when she moved out.

During the first months of their marriage, when Henry had walked the floor nightlong imagining what she might be doing while "playing mah-jongg," he had stopped his tears by painting watercolors. In them her face was always the central figure, which he surrounded with designs, scratches, other figures, other faces, one of which might be his own. The paper was scrawled with bitter words, admonitions, nonsense, cries, written in Japanese, French, Greek, English, German. *Hoki Doki, itchy-koo and Kalamazoo, La Sage-Fou de Big Sur, mushi mushi Schmutzig.* Often the colors were aflame and bloody.

"Not everybody, to be sure, recognizes the anguish I depicted in these water colors."

Slashing her in paint was not enough. He filled pages writing about the fiasco of what had been an unrequited love, knowing all the time that it could not have been otherwise:

Now, of course, I am no longer young—which makes everything all the more disturbing. And, needless to say, all the more ridiculous.

Everybody had her number, it seemed, except me. . . . She was like one of those numbers that are indivisible. She had no square root. And yet, as I say, others could read her. In fact, they tried to explain her to me. No use. There was always a remainder which I could never figure out.

Whatever he writes about her, he also explains about himself:

And so we have this reputedly famous old man (75 no less!) pursuing a young will-o'-the wisp. The old man very romantic, the young songstress quite down to earth because it's her business to make men fall in love, do foolish things, buy expensive gowns and jewels. . . .
It's the Devil in her, of course, that I'm writing about. And it was that which made her so intriguing, so help me God. Her soul was to me angelic; herself, at least as she revealed it, was devilish.

In 1970 he gave the pages and a dozen of the watercolors to Loujon Press, a small workshop printery in Albuquerque, New Mexico, which brought out *Insomnia or the Devil at Large* in seven deluxe editions. The papers of the book were handmade and derived from several sources, and a facsimile of Henry's handwriting was used instead of print. The format of each edition was different from that of the other six, and their prices varied according to their jackets of silver or gold foil, their nameplates of antique brass or copper, or sterling silver or solid gold, and whether or not an original watercolor was included. The price of the cheapest edition was sixty dollars and the costliest, twelve hundred dollars.

In 1974 Doubleday brought out a holographic and watercolor edition for ten dollars.

40

*During all the years that I have been writing I have
steeled myself to the idea that I would not really be
accepted, at least to my own countrymen, until after
my death.*

The Colossus of Maroussi

The reason that Henry Miller gave so many interviews,
allowed his picture to be taken so many times, and appeared on
television shows was because he wanted attention. He had been
rejected in his own country for so many years that popularity was
now irresistible. The single honor that came to him in the United
States was due to Van Wyck Brooks, who presented Henry's name
to the National Institute of Arts and Letters, which elected him
to membership in 1957. In France, where he had already been
named a lifetime associate of the Académie du Périgord, the
French Government awarded him the Legion of Honor in 1976.
But the recognition that eluded him and that he yearned for most
was the Nobel Prize. He often said, "It hurts me not to have been
honored by it. Especially when I think of some of those who have
received the prize."

It was not until Isaac Bashevis Singer had won the Nobel in
1978 that Henry felt the recipient deserved it. Singer was one of
his favorite authors. He kept copies of his books at hand to pick
up and read over and over again. Singer said of Miller that he was
"a man who dedicated his life to fight for literary freedom all over
the world. . . . His life work is of interest to every writer and reader
of today and the future."

Henry's name had been proposed for the Nobel Prize for
Literature and turned down. Upon learning about it he said, "The

committee is made up of nonagenarians, a straitlaced, conservative bunch. My work shocks them. Yet these days writers are applauded for the same things I was put down for."

As the years passed and he was continually overlooked, Henry said, "I have the feeling though that it will be awarded to me just as I am dying." He could not accept the fact that he would never be given the prize.

Publishers welcomed books about Henry. A well-received one, *The Mind and Art of Henry Miller*, had appeared in April 1967. Written by Professor William A. Gordon, it was published by the Louisiana State University Press. Miller disagreed with what Gordon had written about his early work, but he said, "He is sincere, honest, and intelligent—and on my side—but, like all professors, he is too academic." Durrell wrote the foreword to the book, which pleased Henry.

In 1970, a photographer living in Southern California, Bradley Smith, came to Pacific Palisades to interview Henry on tape and photograph him in close-ups as he smoked cigarettes and talked about himself and his work. The result was *My Life and Times*, a Gemini Smith Book that was published by the Playboy Press. In addition to the close-ups, there were numerous other photographs of Henry with his friends and reproductions in color of his paintings. Before the book went to press, Playboy had another photograph made, that of a young woman in the nude, her back to the photographer, playing Ping-Pong with a fully clothed Henry. When asked about the picture later, Henry said that it was Playboy's idea but that he didn't mind. "Nothing comes between me and my Ping-Pong."

Until he was eighty years old, Henry was in good health for a man his age, suffering only from an arthritic hip and other handicaps that were more inconveniences than infirmities. Then, in 1972, he underwent surgery for a circulatory problem. A second operation implanted a plastic vein that his body rejected. During a third operation he went into shock, which brought on a stroke that left him partially paralyzed on the right side and blind in the right eye.

"I was on the operating table fourteen hours for a heart bypass. It was too long, and the optic nerve was affected."

When asked how he felt about death, he answered: "I don't fear death, sometimes I feel I ought to be there. Life must be just as good on the other side. Life goes on, I'm sure. My intuition—feelings—lead me to believe these things exist. Otherwise, it's a waste of time to exist. You live a few years, you're snuffed out. It doesn't make sense."

Yet a few years earlier he had grieved over the deaths of two friends who had meant so much to him. Joe Gray had died suddenly after an illness of only a few days. Walker Winslow had been found dead in his apartment in Pacific Grove.

Following the success of Walker's book, *If a Man Be Mad,* he became a highly respected counselor on the treatment of alcoholism, and was a frequent speaker at hospitals and other facilities where psychiatrists were treating addicted patients. He wrote a third book, *The Menninger Story,* a family saga and history of the famed clinic in Topeka, Kansas. Then, unaccountably, he dropped out of sight and weeks passed before he was located, holed up in an apartment and drinking heavily. For the next six years, Henry saw to it that Walker had hospital or institutional care, and whenever he recovered enough to get along by himself, Henry sent him a generous monthly check that took care of his living expenses. When Walker was sober he tried again to write.

In 1974, Henry was in his 83rd year. His general frailty, and the sclerosis in one of his legs, had made it difficult for him to get around, but he managed with the aid of a walker. Half of the day was spent in bed. When he got up, his usual attire included orthopedic shoes, pajamas, and a bathrobe. He read a little, watched television, or listened to the records of Scriabin, Ravel, Stravinsky, or Wagner. He had reluctantly given up cigarettes.

He had a quotation from the Chinese posted on his front door:

When a man has reached old age and has fulfilled his mission, he has a right to confront the idea of death in peace. He has no need of other men, he knows them already and has seen enough of them. What he needs is peace. It is not seemly to seek out such a man, plague him with chatter, and make him suffer banalities. One should pass by the door of his house as if no one lived there.

It did not keep visitors away. Friends, strangers, magazine and newspaper writers, photographers, aspiring writers, and others asked to come in. He was always "good copy" for the interviewers. If asked what he thought of the current books, he would answer, "A lot of the books today are horrible, especially the sex books. What's wrong with them? Everything. In the first place it isn't literature, it doesn't have any value." If the subject of the current best sellers came up he would say, "I'm not one of the people's favorites. They like Harold Robbins and Irving Wallace, whose work I abhor."

If the subject turned to the Women's Liberation Movement, he said he didn't know what women had against him. "I think that women really are the stronger sex. They have dominated men's thinking for a long time. Men owe a lot to the women who inspired them, their muses." But he knew that he was on their blacklist, "Norman Mailer is number one and I am number two."

The interior of Henry's house was almost as much an attraction as Henry himself. The walls and one ceiling were covered with posters, poems, autographs, astrological data, and quotations in several languages, as well as with his paintings and those of others. Some of the graffiti was irreverent but most of it was amusing, witty, and often sentimental. Henry invited the people he admired to write their names on the walls with colored marking pens.

In 1974 Henry read a book he admired. It was the newly published *Fear of Flying*, which he saw as "the feminine counterpart" of *Tropic of Cancer*. When the book's young author, Erica Jong, came to Pacific Palisades to meet him he was delighted, and a warm friendship resulted.

The next spring, when Henry was asked to be interviewed on the CBS television show *60 Minutes*, he requested that Erica Jong share the interview with him. Mike Wallace brought a television crew to the house to do the interview, which went on the air late in the summer of 1975.

That year another book of Henry's correspondence came out when Grove Press published *Letters of Henry Miller and Wallace Fowlie*, from letters that had been written some thirty years before. Fowlie also wrote a fourteen-page biography of Henry for the

Dictionary of Literary Biography, published by Gale in Detroit, Michigan.

In September 1975, New Directions brought out *The Nightmare Notebook,* a facsimile of the handwritten notes that Henry had kept during his journey across the United States in 1941. The 225 pages included maps, charts, sketches, lists, notes, comments, itineraries, and accounts of money he had spent. The book was limited to seven hundred signed copies, and the price was one hundred fifty dollars.

In 1976, Grove Press published Norman Mailer's book, *Genius and Lust: A Journey Through the Major Writings of Henry Miller.* Henry was disappointed in the book.

He said he didn't like any of Mailer's books. "He's too long-winded. His sentences are too complex and elaborate. I could never finish a thing he wrote." In saying this to his interviewers, he always added that he liked Mailer personally. Mailer visited Henry in 1976. "I like him very much as a person," Henry would say, "he's a charming, seductive individual, but I told him to his face that I find him hard to read. He's a difficult writer, he over-elaborates."

In 1978 more of his correspondence was published when the Southern Illinois University Press brought out *Henry Miller: Years of Trials and Triumph, 1962–1964, The Correspondence of Henry Miller and Elmer Gertz,* edited by Elmer Gertz and Felice Flanery Lewis.

Always Merry and Bright: The Life of Henry Miller, by Jay Martin, was published by Capra Press in 1979. Henry had given Martin permission to read the restricted personal material of his in the Library of Congress, the Special Collections Division at UCLA, and in a dozen other libraries, but he did not authorize the biography. He had told Martin before he started that a biography was unnecessary because he had written his own autobiography in his books. Although the published book was very favorably reviewed, it displeased Henry.

Henry, for some time, had wanted to write a book about his friends, some whom he had known and remembered with affection throughout his life—boyhood chums, schoolgirls he had had a crush on—and about others who had come into his life later. It seemed to him now to be more than he had the strength for.

However, his longtime friend, Noel Young, the publisher of Capra Press in Santa Barbara, encouraged him to try writing the book a hundred or so pages at a time. As they were finished, he would publish them as chapbooks.

Henry went to work. When the first 144 pages were written they were published in 1977 as *Book of Friends.* When Henry finished another 112 pages they were published in 1978 as *My Bike and Other Friends.* The final 123 pages became *Joey,* published in 1979. He said that he would not write more because his hold on life "may break any time now." He was eighty-eight years old.

He gave one last interview for television, with Hugh Downs, for the *Over Easy* show on public-television stations.

Sometime before, Henry's daughter Val had asked her best friend, Twinka Thiebaud, to be her father's live-in housekeeper. She herself was living in the house on Partington Ridge and visiting her father frequently. For a time, Henry's son Tony had lived with his father but he, too, had gone back to Big Sur.

In Paris, in the early thirties, when Henry was working on a book about D. H. Lawrence, many of his notes had been protests against the books that others had written about the English novelist. He felt that J. Middleton Murry, especially, had not understood Lawrence at all.

To support his own ideas, Henry had quoted from Nietzsche, Rank, Swift, Spengler, Dostoyevski, Rabelais, Jung, Boccaccio, Rousseau, and others. As he analyzed, compared, and sought to understand Lawrence, he had organized his notes into "Lawrence the Man," "the Artist," "the Mystic," "the Prophet," "the Philosopher," and "the Saviour." In developing "the Man," Henry had dealt with him as an anarchist, rebel, individualist, heretic, iconoclast, narcissist, satirist, misanthrope, puritan, and phallic worshipper.

In making notes on the homosexual theme in *The White Peacock,* he had written that Cyril's love for George had more reality in it than did any of the love affairs in the book. He made a note: "Distinguish here the nature of his love for man. Yet one can't deny the taint in his 'the sweetness of the touch of our naked bodies against each other was superb.' "

He analyzed Lawrence's mystical imagery of the rainbow, bird, and serpent. He noted Lawrence's appreciation of "the dark, obscene side" of Edgar Allan Poe, and quoted him in writing that Poe was "an adventurer into vaults and cellars and horrible underground passages of the human soul."

Henry saw "the artist's fight with art, with life, with himself . . . the anarchist who rejected all of society's values," and he recognized himself.

"Lawrence is so much myself. And I see my deficiencies, the real nature of the conflict within me."

In Lawrence's love-hate relationship with his wife Frieda, Henry felt that their conflict was not unlike his own with his first wife, Beatrice. Except that Beatrice had not screamed or thrown plates at him.

"I don't believe it was sexual inequality between Lawrence and Frieda. It was Frieda's hungry maw—her obstinacy, pettiness —couldn't suffer him to be greater than her."

"Lawrence's Oedipus complex was the source of his creativity," Henry wrote. He quoted passages to show that the incestuous, homosexual, and castration plots in his books came out of the fear and guilt he felt for his neurotic attachment to his mother.

Catherine Carswell's remark in her book, *The Savage Pilgrimage*, that "Lawrence was never more himself than when he wrote *Lady C.*" was exactly what Henry believed, and he wrote so in his notes.

For months he had been absorbed in his study of Lawrence, analyzing, quoting, comparing. Then he had despaired of ever being able to write a book of his own about his idol and had cast the notes aside. If Anaïs had not gathered them up, sending some to the binders, they would have been lost.

Although in later years Henry took up again his study of Lawrence, still thinking he might write the book, he never did. Finally he added these notes to other material of his that was at UCLA. Now it was suggested to him that his notes be turned over to two writers who would work them into a book bearing his name. When he gave his permission, the task was turned over to Evelyn J. Hinz and Professor John J. Teunissen of the University of Manitoba in Winnipeg. Hinz was an associate professor of English, and Teunissen was a former head of the English Department at the University. Both had collaborated on published articles about Lawrence. The Social Sciences and Humanities Research Council of Canada and the University of Manitoba Grants Committee provided the financial assistance that enabled them to work on the notes, and in two years Hinz and Teunissen produced *The World of Lawrence: A Passionate Appreciation*. It was published by Capra Press but did not appear in time for Henry to see it.

In May 1980 he was very ill, sometimes semiconscious, and no longer aware of the bedroom in which he lay. Those who were looking after him heard him speaking to friends who were not in the room. They realized then that he had returned to the years that had meant so much to him, the Paris years, and was reliving a time that had vanished. It was from the Villa Seurat that he opened the door and stepped to the other side. It was late afternoon on June 7, 1980.

In *Nexus* there is a surrealist scene in which he finds that his heart has been cut out of his body. He wrote: "And the door opened. It was called Death, which always swung open, and I saw that there was no death, nor were there any judges or executioners save in our imagining."

Postlude

As he wished, Henry Miller's ashes were taken to Big Sur to be scattered there. Val kept the copper box that contained them on the mantel over the fireplace in the living room until December 26, 1983, which would have been her father's ninety-second birthday. That day she carried the box down to the sea below Partington Ridge, and released some of the ashes into the outgoing tide. She took the rest back to the house, where they remain.

Notes

Quotations from the published works of Henry Miller in this book are in all cases from the original editions of the works. Pagination given here may therefore vary from reprint editions of the same works.

Page   **1**

3   *Black Spring,* In the past, 143
      Tropic of Capricorn, My people, 13

5   *Tropic of Capricorn,* 54

6   *Tropic of Capricorn,* 323

7   *Tropic of Capricorn,* fired from, 312; feet up, 294

8   *Tropic of Capricorn,* from the moment, 23; a theft, 24; weeping, 33; every ten days, 29

9   *Tropic of Capricorn,* by chance, 33; colossal, 37

10   *Tropic of Capricorn,* 291

  2

11   *Sexus,* Vol. 1, I was at, 9
      Tropic of Capricorn, knowing only, 250

12   *Tropic of Capricorn,* standing, 356; one can wait, 359
      Sexus, Vol. 4, passed for, 106; own wave length, 107

13   *Sexus,* Vol. 4, 187

14   *Tropic of Capricorn,* 256

17   *Sexus,* Vol. 5, grateful, 311; maudlin, 315; then you die, 316

  3

20   *Tropic of Capricorn,* 14

25   *Hamlet,* Vol. 2, inner duality, 306
      Hamlet, Vol. 1, If there is, 16

26   *Genesis of the Tropic of Cancer,* 31

27   *Tropic of Cancer,* damned current, 60

Page   **17**

132   *The Plight of the Creative Artist,* 19

133   *The Air-Conditioned Nightmare,* 20
            Murder the Murderer, 17

134   *Sexus,* Vol. 3, 289

135   *The Power Within Us* (Preface), 1

            18

139   *Big Sur and the Oranges of Hieronymus Bosch,* 122

            19

149   *Black Spring,* whalebone, 203; sand, 176; girl, 175

150   *Black Spring,* grey meat, 186; lost, 198

            20

159   *The Books in My Life,* 28

161   *Hamlet,* Vol. 2, rob the worms, 224; wiggling, 239; words, 241;
                    hungry, 303; rat, 304

162   *Hamlet,* Vol. 2, 242

163   *Circle* 6, gaze into, 45
            Circle 7, in the heart, 136

167   *Money and How It Gets That Way,* 28

172   *Into the Night Life* (privately printed brochure)

            22

174   *Big Sur and the Oranges of Hieronymus Bosch,* 275

            25

200   *Semblance of a Devoted Past,* 5

            26

207   *The Plight of the Creative Artist,* 6

Page

329   *Insomnia or the Devil at Large,* Not everybody, 2

330   *Insomnia or the Devil at Large,* Now of course, 3; her number, 8;
         And so, 5; Devil, 7

         40

331   *The Colossus of Maroussi,* 206

338   *Nexus,* 54

Selected Bibliography

By Henry Miller

Books

The Air-Conditioned Nightmare. New York: New Directions, 1945.

Aller Retour New York. Paris: Obelisk Press (Siana Series No. 1), 1935.

The Angel Is My Watermark. Fullerton, Calif.: Holve-Barrows, 1944. Reprint. New York: Harry N. Abrams, 1962.

Big Sur and the Oranges of Hieronymus Bosch. New York: New Directions, 1959.

Black Spring. Paris: Obelisk Press, 1936. Reprint. New York: Grove Press, 1963.

Book of Friends. Santa Barbara, Calif.: Capra Press, 1976.

The Books in My Life. Norfolk, Conn.: New Directions, 1952.

The Colossus of Maroussi. San Francisco: The Colt Press, 1941. Reprint. New York: New Directions, 1958.

The Cosmological Eye. Norfolk, Conn.: New Directions, 1939.

A Devil in Paradise. New York: New American Library (Signet Edition), 1956.

Hamlet (with Michael Fraenkel). Volume 1. New York: Carrefour, 1939; Volume 2. New York: Carrefour, 1941.

A Henry Miller Miscellanea. Berkeley, Calif.: Bern Porter Books, 1945.

Insomnia or the Devil at Large. Albuquerque, N. Mex.: Loujon Press, 1966. Reprint. New York: Doubleday, 1974.

Into the Night Life (with Bezalel Schatz). Berkeley, Calif.: privately published by Henry Miller and Bezalel Schatz, 1947.

Joey. Santa Barbara, Calif.: Capra Press, 1979.

Just Wild About Harry (a play). New York: New Directions, 1963.

Maurizius Forever. Waco, Tex.: Motive Press, 1946, and San Francisco: The Colt Press, 1946.

Max and the White Phagocytes. Paris: Obelisk Press (Villa Seurat Series, No. 2), 1938.

My Bike and Other Friends. Santa Barbara, Calif.: Capra Press, 1978.

My Life and Times. Chicago: Playboy Press (a Gemini Smith Book), 1972.

Nexus (Book 3 of *The Rosy Crucifixion*). Paris: Correa, 1960. Reprint. New York: Grove Press, 1965.

Nights of Love and Laughter. New York: New American Library, 1955.

On Turning Eighty. Santa Barbara, Calif.: Capra Press, 1972.

Order and Chaos Chez Hans Reichel (with an Introduction by Lawrence Durrell). Tucson, Ariz.: Loujon Press, 1966.

Plexus (Book 2 of *The Rosy Crucifixion*). Paris: Olympia Press, 1953. Reprint. New York: Grove Press, 1965.

Quiet Days in Clichy. Paris: Olympia Press, 1956. Reprint (with *The World of Sex*). New York: Grove Press, 1978.

Reflections (Twinka Thiebaud, editor). Santa Barbara, Calif.: Capra Press, 1981.

Remember to Remember. New York: New Directions, 1947.

Reunion in Barcelona: A Letter to Alfred Perlès. Northwood, England: Scorpion Press, 1959.

Semblance of a Devoted Past. Berkeley, Calif.: Bern Porter Books, 1945.

Sexus (Book 1 of *The Rosy Crucifixion*). Paris: Obelisk Press, 1949. Reprint. New York: Grove Press, 1965.

The Smile at the Foot of the Ladder (with a Preface by Edwin Corle). New York: Duell, Sloane and Pearce, 1948.

Stand Still Like a Hummingbird. Norfolk, Conn.: New Directions, 1962.

Sunday After the War. Norfolk, Conn.: New Directions, 1944.

The Time of the Assassins. Norfolk, Conn.: New Directions, 1956.

To Paint Is to Love Again. Alhambra, Calif.: Cambria Books, 1960.

Tropic of Cancer (with a Preface by Anaïs Nin). Paris: Obelisk Press, 1934. Reprint. New York: Grove Press, 1961.

Tropic of Capricorn. Paris: Obelisk Press, 1939. Reprint. New York: Grove Press, 1962.

Why Abstract? (with Hilaire Hiler and William Saroyan). New York: New Directions, 1945.

The Wisdom of the Heart. Norfolk, Conn.: New Directions, 1941.

The World of Lawrence (compiled by Evelyn J. Hinz and John J. Teunissen). Santa Barbara, Calif.: Capra Press, 1980.

The World of Sex. Chicago: privately published by Ben Abramson, 1940. Reprint. Paris: Olympia Press, 1959. Reprint (with *Quiet Days in Clichy*). New York: Grove Press, 1978.

Zev. Paris: Edition Galerie Furstenberg, 1955.

Brochures, Pamphlets, and Miscellaneous Items

The Amazing and Invariable Beauford DeLaney. Yonkers, N.Y.: Alicat Book Shop, 1945.

Echolalia (a portfolio of watercolors by Henry Miller). Berkeley, Calif.: Bern Porter Books, 1945.

Into the Night Life (illustrated booklet). Los Angeles: privately published by Henry Miller and Bezalel Schatz, 1947.

Money and How It Gets That Way. Paris: *Booster Broadside* No. 1, 1938. Reprint. Berkeley, Calif.: Bern Porter Books, 1946.

Murder the Murderer. Berkeley, Calif.: Bern Porter Books, 1944.

Obscenity and the Law of Reflection. Yonkers, N.Y.: Alicat Book Shop, 1945.

Of, By, and About Henry Miller (Oscar Bardinsky, editor). Yonkers, N.Y.: Alicat Book Shop, 1947.

Patchen, Man of Anger and Light. New York: Max Padell, 1946.

The Plight of the Creative Artist in the United States of America. Berkeley, Calif.: Bern Porter Books, 1944.

Scenario (with Frontispiece by Abraham Rattner). Paris: Obelisk Press, 1937.

Un Etre Etoilique. Paris: privately published by Henry Miller, 1937.

Varda, the Master Builder. Berkeley, Calif.: Circle Editions, 1947.

The Waters Reglitterized. San Jose, Calif.: John Kidid, 1950.

What Are You Going to Do About Alf? Paris: privately published by Henry Miller, 1935. Reprint. Berkeley, Calif.: Bern Porter Books, 1943.

Magazines

The Booster (co-edited by Henry Miller). Paris: all issues, September 1937 through December 1938.

Circle. Berkeley, Calif.: all issues, 1 through 10, 1944–1948.

Death, A Literary Quarterly. New York: Vol. 1, No. 1 (Summer 1946).

Delta (co-edited by Henry Miller). Paris: issue of Christmas 1938.

Henry Miller Literary Society Newsletters (Edward P. Schwartz, editor). Minneapolis: issues 1 through 13, 1959–1964.

Horizon, A Review of Literature and Art. London: Vol. 20, No. 115 (July 1949).

The Phoenix. Woodstock, N.Y.: Vol. 1, No. 1 (March-April-May 1938).

Soviet Literature. Moscow: June 1950.

Records and Films

Folkways Records. New York: a radio interview between Audrey June Booth and Henry Miller in Minneapolis, June 7, 1962.

Henry Miller Recalls and Reflects (two-part album). New York: Henry Miller with Ben Grauer; Riverside Modern Voice Series, 1956.

Just Wild About Harry (album). New York: Spoken Arts, 1963.

Sound Portraits (album). New York: Henry Miller reading from his writings and commenting extemporaneously; produced by Louis and Bebe Barron, 1949.

Other Sources Consulted

Bezalel Schatz. San Francisco: San Francisco Museum of Art, 1949 (issued with exhibition of oil paintings, August-September 1949, with a Foreword by Henry Miller).

Bufano Society of the Arts. *Bufano* (with an Introduction by Henry Miller). San Francisco: undated.

California History. San Francisco: California Historical Society, Summer 1980.

The Coast. San Francisco: issue of December 1937.

Dibbern, George. *Quest.* New York: W. W. Norton, 1941.

Durrell, Lawrence. *The Black Book.* Paris: Obelisk Press, 1938 (manuscript in author's collection, dated 1937).

——— (editor). *The Henry Miller Reader.* New York: New Directions, 1959.

———, Miller, Henry, and Perlès, Alfred. *Art and Outrage* (correspondence). New York: E. P. Dutton, 1961.

Fowlie, Wallace, *Aubade, A Teacher's Notebook.* Durham, N.C.: Duke University Press, 1983.

———. *Clowns and Angels.* New York: Sheed and Ward, 1943.

———. *The Clown's Grail.* London: Dennis Dobson, 1948.

———. *Journal of Rehearsals.* Durham, N.C.: Duke University Press, 1977.

——— (editor). *Letters of Henry Miller and Wallace Fowlie, 1943–1972.* New York: Grove Press, 1975.

Fraenkel, Michael. *Bastard Death.* New York: Carrefour, 1936.

————. *Death in a Room.* Waco, Tex.: Motive Press, 1947.

————. *Death Is Not Enough.* London: C. W. Daniel, 1939.

————. *Genesis of the Tropic of Cancer.* Berkeley, Calif.: Bern Porter Books, 1946.

Gertz, Elmer. *A Handful of Clients.* Chicago: Follett, 1965.

———— (co-editor with Felice Flannery Lewis). *Henry Miller: Years of Trials and Triumph, 1962–1964* (correspondence between Henry Miller and Elmer Gertz.) Carbondale, Ill.: Southern Illinois University Press, 1978.

————. *To Life.* New York: McGraw-Hill, 1974.

Gordon, William A. *The Mind and Art of Henry Miller.* Baton Rouge, La.: Louisiana State University Press, 1967.

Gray, Eunice T. *Cross Trails and Chaparral.* Carmel, Calif.: Seven Arts, 1925.

Hordequin, Paul. *Le Temps des Cerises* (with a Preface by Henry Miller). Paris: La Table Ronde, 1951.

Jeffers, Robinson. *The Selected Poetry of Robinson Jeffers.* New York: Random House, 1927.

Lawrence, D. H. *Lady Chatterley's Lover.* Florence, Italy: privately published, 1928. Reprint. New York: Grove Press, 1959.

Long, Haniel. *The Power Within Us* (with a Preface by Henry Miller). London: Drummond, 1946.

Maine, Harold (Walker Winslow). *If a Man Be Mad.* New York: Doubleday, 1947.

Manchester, William. *Disturber of the Peace.* New York: Harper, 1950.

Martin, Jay. *Always Merry and Bright: The Life of Henry Miller.* Santa Barbara, Calif.: Capra Press, 1978.

Mathes, W. Michael. *A Brief History of the Land of Califia.* La Paz, Mexico: Patronado del Estudiante Súdcaliforniano, 1977.

Mezzrow, Milton (with Bernard Wolfe). *Really the Blues.* New York: Random House, 1946. Paris: Correa, 1950 (French translation entitled *La Rage de Vivre,* with a Preface by Henry Miller).

Moore, Thomas H. *Henry Miller on Writing.* New York: New Directions, 1964.

———— (editor). *Bibliography: Henry Miller.* Minneapolis: Henry Miller Literary Society, 1961.

Murphy, Marion Fisher. *Seven Stars for California: A Story of Its Capitals.* Sonoma, Calif.: privately published, 1979.

New Directions Year Books (James Laughlin, editor). New York: New Directions, 1936–1950.

Nin, Anaïs. *D. H. Lawrence: An Unprofessional Study.* Paris: Edward W. Titus, 1932.

——. *The Diary of Anaïs Nin,* Vol. 1, 1931–1934; Vol. 2, 1939–1944 (edited and with an Introduction by Gunther Stuhlmann). New York: The Swallow Press and Harcourt, Brace, 1966 and 1969.

Orwell, George. *Inside the Whale.* London: Gollancz, 1940.

The Paintings of Henry Miller. San Francisco: Chronicle Books, 1982.

Paris des Rêves. Lausanne, Switzerland: La Guilde du Livre, 1950 (a book of photographs and comments with three pages devoted to Henry Miller).

Perlès, Alfred. *My Friend Henry Miller: An Intimate Biography* (with a Preface by Henry Miller). London: Neville Spearman, 1955. New York: John Day, 1956.

——. *Reunion* in *Big Sur: A Letter to Henry Miller in Reply to His Reunion in Barcelona.* Northwood, England: Scorpion Press, 1959.

Porter, Bern (editor). *The Happy Rock.* Berkeley, Calif.: Bern Porter Books, 1945.

—— (compiler). *Henry Miller: A Chronology and Bibliography.* Berkeley, Calif.: Bern Porter Books, 1945.

Ross, Lillian Bos. *The Stranger.* New York: William Morrow, 1942. Paris: Denoel, 1948 (French translation entitled *Big Sur,* with a Preface by Henry Miller).

Schorer, Mark. *Sinclair Lewis: An American Life.* New York: McGraw-Hill, 1961.

Shapiro, Karl. *In Defense of Ignorance.* New York: Random House, 1960.

Spearhead: Ten Years of Experimental Writing in America. New York: New Directions, 1947.

Stuhlmann, Gunther (editor). *Henry Miller: Letters to Anaïs Nin.* New York: Putnam, 1965.

Thoreau, Henry David. *Life Without Principle: Three Essays* (with a Preface by Henry Miller). San Francisco: James Ladd Delkin, 1946.

White, Emil (editor). *The Big Sur Guides: The Monterey Peninsula and Big Sur.* Big Sur, Calif.: Emil White, 1955.

—— (editor). *Carmel-by-the-Sea.* Big Sur, Calif.: Emil White, 1967.

―――― (editor). *Henry Miller: Between Heaven and Hell* (symposium). Big Sur, Calif.: 1961.

Wickes, George (editor). *Lawrence Durrell and Henry Miller: A Private Correspondence.* New York: E. P. Dutton, 1963.

Works Projects Administration Writer's Project. *California: A Guide to the Golden State.* New York: Hastings House, 1967.

Index